But Wait...
THERE'S MORE!

REMY STERN

But Wait...

THERE'S MORE!

TIGHTEN YOUR ABS, MAKE MILLIONS, AND LEARN HOW THE $100 BILLION INFOMERCIAL INDUSTRY SOLD US EVERYTHING BUT THE KITCHEN SINK

COLLINS BUSINESS
An Imprint of HarperCollins Publishers

To Mom

HarperCollins books may be purchased for educational, business, or sales promotional use. For information, please write: Special Markets Department, HarperCollins Publishers, 10 East 53rd Street, New York, NY 10022.

FIRST EDITION

Designed by Renato Stanisic

Library of Congress Cataloging-in-Publication Data

Stern, Remy.
   But wait . . . there's more! : tighten your abs, make millions, and learn how the $100 billion infomercial industry sold us everything but the kitchen sink / Remy Stern.
      p. cm.
   Includes bibliographical references and index.
   ISBN 978-0-06-126055-1
1. Television advertising—United States. 2. Infomercials—United States. I. Title.

   HF6146.T42S842 2008
   659.14'30973—dc22   2008024017

09 10 11 12 13 OV/RRD 10 9 8 7 6 5 4 3 2 1

CONTENTS

ACKNOWLEDGMENTS

In some ways, this book began twenty years ago when I found myself watching television in my room late at night when I really should have been doing homework or sleeping. So I suppose I should start off by thanking my mom and dad for buying me a TV at the age of thirteen against their better judgment.

I was fortunate to talk to many, many people who work in the trenches of the infomercial and home shopping industries as part of my research. From inventors to marketers, entrepreneurs to production personnel, I'm enormously grateful to the people who took time out of their busy schedules to sit down and talk with me about what they do every day. This is an industry that rarely gets much positive attention in the mainstream media and, understandably, some were reluctant to pull back the curtain. I think my personal passion for the material gave many of them confidence that I could cover the subject fairly and address both the positive an the negative. I hope I've done that.

I owe a debt of gratitude to my agent, Dan Lazar, who had a vision of this book from the very start and has been exceptionally supportive every step of the way. My deepest thanks to everyone at HarperCollins, in particular Ethan Friedman, who acquired the book for Collins and edited the first draft, and Matthew Inman, who edited the final manuscript and shepherded the book to print. Emma Garman read the manuscript more times than I can count and offered invaluable input and guidance. Pulling together thousands of pages of documents was no small task and I was fortunate to have Ellen Wernecke assist me during the research process. Maer Roshan has been a mentor and friend as well as a source of inspiration. Thanks to Mariel, Shawee, and Karen for their love and support. My late grandfather, Marc Martin, never watched an infomerical in his life, but as an engineer and inventor he instilled in me a love for gadgets and gizmos at an early age. My late uncle, Henry Lange, encouraged me to pursue my writing when I wasn't so sure myself. Finally, thanks to my mom. This is for you.

INTRODUCTION

I'll come right out and confess the truth. There was a point in my life when I watched infomercials with alarming regularity. I didn't sit up all night and watch them, mind you. And I wasn't a shopping addict, running up my credit card with the purchase of countless mops, blenders, self-help books, and cubic zirconia rings. But I did find myself often turning on the TV late at night and bypassing the other shows on television to watch Ron Popeil try to sell me on a pasta maker, Tom Vu explain how I could make millions in real estate, and Tony Robbins convince me that he could help me chart a new career direction and get along better with my wife. The fact that I was a high school student who didn't have any interest in cooking, had no career to speak of, and wasn't even of legal age to get married or purchase real estate hardly mattered. These were some of the most amusing characters on television in the wee hours of the morning.

Of course, there wasn't much competition at the time. I didn't have a digital cable box with 1,102 channels, thousands of hours of video on demand at my fingertips, a TiVo capable of storing my favorite shows, or a subscription to Netflix. There were a couple dozen channels, and almost all of them seemed to magically turn into a flea market late at night as smarmy men took to the airwaves with their dubious wares. A few hours earlier, these same channels had been broadcasting sitcoms, dramas, and weighty news programs. When night turned into early morning, they became home to people like Tony Little, a manic ponytailed personal trainer, and Matthew Lesko, an equally hyperactive man famous for his suits decorated with gigantic question marks who assured audiences that he had the secret to extracting free money from the government.

As it turns out, my interest in infomercials coincided with the golden age of the medium. In the late 1980s and early '90s, the airwaves were flooded with products, many of which were about as dubious as the notion that the government had billions of dollars sitting in a bank account somewhere that they were just itching to hand over to me as long as I filled out the right form. The advent of cable had unleashed dozens of new stations, many of which had little in the way of original programming. Deregulation of the industry had given broadcasters the right to sell the airtime to advertisers. And buying time on these channels was cheap, which meant that almost any marketer could come along and offer, say, a car wax so powerful you could set your luxury vehicle on fire without doing any damage. As this new phenomenon of paid programming flooded the airwaves, Americans responded by doing what they've always done best: they opened up their wallets and went shopping.

I wasn't the only one fascinated by this parade of bizarre late-night pitchmen. There were millions of perfectly intelligent people tuning in to these characters. What led me—and so many others from my generation—to this wacky world was an affection for the campiness of it all. Like other kitschy staples from the '80s, the infomercial quickly became a fixture on the American pop culture landscape. But we weren't just sitting back and laughing. We were picking up the phone to order these products, too. When I mentioned to an editor at a fashion magazine that I was working on a book about infomercials, she whispered that she'd purchased the Showtime Rotisserie oven a decade earlier but had made sure to keep it hidden away. An investment banker described how he purchased a get-rich-quick program as a teenager. Before realizing that Wall Street would be the quickest path to making millions, he briefly thought that Dave Del Dotto held the key to everlasting riches.

The first product I ever purchased was Didi Seven, a stain remover that came in a small tube and was imported from Germany. Didi Seven inundated the airwaves in the late '80s with a demonstration that is much like the one you can see today in commercials for OxiClean, InstaGone, and OrangeGlo. A large bowl of filthy water turned clear instantly when a bit of Didi Seven was added to the mix. Grass stains and mustard splotches disappeared instantly; yellowed curtains that hadn't been cleaned in three decades looked brand new. Didi Seven could remove iodine and blood stains, the infomercial assured viewers. I still have no idea who handles iodine on such a regular basis that they need to have an iodine cleanser on hand at all times (and I'd venture to say that if you're drenched in your own blood—or anyone else's—you probably have bigger things to worry about than a ruined shirt), but as the host ran through all the potential uses for the product, each one seemed to serve as ample proof that *not* having a tube of Didi Seven in the house would be a major liability. And so off I went with my father's credit card. A week later it came in the mail, and I went around the house ready to conquer every blemish in sight. I still don't know what Didi Seven's active ingredient was (it remains a secret even though you'd be hard-pressed to find Didi Seven these days), but I can't imagine it was all that different from bleach. I left a half dozen white splotches on the carpet in my bedroom and on several pairs of pants hanging in my closet before I tossed it in the garbage.

My Didi Seven experience should have taught me the defining lesson of the infomercial industry: if it's too good to be true, it probably is. But it wasn't the last product I ordered on the phone. Not long after that, Ron Popeil convinced me to plunk down my parents hard-earned money on a Ronco Automatic Pasta Maker, despite the fact that I didn't have any interest in cooking regular, prepackaged pasta, much less making pasta from scratch. (It was Ron's demonstration of chocolate pasta that hooked me, I'll admit it.) About a year later, I convinced my grandmother that we desperately needed to order the Juiceman, a device that the white-haired inventor of the product, Jay Kordich, promised was the "greatest insurance policy in the world." After regurgitating a few facts I'd gleaned from the infomercial, I successfully made my case; several days later I was the proud owner of a hulking piece of plastic that took up half the counter space in our kitchen and sounded like someone had placed an industrial wood chipper in the middle of the room every time I turned it on. I probably ended up using it three or four times before burying it in the closet, where it remained for a decade before someone had the decency to throw it out. Filling up a grocery basket full of produce to extract a couple of glasses, it turned out, was a pain and not particularly cost-effective. And despite Kordich's claims to the contrary, parsley and beet juice tasted awful.

Once again, I wasn't alone. While I was spending money on "revolutionary" gizmos, just as many people were responding to the notion that for $59.99 you could change your life in an instant. Many of the shows seemed to provide cure-alls to life's most challenging problems. There were potions to cure your acne and regrow your hair and various regimens, pills, and devices to help you lose weight instantly. Get-rich-quick programs offered viewers a way to solve all their financial problems in a matter of weeks. All of them promised to change lives. And millions of Americans succumbed, spending millions—and, later, billions—dialing up 800 numbers to place their orders.

It's been twenty-owe years since the first modern-day infomercials appeared on television, and it has since become a massive industry. Today direct response marketing—which includes infomercials, home shopping, and online commerce—is a $300 billion industry, which makes it larger than the film, music, and video game industries combined. Infomercials alone, which represent nearly a third of the overall total, managed to convince one out of every three Americans to pick up the phone and place an order in 2007. Each month, more than 300,000 infomercials air on stations in the United States and Canada. It's a business with many moving parts. At the tip of the iceberg are the people who create these products and market them on the air. Then there are vast manufacturing facilities that turn out these items: as you read this, there are thousands of men and women in China sitting in a factory assembling the junky product that is now being pitched as "state of the art." Telemarketing firms earn billions every year fielding the calls that flood into call centers. Cable networks remain solvent thanks to the airtime they unload to the highest bidder every night. Even large chain retailers earn billions every year marketing the products that became famous after they became television staples.

Built on the hopes and dreams of Americans, it's also become an extraordinarily sophisticated business. Thanks to years of experience—and a good deal of testing—the creators of direct response programming have become some of the savviest marketers around. They've figured how to get lethargic telecitizens off the couch in the middle of the night to pick up the phone and order mops, rotisserie ovens, blenders, vacuum cleaners, and beef jerky machines. They've managed to tap into the minds of consumers in ways traditional retailers haven't dreamed about with a never-ending stream of upsells, cross-promotions, special offers, and continuity programs.

Of course, infomercial marketers rarely get any credit for any of this. You won't see any of them appear on the cover of *Fortune*. The ad industry sneers at them—as do most Americans. Perhaps for good reason. The blender you purchase may not actually work when it arrives on your doorstep. The exercise machine that looked so sturdy on television may crumble to pieces when your fourteen-pound baby climbs on top of it. You won't find a get-rich-quick no-money-down real estate program that will allow you to retire by next week. And there are dozens of people who have gotten very rich very quickly thanks to fraudulent infomercials who are sunning themselves in the Cayman Islands when they really should be confined to an eight-by-eight prison cell in Guantanamo Bay. More than two decades after it exploded, the infomercial industry still has its fair share of sleazy types who will do anything, say anything, and sell anything to make a buck; a business where ex-cons happily move from one scheme to another, all the while funneling cash to their offshore bank accounts. It's an industry where a sheetrock salesman became a real estate expert overnight and made millions selling a get-rich-quick package to the public before retiring to a life of peaceful tranquility on a Napa Valley vineyard; where a doctor who had his license suspended for sexually assaulting a patient found a new career marketing the fountain of youth. As one veteran of the trade joked, it's an industry where you never, ever ask what people were doing before they got into infomercials.

When I was watching these shows back in the day, the seamier side wasn't all that apparent. Sure, I had difficulty believing that a Vietnamese immigrant standing awkwardly in front of his chocolate brown Rolls-Royce and the "waterfall" on his front lawn really had the key to making millions. Part of my skepticism may have had to do with the fact that what he was calling his "waterfall" was actually a water fountain, and I figured if he didn't know what it was, he probably didn't own it either. But it was precisely because it was so preposterous that I couldn't turn away. I was just transfixed by the zany nature of it all.

This is a book about this weird world of late-night entertainment. It's also a book about one of the largest, most sophisticated industries in America that you're probably familiar with, yet know nothing about. It's also a book about spray-on hair, fishing rods that fit in your pocket, porcelain collectibles, and hydroponic vegetable gardening kits. Oh, and the cure for cancer, too.

CHAPTER 1

County Fair to Cable Fare

R on Popeil's assistant had sent me directions to his home in Beverly Hills, but as I climb the steep streets above Los Angeles, I'm having trouble finding the dead-end street off Coldwater Canyon.

If there's one person that Americans associate with a late-night TV pitch, it's Ronald S. Popeil. He's been on the air in one form or another for a half century. If you've watched any TV at all over the past, say, three decades, it's unlikely you've missed him. Popeil is the man who pitched Mr. Microphone, the Ronco Food Dehydrator, and the Showtime Rotisserie. He's the man who introduced the world to spray-on hair. He's the guy who popularized ubiquitous catchphrases like "Operators are standing by" and "But wait, there's more," and made the names Popeil and Ronco synonymous with gadgets and gizmos. Popeil is the grandfather of the infomercial, not because he was the first or has made the most money, but because he's the most famous TV pitchman that has ever come along. It was Ron who inspired Dan Aykroyd's famous "Bass-O-Matic" skit on *Saturday Night Live* in the 1970s. He's played himself on *The Simpsons*. "Weird Al" Yankovic even wrote a song about him. Still not jogging your memory? Turn on the TV. Although he hasn't filmed an infomercial for nearly a decade, there's a good chance the infomercial for his Showtime Rotisserie will air on some distant cable channel this evening.

Popeil is now in his early seventies and semiretired. He no longer runs the company he founded, Ronco, having sold his stake to a group of investors in 2005. He spends his time with his youthful wife and their young children on an estate he's owned for years. He's supposedly hard at work on a new invention, which may be the rousing finale to his six-decade career or may never see the light of day, depending on whether he sorts out the legal and financial issues that have thus far kept the project in limbo.

After nearly getting lost trying to find Popeil's house, I make a couple of quick turns and find my bearings. I pull on to the small street and arrive at a tall wooden gate. After ringing the buzzer, the gate opens, and I park my rental car in the driveway. A maid meets me at the door and escorts me inside, where I find the infomercial king sitting in the kitchen eating a bagel. I'm hardly surprised. What other room would Ron Popeil be in?

Ron looks a bit older since he last appeared on television with his rotisserie oven in the late 1990s, but he's in excellent shape. His thinning hair is painted a dark shade of brown. His skin is tan and wrinkle-free. As he bounds up from the kitchen table to greet me with a mouthful of lox, he doesn't seem to have lost a bit of the energy that propelled him to once stand on his feet for sixteen hours a day and demonstrate kitchen products in front of crowds at the Woolworth's in Chicago.

For the past sixty years or so, Popeil has been thinking of things to invent and sell. It's a family tradition: his father, uncles, and many cousins all did precisely the same thing. His approach hasn't wavered much over the years. He takes notice of life's small annoyances and minor inconveniences—the sort that you didn't even know you had until you flipped the channel one night and landed on one of his programs—and then heads home to his garage-cum-workshop to figure out a solution. Unlike other men with big dreams who tinker away in their garage, Popeil has never been the sort of inventor to engage in flights of fancy. He's never tried to build a jet pack or a robot. He's never tried to construct a time machine or find a cure for cancer. He has, however, spent years obsessing over how to improve the spatula.

Few of his products have been revolutionary. Many of his most successful items were updated versions of products his father and great-uncle once sold; others were around long before Ron came along and slapped them up on television. But his gift for packaging products and marketing them to the public with catchy ads and slogans has made him both very famous and very rich. His perfect timing has helped! When he noticed people becoming increasingly concerned about the threat of secondhand cigarette smoke in the '70s, he debuted the smokeless ashtray, which collected the smoke in a filter. The growing popularity of the bagel three decades ago led him to come up with a bagel cutter, which, rather appropriately, he named the Bagel Cutter.

Popeil has had his share of losers, to be sure. He was clearly on to something in the mid-'70s when he came up with Hold-Up, a bulletin board that was covered with adhesive that you could use to attach notes and other little reminders. Unfortunately, 3M introduced Post-it Notes around the same time, relegating Ron's invention to the dustbin of infomercial history. His Glass Froster was a clever concept: inspired by a beer commercial, Popeil came up with a device that applied a thin layer of frost to your favorite mug. Alas, the gizmo relied on Freon, the environmentally toxic coolant that was later banned by the government. (These days Ron frosts his glasses the old-fashioned way: he dunks them in water and puts them in the freezer.) But he's had more hits than failures. Over the course of his career, he estimates he's sold well over $2 billion in products, and many Popeil products continue to sell, even though they haven't been marketed in decades. Popeil's Pocket Fisherman, for example, which Ron's father was responsible for inventing, can still be found at Ronco.com for $29.99. (Adjusted for inflation, it's a relative bargain: it retailed for $19.99 when it debuted in 1972.)

After walking through the kitchen—and after Ron shows me his stash of olive oil, which he claims is one of the largest collections in the world—we retreat to his office, a room that provides further evidence of Ron's obsession with all things cooking related. A giant bookcase that reaches up to the ceiling is stocked with every condiment, sauce, and marinade imaginable, which Ron explains he keeps on hand for when he's testing out one of his kitchen inventions. The other corner of the room shows off his other primary occupation: there's a giant stack of videotapes and a professional video camera mounted on a tripod.

As he sinks into his office chair and starts to spin yarns from the television battlefield, it's clear he still possesses the consummate sales charm that has made him so successful for so many years, which, as anyone who has fallen for his pitch (myself included) knows all too well. (Ron seems to know this, too: he humbly titled his 1995 autobiography *The Salesman of the Century*.) I'm quite convinced that even now you could drop Ron on any street corner in America with a folding table and a giant box full of just about anything and he'd amble off a couple of hours later with a stack of bills in his hand. He's both intensely charismatic and extraordinarily skillful at guiding the conversation away from subjects he doesn't want to talk about (his bankruptcy years ago, his first wife) and focusing on, say, all the genius products he's invented over the years. I ask him a question about his childhood, and a moment later we're talking about how his rotisserie oven revolutionized cooking in America. I'm sure that if you'd approached him on the streets of Chicago when he was demonstrating a vegetable chopper and queried him on the specifics of the money-back guarantee, within about ten seconds you'd have been discussing how to slice up an apple to prepare the perfect Waldorf salad.

The stories of Popeil's sales prowess in the 1940s and '50s are largely apocryphal at this point. Ron tells me the tale—which he's recounted on numerous occasions over the years—of how he faced off against the man who was once regarded as the consummate pitchman of the era, Frosty Wishon. Along with his cousin Arnold Morris, Popeil proposed a competition in which all three men would take turns selling the same item and see who did the best at the end of the ten-day fair. Given the joy Ron takes in retelling the story, it's probably unnecessary to mention that Ron handily beat them. "Frosty looked at me and said, 'Ron, I will never work with you as long as I live from this point going forward.' And he never did!" He leans back in this chair, beaming with delight.

You can't quibble with Ron's skill as a salesman, but it's been quite a while since it's been on display on television. His most recent infomercial was for the Showtime Rotisserie & BBQ, which was introduced in 1998. Like all of his products from the '90s, Ron was also the star of the infomercial, which you probably know all too well since the show has aired about a gazillion times over the past decade. Clad in a green Ronco apron, Popeil's pitch featured him cooking up chicken kebabs, lobster tail, and pork loin roast amid the near-constant refrain "Just set it and forget it!" It's since turned out to be his most successful product: By his own estimation, he's sold seven million of them, racking up more than $1 billion in sales. Since then, though, he's been out of the mix. But as everyone in the industry knew full well, he hadn't simply retired to a life of gardening or golfing. He'd been laboring on a new gizmo, a deep fryer that he hoped would be the big follow-up to his rotisserie oven.

When I'd first read that Popeil was working on a fryer, I was somewhat surprised. Part of the allure of the Showtime was that the oven allowed the fat to drip off the food, and I couldn't think of anything less appealing to the public at large—particularly in this health-conscious era—than a device that submerges food in a vat of boiling hot oil. Given Popeil's knack for tapping into the zeitgeist with his TV products, it seemed like an odd choice. But I also knew that whatever reservations I had would be put to rest instantly if I gave Ron sixty seconds to explain.

"There are more people who fry food than don't fry food," he started when I broached the subject. "And when you get out of this country the word *more* takes on new meaning, because if you go to China, South America, Mexico—that's all they do! Fry food! That's it! Don't you know that there are two million people who fry whole turkeys in this country?"

After explaining to me how much healthier it was to fry food rather than sauté it, he turned to what he described as the "giant problem" with the industry. As with most of Ron's products—and most of the products marketed on television in general—there always needs to be a problem that requires a fix.

"I should show you tapes of these kitchens blowing up," he starts, reminding me of those perennial Thanksgiving local news stories when people burn down their homes because they tried to deep fry a whole turkey. Ron's pitch, of course, is that his device will allow you to drop a sixteen-pound bird into a boiling vat of oil without giving it a second thought.

"No fires, no splashing! The food cannot go into the oil if the lid is not on," he says, starting to gesticulate wildly. "That's why it won't do tempura! Because you've got to drop those things in hot oil. Splash! You can't do that with my machine. My deep fryer does a sixteen-pound turkey. The others don't do that. I took a one-third frozen turkey and dropped it in my machine. Nothing. Fifty percent frozen? Nothing. One hundred percent frozen? Nothing!"

It was beginning to sound a lot like the basis for a pitch he might use one day in front of a TV camera and studio audience. Sure enough, he immediately turns the table and starts to ask me questions, which, as anyone who has been subjected to a savvy sales pitch knows, is a surefire way to engender support. Engage the customer, as they say.

"Do you cook at all?" he asks.

I explain to him that I rarely cook, although I also point out that my disinterest in the culinary arts hardly stopped me from purchasing his Ronco Automatic Pasta Maker years ago. Ron stops his shtick for a moment to smile and thank me for my purchase. He knows full well that it's his sales routine that often hooks consumers, not the actual product on display. In his memoir, Popeil recounts a story about his cousin, who sold little gizmos on the boardwalk in Atlantic City in the '50s. One day, his cousin noticed that a man was buying every single item he demonstrated in front of the crowds. When he took a break a few hours later, he noticed the man dropping two large shopping bags full of his newly purchased merchandise in a garbage can. He couldn't resist the sales pitch.

"What kind of food do you like?" Ron continues, perfectly aware that you don't need to know how to cook to be a potential customer. I tell him I like french fries.

"My machine will do four and a half pounds of french fries in one shot. Four and a half pounds! So it does a lot of food—and it does it safely. And it's small enough to fit in your kitchen cabinet. If you have to store it away in a cabinet or in your garage every time you use it, you wouldn't use it. It's got to be handy! And it has to be easy to clean! It's really the greatest fryer that's ever been invented," he adds.

As he punctuates the air with his finger for emphasis, I'm immediately reminded of my poor Ronco pasta maker. I probably used it only once or twice before putting it away in the cupboard, where it spent several years collecting dust alongside the Juiceman before my mother threw them both in the trash. It dawns on me that I never even got to sample the delicious-looking chocolate pasta that had led me to order it in the first place.

Ye Olde Days

The infomercial first entered the public consciousness in the mid-1980s, when cable deregulation eliminated the rules that had previously restricted the number and length of commercials that could be broadcast in an hour. When the rules were set aside in 1984, the floodgates opened. Combined with the explosion of cable—and the thousands of hours of airtime that were created as a result—paid programming was unleashed with a fury on an unsuspecting American public. But infomercials weren't necessarily all that new when they arrived on the scene. Lengthy "product demonstrations" had aired during the 1950s and early '60s, and the tactics used in infomercials had been around for generations.

Long before television or radio existed, charismatic salespeople would set up stalls at carnivals or state fairs, spread their wares out, and launch into an elaborate pitch. The demonstrations first became popular in Europe (England in particular) in the nineteenth century and soon migrated to the States. (Of course, the pitch goes back further than that: there were probably Neanderthal salesmen putting on shows to demonstrate the latest and greatest loincloth.)

The early practitioners—known as pitchmen, grafters, snake oil salesmen, or medicine men (although there were occasionally women who performed as well)—would put on a dramatic show to get a crowd to gather round as they offered up remedies for various common ailments. Throughout the nineteenth century, colorful spectacles took place in small towns all over America as men like John "Doc" Healy and Charles "Texas Charlie" Bigelow, the founders of the Kickapoo Indian Medicine Company, toured the country, promising cures for everything from consumption to "female weakness" to everyday aches and pains. Most of the products were high in alcohol, which explains why so many people seemed to feel better after a generous swig. And deceit was often part and parcel of the pitch. In Mark Twain's *Huckleberry Finn,* the "doctor" is assisted by a shill in the crowd who swears that the potion has cured him of his ills. Circus-like fanfare was often used to attract an audience, as were elaborate stunts featuring giant hookworms in glass bottles and rattlesnakes that were strangled and used to produce an elixir, which was then sold to the crowd. (That's where the term *snake oil* comes from.) The Pure Food and Drug Act of 1906 helped curb some of these practices, but the demonstrations continued well into the twentieth century and, perhaps not surprisingly, alcohol-infused tonics enjoyed a revival during Prohibition.

The first radio "infomercials" came along in the 1920s. One of the earliest was produced by a quack named John R. Brinkley, who hawked a remedy for male impotence that involved surgically implanting goat testicles into the scrotums of his "patients." Brinkley first started promoting the procedure with newspaper ads; in 1923 he started broadcasting on KFKB, the first radio station established in Kansas, advertising his barbaric treatment and mixing in fundamentalist religious teachings and the occasional bedtime story for children. For more squeamish men, Brinkley offered Formula 1020, a mysterious blue liquid that could be taken orally. (It later turned out to be colored water.)

After the state of Kansas revoked Brinkley's medical license in 1930 (and after he ran an ill-fated campaign for governor as a write-in candidate), Brinkley settled in Del Rio, Mexico, in 1932, where he set up a powerful radio transmitter and beamed his messages into the United States. Brinkley operated a thriving practice during the half decade he spent south of the border: by one estimate, he collected a total of $12 million from his patients—an astounding sum for the time—before ultimately returning to the States to revive his practice in Arkansas. Brinkley's career ultimately ended in disgrace, however. A series of lawsuits left him bankrupt before his death in 1942.

While unorthodox medicinal remedies earned the ire of the authorities, selling legitimate products and services on the radio wasn't nearly as controversial. The first radio commercial debuted in 1922 for an apartment complex in the borough of Queens, in New York City; by modern standards, though, it was really an infomercial: the show was ten minutes in length and was structured as an "informational program" with the name of the advertiser, Queensboro Corporation, mentioned only once. Radio would quickly become a haven for product pitches, but in-person demonstrations thrived throughout the early part of the twentieth century at county fairs, on the boardwalks of the eastern seaboard, and in the market districts of big cities like Chicago. Pitchmen were especially popular during the Depression, when frugal Americans proved particularly receptive to the notion that a simple, inexpensive gadget such as a vegetable slicer had the power to make their lives simple and worry-free.

It was from this milieu that Ron Popeil emerged; his ties to pitching date back two generations. Nathan "Nat" Morris, Ron's great-uncle, started his sales career on the boardwalk of Asbury Park, New Jersey, and became enormously successful pitching kitchen products at county fairs up and down the East Coast, ultimately establishing a factory in New Jersey to manufacture the gizmos himself. Nat later inducted his sons into the business, Lester and Arnold "the Knife" Morris, who gained his nickname for his extraordinary prowess demonstrating knives. (Nat also gave a teenage Ed McMahon, of Publishing Clearinghouse and *The Tonight Show* fame, his first job, demonstrating the Morris Metric Slicer on the Atlantic City boardwalk.) One of the most formidable families operating in the business at the time, the Morrises recruited a handful of cousins to join the pitch business over the years.

Ron's father, Samuel Popeil (or S. J.), got into the business by accident: at seventeen, he filled in for one of his uncles, Irving Rosenbloom, when he was out sick, stepping in for him at a demonstration at Macy's. S. J.'s first encounter with the business wasn't terribly successful (apparently he sliced open his finger during the presentation), but he soon got the hang of it, and like other members of the clan, he started touring county fairs and working the Jersey boardwalks during the 1930s.

It was hardly a given, though, that Ron would follow in his father's footsteps. By all accounts, he had a miserable childhood. His parents divorced when he was young, and S. J., who had a reputation as a gruff, cold man, sent Ron and his brother, Jerry, to live at a state-run boarding school in upstate New York. Their grandparents eventually came to retrieve the two boys and took them to Miami to raise them. But life with his grandparents wasn't much of an improvement. A onetime garment industry worker, Isadore Popeil was physically abusive and emotionally distant. Ron claims neither he nor his brother ever had a birthday party while growing up.

Ron reconnected with his father at the age of thirteen, when his grandfather relocated the family to Chicago so he could help out S. J. with the manufacturing business he'd founded several years earlier. After learning the ins and outs of the business from Nat Morris, S. J. had moved to the Windy City with his brother, Raymond, to take advantage of the fertile new territory of the Midwest, initially distributing products on behalf of the Morrises and later starting up a manufacturing business of his own, Popeil Brothers. (His decision to manufacture items that were very similar to the ones the Morrises produced led to years of tension between the Popeils and the Morrises, as well as a very public lawsuit in 1958.)

S. J. plowed ahead with his business. After producing a series of inexpensive kitchen gadgets like shredders, juicers, and pan scrapers, Popeil Brothers entered the exciting world of plastic in the 1950s with O-Matics. There was the Chop-O-Matic, a food processor, which debuted in 1956. Then came the Dial-O-Matic two years later, which featured a blade guard to prevent people from accidentally cutting themselves. Next was the Veg-O-Matic, which proved to be the biggest success of S. J.'s career. Touted in ads as "the most revolutionary kitchen appliance of the century," the device promised it could create 700 french fries in a minute.

S. J.'s gadgets were hardly high tech, but they earned attention for their sleek designs. Timothy Samuelson, the former curator of architecture and design at the Chicago Historical Society and now the cultural historian for the city of Chicago, is the owner of one of the largest collections of Popeil products from the era. Samuelson published a book in 2002 to celebrate the Popeil design aesthetic and declared the items from the O-Matic line as "some of the classic contemporary designs of the times."

S. J.'s focus on form and function would later be passed on to his equally entrepreneurial son. But like every other member of the Morris–Popeil clan, Ron got his start learning the art of the pitch. Ron was sixteen when he first started heading down to Chicago's raucous Maxwell Street, where vendors set up tables elbow to elbow, each with a different item on display. Purchasing his father's slicers and dicers at wholesale prices (which guaranteed his father a profit), he showed up at the crack of dawn with a portable microphone, folding table, and mound of vegetables that would get sliced to pieces by the end of the day. Clearly, he'd inherited the family's gift of gab: not long after starting out, he was raking in $500 a day, an impressive sum considering many of the products retailed for only a dollar or two. He soon moved to the Woolworth's at State and Washington streets, then the largest location in the chain of department stores.

It was at the five-and-dime that Ron really honed his pitch, which, if you've ever seen it in person—and by the right pitchman—is indeed performance art. It's scripted, but loosely so, and a good pitchman knows how to build momentum and excitement until it's time for the all-important "turn," the moment when it's time to ask for the money. It also happens to be extremely hard work. A pitchman may spend twelve hours or more repeating the same spiel again and again, with slight variations, from morning till night.

Ron's tactics weren't new—the tricks has been around for years—and had been performed by his father, great-uncle, and cousins on the boardwalks of Atlantic City. But Ron was especially gifted. All the time-tested strategies were on display: he offered bonuses or freebies as incentives, and heightened tensions by warning people that he only had a certain number of units on hand ("Supplies are limited!"). He assigned numbers to his customers—"You're number eight, you're number nine," and so on—which gave the impression that you had to get on line to take advantage of the great deal he was offering up. He employed the classic countdown technique, where he systematically lowered the price as he neared the end of the pitch. And when he was at the very end and started accepting cash, he avoided selling the item to the last batch of eager customers, instead launching into a fresh pitch. To get new people to come over to watch a demonstration, it requires that other people be standing in rapt attention. "Wait, there's something else I'd like to show you before you take this home with you," he might say to hold on to a small crowd as he started the pitch all over again. He also paid careful attention to the environment around him. When he pitched at county fairs on the weekends or on vacations, he often located his booth near the women's restrooms, which guaranteed that there would be a group of women lingering by his booth full of kitchenware at all times. Popeil's gift for gab soon had him outearning the manager of the Woolworth's store (or so he says), and he earned a rep as such a charismatic salesman that secretaries from nearby office buildings would come to the store during their lunch breaks to watch the dashing, young Popeil dazzle the crowds.

Ron wasn't the only bright talent on the circuit at the time. A wonderful documentary on the early origins of the business, 1999's *Pitch People* by Stanley Jacobs, features interviews with a handful of legendary pitchmen from the era, many of whom have since passed away. There was Chet Nairne, who got his start pitching medicinal remedies; Harry Mathison, who was one of London's most famous street salesmen in the post–WWII era before coming to the United States; and Wally Nash, who worked the fairs of England in the '50s and '60s before moving to the States. (Amusingly, Nash tried to use his pitching abilities to win elected office in 2004, campaigning for Washington State's House of Representatives. He lost.)

Of course, television would change everything for the pitch business. Although direct response ads had been used on the radio for years, you couldn't very well demonstrate a kitchen appliance with audio alone. And television became such an exciting new phenomenon in the homes of Americans in the 1950s that combined with the pitches of skillful salesmen, the effect was mesmerizing. "At some magical point in the 1950s, television ceased to be just an odd-looking gizmo—a radio running a picture-track—and entered the bloodstream. It became part of our nervous system. It is who we are. It is what we do," writes James Twitchell, a professor at the University of Florida and the author of *Lead Us Into Temptation*. Families that eagerly gathered around the tube for the next installment of their favorite show could now get as equally excited about a new gizmo spinning slowly on a turntable.

For pitchmen, the advantages of the medium were pretty obvious: a pitch could be recorded once, edited, and then repeated endlessly on TV stations all over the country. Instead of spending sixteen hours cajoling customers to fork over their cash one by one, people like Ron Popeil could sit back and wait for the money to roll in.

Once again, though, Ron was not the first—or even the first member of his family—to use TV to his advantage. It was Ron's uncle, Arnold Morris, who was responsible for the very first half-hour infomercial, although at the time they were known as "product demonstrations." They weren't that different from the infomercials that air today: they typically featured half-hour segments in which a pitchman sliced and diced vegetables with some kitchen device.

Morris's first program advertised a glass knife called Arnold's Kitchen Gourmet. It was a product that played to his strong suit: Morris's knife demonstrations on boardwalks and at county fairs were legendary. They'd play out over the course of twenty minutes or more as he sliced vegetables, fruits, and loaves of bread before concluding, naturally, with a hammer, shoe, cinder block, or some other item that the knife wasn't expected to cut, which demonstrated to would-be customers that the knives were virtually indestructible:

> *Watch this! Here's a steel hammer. Now I'm going to cut a notch out of that hammer right now! This could be a chicken bone. It could be a ham bone. Frozen foods. What would happen if your child took your best knife and started sawing down a cherry tree with it? This is steel against steel! Take a look at this! Something has to give. You see those filings over here? Now, there's only one way to find out if that knife is still razor sharp. Take a look. You go back to the same tomato. Look at this! Today, tonight, tomorrow, next week, next year, for the rest of your life, you never—ever!—have to sharpen this knife.*

The knife set was a hit when it debuted on television, and Arnold and his brother, Lester, followed up with a slew of successful products over the years like the Roto-Broil and, much later, the Crazy Straw. But plenty of other now legendary direct response gurus got their start with television product demonstrations, including Alvin "Al" Eicoff and Lester Wunderman, both of whom are often described as the fathers of the direct response industry.

The Montana-born Eicoff learned about sales from his shopkeeper father before settling in Chicago in the 1940s and starting his career selling radio time. He soon turned to TV: one of his first TV spots was for an early food processor called Vita-Mix.

He later marketed products like rat poison, fly repellent, and his own iteration of that boardwalk favorite, the glass knife. Over the course of his career, Eicoff created hundreds of television spots as part of the firm he founded, A. Eicoff & Co., generally recruiting his television pitchmen from the boardwalks of Atlantic City or the street fairs of Chicago. "We figured if these people could sell five out of ten people in person, they could easily sell five hundred out of a thousand if broadcast in front of a mass audience," he once said.

One of Eicoff's early discoveries was that his products tended to perform better when they were marketed late at night. Airtime was cheaper, too, but Eicoff also recognized that viewers' defenses started to topple as they grew sleepy. This was a new discovery: live pitchmen usually performed during daylight hours and never had much of a chance to try out their routines at one o'clock in the morning. "People are less resistant at that hour," Eicoff later remarked. "If they are tired, their subconscious will accept without their consciousness fighting it." Eicoff also realized early on that boredom played a critical role in how well his spots performed. When he placed sixty-second commercials during a hit show, the responses were unimpressive. When the programming was lousy, many more people purchased products. Eicoff had stumbled across a curious discovery: more desirable airtime wasn't necessarily better when it came to selling goods on TV.

Ron's first appearance on television came in 1956, when the Grant Company selected the Popeil Brothers' Chop-O-Matic for a TV promotion they planned to run. S. J. asked Ron, who was twenty-one at the time, to host the show. Wearing a tie and a white lab coat, he pitched the Chop-O-Matic for $3.98:

Everyone likes cole slaw—everyone, that is, except
Mother. The reason she doesn't like it is because she's

*the one who's got to make it on that old grater—and
oh, the scrapes on her poor knuckles. Well, here's where
your Chop-O-Matic comes to the rescue. Place that cab-
bage under the container and start tapping. You know,
why even the youngsters will be glad to help if you let
them. And just look at how fine this cole slaw is made!*

Ron's debut was just four minutes long—not a half-hour
product demonstration—but in those days there was no restric-
tion on the length of TV ads. This was the '50s, after all, when
advertisers had their fingers in every aspect of television programming. Ad agencies hired writers and wrote the scripts, and
almost every TV show during the era was linked to a sponsor.
These were the days of Geritol's *Twenty-One, The Colgate Comedy
Hour,* and the *Texaco Star Theater.*

Things changed in the aftermath of the quiz scandals, which
focused attention on the interference of advertisers in broadcasting.
Vance Packard's 1957 exposé, *The Hidden Persuaders,* heightened the
drama, identifying TV as the province of dangerous corporations
that used psychological techniques and subliminal tactics to manipulate the masses. The groundswell culminated in 1961, when
Newton Minow, the new chair of the Federal Communications
Commission (FCC), delivered his famous "Wasteland" speech,
which railed against television for excessive violence and the undue
influence of advertisers, solemnly warning that "when television is
bad, nothing is worse." (His distaste for television did earn him one
notable distinction: Sherwood Schwartz, the creator of *Gilligan's
Island,* named the show's ill-fated ship the SS *Minnow* in his honor.)
By 1963 the FCC had forced the networks to adopt a cap on the
number of minutes devoted to commercials in a given hour, as well
as a two-minute limit on any single commercial. The era of lengthy
product demonstrations came to an end.

People like Eicoff and the Popeils didn't disappear, of course. They simply turned to "short-form" spots in the 1960s and '70s, which lasted up to two minutes, as opposed to lengthier product demonstrations or, beginning in the '80s, "long-form" infomercials, which occupied a half hour. Eventually, what both short-form spots and long-form infomercials shared in common was a "call to action," a solicitation that the viewer take action and place an order that very instant. Naturally, in those days, there were no 800 numbers to call. Viewers were expected to head down to a participating department store to pick up the item or send in a check or money order.

Both Ron and his father, S. J., kept busy during the days of short-form spots. They did not, however, work together. In 1964 Ron went out on his own, teaming up with Mel Korey, a friend from his brief stint at the University of Illinois. They launched their first product the same year, the Ronco Spray Gun, which promised to clean your car, wash your windows, and water your lawn. The high-powered hose came with little chemical tablets you'd insert between the hose and nozzle, depending on whether you were, say, hosing down your car or applying fertilizer to your lawn. (The tablets weren't accidental: Ron and Mel realized they would force customers to keep coming back to buy more of them.)

The duo sold more than a million Spray Guns before moving on to other products, such as a brand of nylon stockings called London Aire, which were, in fact, manufactured in North Carolina. S. J.'s Popeil Brothers debuted products like the now-legendary Pocket Fisherman, although to complicate matters, during his early career Ron not only introduced his own products but also acted as a distributor of his father's items, which meant that some of the commercials for S. J.'s products—such as several of the spots for the Pocket Fisherman—featured Ron's voice.

One of the factors that worked in Ron's favor was that he was never known as the sort of pitchman who needed a long windup. Some live demonstrators took a good deal of time going through a presentation, showing feature after feature, all the while creating a sense of anticipation before the all-important "turn." Ron's pitches were succinct. He'd learned to move through his act quickly when he worked at Woolworth's since people typically rushed through the store during their lunch breaks. This ability worked in his favor during the short-form era, and although his ads weren't very glamorous and didn't boast high production values, they earned plenty of attention (and a measure of annoyance) thanks to their in-your-face salesiness.

Not that it was all that hard to make a buck in the early days. Americans weren't the savvy consumers they are today, nor were they bombarded with commercial messages everywhere they turned. "I could have sold empty boxes and made a fortune," Popeil once said. In 1969, buoyed by its success, Ronco went public, with Korey and Popeil walking off with $2.5 million apiece. S. J.'s Popeil Brothers followed suit a few years later. Both father and son enjoyed the fruits of their success. S. J. was ferried around town in a chauffeur-driven Cadillac and lived in a fancy high-rise apartment with a view of Lake Michigan. Ron bought a sailboat and a Rolls-Royce, dined daily at Chicago's fanciest eateries, and moved the company's offices to the Playboy building on tony North Michigan Avenue.

Plenty of others earned their stripes during the 1970s, too, people like Arthur Schiff, who would go on to become one of the most famous direct response gurus of the era. During his thirty-year-career, Schiff created an estimated 1,800 direct response campaigns, popularizing phrases like "Act now and you'll also receive . . . " and "Now, how much would you pay?" (Who in fact originally coined many of these phrases has been up for debate for years, particularly since—like the products themselves—pitchmen have long had a tendency to "borrow" successful lines from others in the business. Schiff, for example, is often given credit for coming up with the ever-popular "But wait, there's more!" but Popeil has been credited with inventing it, and still many others have said it came long before both men arrived on the scene.)

Schiff's greatest creation, though, was his series of ads for the Ginsu knife. In the 1970s, he was a copywriter for an ad agency in Providence, Rhode Island, when he teamed up with Ed Valenti and Barry Becher to promote products via direct response. Their first collaboration resulted in the Miracle Painter, which was touted as a drip-free brush. (To convey the point, Schiff's ad featured a man dressed in a tuxedo painting his ceiling.) The Ginsu came along in 1978, although that wasn't the name of the knife when they first came upon the product. It was called the Quikut and manufactured in Fremont, Ohio. No, there was nothing remotely Japanese about the knife. Nor was the knife revolutionary—doubled-edged blades had been around for years. But the marketing gimmick made it one of the most recognizable brands of the era.

Schiff says he came up with the Ginsu concept while he was sleep. "And then it happened!" Schiff later recalled in a promotional piece for his marketing firm. "I bolted out of bed at three o'clock in the morning and yelled, 'Eureka! I've got it. Ginsu!' I wrote the bizarre word down on a piece of paper and went back to sleep. When I got up again four hours later, the paper was still there, and that strange word was still on it." Of course, the word sounded Japanese, and viewers couldn't help but make a connection to samurai swords or even the Benihana steakhouse, which had taken off around the same time. Schiff and his partners hired a Japanese exchange student as the commercial's "chef," and the three created one of the most famous ads of the twentieth century, which opened with a hand karate chopping a wooden board. "In Japan," the commercial went, "the hand can be used like a knife. But this method doesn't work with a tomato," the narrator said, as a hand squashed a tomato. The commercial not only made Ginsu one of the most successful direct response ads of the decade, it also led to parodies on programs like *The Tonight Show* and *Saturday Night Live*.

Ron Popeil was on a blitz himself throughout the '70s and early '80s, introducing countless new products via short-form spots that he generally narrated himself. There was the Inside-the-Shell Electric Egg Scrambler, which inserted a small needle into the egg and, yes, scrambled the egg before you cracked it open. He released a slew of battery-powered devices, including Power Scissors, Garden Trimmer, and Miracle Broom, although since he didn't care much for the word *battery,* he called them "cordless electric," which sounded much more glamorous. There were a handful of compilation albums, like *Disco Super Hits,* and a collection of crafts-oriented products, like the Ronco Bottle and Jar Cutter. Ronco Ornamental Ice fulfilled that desperate need that so many Americans had at the time: to create little ice sculptures using a set of custom molds. A bit more useful was his Tidie Drier, a compact desktop dryer that was pitched to women to dry their bras and underwear so they wouldn't have to do a trek to the Laundromat. Then there was one of his most famous products from the day, Mr. Microphone, which served no useful purpose except for allowing kids the enormous thrill of hearing themselves on the radio. (When you tuned your radio to a specific frequency, you could hear yourself when you sang into the microphone.) Like most of Ron's products, he didn't invent the technology. He saw a crummier version of it at a toy store before hiring an engineer to come up with something that was more appealing. Thanks to his now-iconic commercial—which featured the line "Hey, good lookin', I'll be back to pick you up later!"—he ended up selling a million units before the market was saturated with knockoffs and he had moved on to greener pastures.

By the late '70s, change was clearly afoot in the direct response industry. Up until then, marketers generally had to rely on the U.S. Postal Service to collect checks or money orders from their customers, a process that had its obvious drawbacks: people sent cash in the mail, checks would bounce, and marketers needed a small army of people to open envelopes. The advent of the 800 number, which was introduced by AT&T in consultation with Al Eicoff, changed that. First developed in the late '60s, the 800 number didn't come into wide use until nearly a decade later, but its benefits were substantial: viewers could pick up the phone and order products directly. (You couldn't get a vanity number at the time: it wasn't until telephone deregulation in the early '80s that marketers could pick their numbers to create easy-to-remember words.) Thanks to the growing proliferation of credit cards, you could now pay for a product on the phone, too.

Ron's great ride, however, ended in 1984. After a series of products failed to drum up sales and after taking on millions in debt to fund the expansion of his business, Ronco was forced to file for bankruptcy. It was a stinging defeat. But Ron managed to walk away from the carnage unscathed and ever the cunning businessman, he later purchased Ronco's inventory from the company's creditors using his own money and he returned to the demonstration circuit, where he sold it all off at a profit. By the late 1980s, he'd settled into (temporary) retirement, retreating to Las Vegas, where he puttered around the Mirage Hotel for a couple of years, having been named to the board of the company by his pal Steve Wynn.

The Modern Era

Ironically, it was right around the time that Ron disappeared from the scene that the direct response industry was revived in a big way. In 1984 the cable industry was deregulated, paving the way for the thirty-minute infomercial to return with full force.

Although industry lore has it that the first infomercial was a ninety-minute "rally" for Herbalife on the USA Network in the fall of 1984, the truth is infomercials had been airing for a couple of years before cable deregulation. Soon after President Ronald Reagan was elected, he nominated a former broadcast industry lawyer named Mark S. Fowler to serve as chairman of the FCC. It was clear from the outset that Fowler planned to adopt a more lenient approach to the industry. He was, after all, a man who once referred to TV as nothing more than "a toaster with pictures," a clear indication he didn't view television as a sacred "public trust" that had to be vigorously guarded by the government. In 1981 Fowler deregulated the radio industry, and although his efforts to do the same with broadcast television didn't come for another three years, Fowler was noticeably lax about the programs that emerged that treaded the line, such as children's shows *GI Joe, He-Man,* and *Thundarr the Barbarian.* These were produced in many cases by the toy manufacturers themselves; they presented a win–win for both the companies interested in boosting sales of their games and action figures as well as broadcasters, who were handed popular programming that they didn't, in many cases, have to create themselves.

Given what seemed to be significant leeway on the part of the FCC, it wasn't long before people came along to push the envelope even further. One early trailblazer was Frank Cannella, a media buyer at Al Eicoff's ad agency, who had been buying big blocks of time from the networks to divide into 60-

and 120-second commercials for the agency's clients. Cannella simply started bundling the time together to create half-hour spots. If *GI Joe* got a half-hour program to promote its line of action figures, the reasoning went, why couldn't you air a program that promoted a balding remedy? And if televangelists like Oral Roberts were permitted to purchase half-hour blocks of time to solicit donations to their churches, why couldn't you purchase the same block of time to sign up attendees to a real estate seminar?

In 1982, despite the fact the FCC had yet to officially give the green light, Cannella went ahead and started airing half-hour spots for Bob Murphy, who pitched a balding formula called New Generation. An unemployed motel manager, Murphy was living at home with his mother at the time, reportedly mixing up his formula in his mom's kitchen sink. Set up as a talk show, the infomercial looked a lot like normal television programming and aired on both local stations and cable networks. The FCC didn't blink.

It was on June 28, 1984, that Fowler officially repealed the rule that prevented broadcasters from scheduling more than sixteen minutes of commercials in an hour. This "removes an unnecessary layer of Government involvement in the television program decisions of the American people," Fowler summed up in an official statement. Network executives, who had lobbied hard for the change, were thrilled: they now had the right to sell airtime to the highest bidder. Critics were decidedly less enthusiastic, arguing that the decision would lead to a lowering of standards on TV.

With the floodgates wide open, a series of infomercials soon flooded the air. Many of the early entrants were men pitching real estate courses, people who had previously been required to travel from city to city delivering seminars. Now they could

film an infomercial and broadcast it nationwide. In the fall of
1984, in addition to the Herbalife infomercial, a producer named
Nancy Marcum introduced audiences to real estate impresario
Paul Simon. Ed Beckley, who had been a mentor to Simon, followed soon after with a real estate course called "The Millionaire Maker."

It was under the tutelage of Beckley that a handful of now-
industry titans got their start, including Tim Hawthorne, who
now runs one of the largest infomercial production companies,
Hawthorne Direct Inc., and Katie Williams, who runs Williams
Worldwide Inc., a major media buying agency. (Following the
success of New Generation, Cannella also teamed up with Beckley.) Both Beckley and Simon generated smash hits when they
took to the airwaves; according to Hawthorne, Beckley generated $60 million in sales in fifteen months. Simon sold so many
packages that the man charged with duplicating his audiotapes,
Bill Guthy, who would go on to found infomercial powerhouse
Guthy-Renker, could hardly keep up.

Their only mistake—and one made by countless others during
the 1980s—was linking up with the wrong set of clients during
the nascent days of the industry. Beckley would later turn out to
be one of the industry's first scam artists. A couple of years after
his first appearance on the air, the Iowa attorney general's office
conducted an investigation and sued Beckley for $2.8 million
on behalf of some eight thousand customers who had paid $295
apiece for home-study investment programs. Beckley agreed to
a settlement, but instead of returning the money, he filed for
bankruptcy and moved out of state. When he returned to the
scene several years later, he was arrested on a series of federal
charges, including mail fraud, and ended up spending fifteen
months in prison. Murphy, too, ran afoul of the authorities. In
1988 the Federal Trade Commission (FTC) filed suit in U.S.

District Court in Reno, Nevada, charging Murphy with false advertising. The court later required Murphy to hand over $2 million and barred him from marketing balding remedies in the future. (The judgment was reduced to $1.875 million on appeal.) The "magic" potion in his bottles? It turned out to be polysorbate 60, which, among hundreds of other uses, is what keeps a three-year-old Twinkie from going stale.

That many of the early promoters turned out to be crooks isn't all that surprising. After all, it was a new medium without any proven commercial success; it certainly wasn't going to be a big brand like Coke or Ford that was going to be the format's guinea pig. Besides, it wasn't entirely clear what was and wasn't permissible on television. Even the networks themselves had difficulty making sense of the emerging market. In the early days, many of Nancy Marcum's media buys were classified as religious programming because there was no other category to place it in. Yet one of the unfortunate by-products was that it cast suspicion on the industry right from the start. It would take a few more years of similar scandals before a group of industry executives would form a trade group to try to shape up the industry.

It wasn't long after the real estate pitchmen hit the air that physical products followed fast and furious. The legendary British pitchman Wally Nash turned up on an infomercial for The Great Wok of China in 1985. Marcum soon introduced the world to Mike Levey, who attained late-night TV fame as the "Sweater Man" for his colorful duds. It was Levey who, along with the British pitchman John Parkin, famously set a Rolls-Royce on fire to demonstrate the effectiveness of Auri car polish, an act that lives on—in multiple languages—on YouTube.

The late 1980s and early '90s proved to be the industry's golden age, albeit in financial (and perhaps pop culture) terms, not necessarily in terms of product quality. Within two years, a

$2 billion-a-year business had materialized. It was also during the 1980s that home shopping networks pervaded the airwaves, making cubic zirconia a household name. Not every infomercial product was a hit, of course, but success rates were extraordinarily high. For every show that failed, a show succeeded. (These days one in fifty might be a hit.) Plus, the costs were incredibly low. The television networks hadn't really figured out just how much the time was worth, which meant that people like Frank Cannella could buy twelve hours of time on the Financial News Network (the precursor to CNBC) for $500, and Tim Hawthorne could pick up an hour on the Discovery Channel for $50.

With barriers so low, marketers could afford to try anything. Since they didn't have a good idea of what would work or not, some of the silliest, craziest products made their way to TV during the late '80s. A small vacuum cleaner–like apparatus that you could use to cut your own hair? Bring it on. A Vietnamese immigrant who barely spoke English selling a get-rich-quick program? Why not? Because it wasn't entirely clear just how far infomercials could go in blurring the line between commercial and regular programming, several producers quickly tested the limits. In the late '80s, a longtime direct response entrepreneur named Joe Sugarman filmed an infomercial for BluBlocker sunglasses, which he billed as an "independent consumer news program conducting an objective investigation into sunglasses." I'll leave it to you to guess which brand of sunglasses came out on top.

Much like Beckley and Murphy before him, Sugarman ran afoul of the FTC and paid a fine to settle the case. The rising tide of shady infomercials eventually prompted Congress to launch an investigation in 1990. To stanch the criticism and avoid potential government regulation, a group of nine direct response pros—including Greg Renker, Tim Hawthorne, Katie Williams, and industry attorney Jeff Knowles—came together to form the National Infomercial Marketing Association and vowed to tame the Wild West mentality that pervaded the industry. (The group later changed its name to the Electronic Retailing Association, ERA.) Some of the most outlandish programs faded by the early '90s. But plenty of dreck continued to make it to late night, too.

It would be nearly a decade before Popeil would once again become a leader in the industry he helped create. There was nothing that forced him to make a comeback; he wasn't exactly hurting for cash. His return, I imagine, had a good deal to do with the two sides of his personality. He's always been passionate about coming up with new gizmos, and probably he'll be tinkering with things in his garage until the day he dies; but he's also the kind of person who can recall the day he ponied up for his first Rolex watch. It's easy to see how Popeil must have felt left out when, just a few years after he exited the scene, infomercial millions started to fall from the sky.

Popeil plunged back into the business in 1989, when he negotiated a deal with Fingerhut to sell it 20,000 Ronco Electric Food Dehydrators. The mail-order company planned to offer them on a home shopping channel; when they changed their plans, Popeil decided to shoot an infomercial and promote the Dehydrator himself. It was the beginning of the second act, and unlike the 1970s, he had a half hour to work with. Ron deployed all the tactics he'd used on the live pitch circuit years earlier. He used a dramatic countdown at the end of the program, systematically lowering the price. He threw in giveaway after giveaway. He suggested that he would only offer the Dehydrator at such a reasonable price point to people who promised to "tell a friend" about the "incredible offer"—a classic tactic designed to make the audience feel indebted to him for his act of generosity, which, naturally, they could reciprocate by making a purchase.

The Dehydrator was a hit; he sold 1.3 million of them in the first three years, thanks to infomercials and regular appearances on QVC. He followed up with one of the most memorable products of the early '90s, GLH Formula No. 9. Popeil's pitch for spray-on hair generated a torrent of attention for its sheer ridiculousness, but few could turn away from the infomercial, which featured Popeil spraying the heads of countless bald men in one of the nine colors Ronco offered.

Sitting in his office, I mentioned to Ron that I'd purchased the product for kicks a few months earlier, spraying it on a half dozen friends to see how it looked. I'd guessed it was like spray paint and had trouble grasping how it managed to look so natural on the show. What I learned (and as Ron had explained on the infomercial) was that it's a slightly foamy substance that mimics the fuzz of hair. But the product had some limitations, too. I noticed that when you sprayed it on someone's scalp and then touched his head, your hands turned brown. It was clear that if someone wearing it started to sweat or, say, got caught in the rain, he'd end up in a colored puddle.

"You put too much on," Ron said when I explained the problem.

"Is that what I did?"

"You put too much on, that's the problem. Now, let's talk about hot days. How many super-hot days do we have in a year?"

It seemed like Ron had been down this path before.

"Let's segment it because you don't want to judge the product based on a thirty-day period out of twelve months in a year. First, forget about gyms—they're all air-conditioned. That's not the problem. And I've used it on people with very serious, big, gigantic bald spots. There was that one guy who was in the infomercial, and he was almost totally bald. And I just sprayed the hell out of him, and he looked great in the end and he was fuckin' amazed! Sure, if it was one of those thirty days when you have temperatures of 100 degrees and no air conditioning, you might see a little coming down. But the average person? I could spray anyone's head now, and they'd have no problem whatsoever. That's the problem, putting too much on. Put too much ketchup on a piece of meat, it'll slide off your plate."

Following hot on the heels of GLH (which, in case you're wondering, isn't the acronym for some chemical formula; it stands for "Great Looking Hair"), Popeil unveiled the Ronco Automatic Pasta Maker. His Showtime Rotisserie followed in 1998. Unlike in his early years when he rarely focused on designing products and preferred to take existing items and repackage them, Popeil paid a good deal of attention to the design of the pasta maker and rotisserie oven. Unlike his father, who produced the items at his own factory, he didn't manufacture them himself, but he did pay much more attention to aesthetics. Not only did he want his products to work, but he also wanted to *show* people how they worked. Using the device, Ron argued, had to provide some sort of thrill, which also served to promote the product when it was demonstrated on TV. I knew this from the pasta maker infomercial—clip after clip of the pasta flour churning in the mixer, accompanied by oohs and aahs from the audience for added effect, was part of what made the show so entertaining.

Over the years, Ron has claimed that he was inspired to create the Showtime after seeing people at the grocery store lining up to buy rotisserie chicken. It wasn't quite as novel as he made it out to be. As both Stan Jacobs and Timothy Samuelson point out, the Showtime bore a strong resemblance to Nat Morris's

Roto-Broil in the 1950s. Ron improved on the design by adding new features and making it much more compact. Then there was his extraordinary pitch, which made it irresistible. The infomercial featured shot after shot of juicy hunks of meat moving in slow motion and Popeil's insistent reminder that you could "set it and forget it," which meant it's on a timer, not that you should leave your house and go to the beach while a ten-pound pork loin is sizzling away in your kitchen. His countdown in the final seconds of the show was sales magic:

> *You know you're not going to have to spend $400 for it.*
> *Not $375 or $350.*
> *Not $325 or even $300.*
> *Not $275 or $250.*
> *Not $225 or $200 like you may all be thinking.*
> *Not $190.*
> *Or $180.*
> *All you send for this fabulous machine—an over $400 value—all you send is four, easy monthly payments of $39.95.*

It was an extraordinary pitch, which explains why Ronco has since sold so many of them. But as I sat with him, I had to wonder if he'd ever get to perform his shtick on television again. In 2005 he sold Ronco for $55 million and negotiated an arrangement whereby the company had the right to acquire the fryer for $3 million, plus a percentage of the profits. But in July 2007, with no new products in the marketplace, Ronco filed for bankruptcy protection. Making money with infomercials, it's clear, isn't as easy as it once was. Then again, people have counted him out before.

I press Ron for details about his latest creation.

"Will it be as big as the rotisserie? Absolutely not," Ron admits. "There is nothing that will be as big as the rotisserie. But it will still be big," he says as he takes me over to the video camera in the corner of the room to show me footage of the device in action.

Ron, it turns out, tapes hours of footage of himself cooking various foods using both his own machine and his competitors' devices. He tells me it's all part of the research process. Does the surface of the fryer reflect back at the camera on TV? (Bad.) Can you hear the sizzle of a frying turkey on tape? (Good.)

On the video, Ron is shirtless. His torso is covered by a green Ronco apron. It's clear the footage was filmed at night, and I can picture the restless Popeil whiling away the late-night hours in his massive Beverly Hills garage, frying frozen turkeys high above the streets of Los Angeles as he makes notes about what to change, fix, and improve, which he'll pass along to his product development team.

As he shows me the video, I broach whether I might get to see the top-secret prototype in person. Ron had warned me earlier in the conversation that the machine was under wraps, but my enthusiasm for kitchen appliances seems to have warmed him up, and we dart out to the garage. He points to the prototype in the corner. "Don't get too excited," he says. It's a fairly rudimentary affair, primarily, he says, because he hasn't settled on some of the outstanding design issues. I try my best not to look disappointed.

Moments later, Ron's wife, Robin, strolls over. A former model for Frederick's of Hollywood, she's nearly forty years Ron's junior. She's his fourth wife and the mother of their two young daughters. (He has another three daughters from his previous marriages.)

It's not the least bit surprising that Popeil's had a rather rocky personal life. After all, this is a man who, when asked about his greatest regret in life, alternates between not having invented Velcro and not having invented The Clapper. His single-minded pursuit of the latest gadget has never left much room for anything else.

An eventful romantic life seems to be a Popeil family tradition. In the 1970s, S. J.'s second wife, Eloise, was implicated in a plot to kill him. They divorced, and she went to prison for nearly two years. After she was released, S. J. took her back, and they remarried. Much like S. J., Ron, famously tough and tightfisted, has also had contentious relationships with his employees and business partners over the course of his career. More than a few people in the industry who praised him as a pioneer added that they'd never work with him again in their lives.

As the three of us walk out of the garage, I have my doubts that the public will ever get to see a green-aproned Ron demonstrate the turkey fryer in all its glory. But I also know that his talent lives on with the newer generation of pitch people. Although infomercials don't dominate like they used to, products don't sell themselves. In the end, the pitch is still the pitch. The demonstration may happen on the Web or on a cell phone, but someone's got to show you how the thing works. And someone's got to convince you to buy it. The street-pitchman-turned-millionaire-TV-entrepreneur lives on. Billy Mays, the rotund, bearded man who now hawks OrangeGlo, OxiClean, and Kaboom, spent fifteen years working state fairs and trade shows before he was discovered on the boardwalk of Atlantic City and migrated to TV. As Mays puts it, "If you can sell in Atlantic City, you can sell anywhere."

As I walk to my car, a giant truck pulls into the driveway, roughly the size of a moving van. "My avocado trees!" Ron exclaims as the man unloads several giant plants that will be meticulously replanted in Ron's garden, which has a dazzling view of the city of Los Angeles below.

"You should see what I do with those avocados when I'm in the kitchen," Ron says as I get into my car.

I have no doubt.

CHAPTER 2

Late-Night Carnival

As you undoubtedly know if you've spent any time watching TV over the past twenty-five years, just about everything imaginable has been sold on television since the mid-'80s. Some have been absurdly low-tech, such as Doggy Steps, a carpeted stepladder for owners of obese or arthritic dogs who need help climbing up to the sofa or bed. There's been the bizarre, like the colon cleanser marketed by a nutty Christian evangelist who somehow manages to equate intestinal health with following the biblical teachings of Jesus. There's been the downright scary, too: for years, various electrical muscle stimulation contraptions were pitched to the public, each promising that if you gently electrocuted yourself with a gizmo made in China for pennies, you'd see a six-pack suddenly materialize as you sat on your couch and gobbled down fried chicken. So where do all these products come from? Do any of them work? Is there anything real that gets sold on late-night television?

Most of the items you see on TV are not, in fact, all that original, at least in spirit. The categories that have worked since the dawn of time—health and beauty products, get-rich-quick products, various items for the kitchen—continue to dominate the airwaves. This isn't because infomercial makers (necessarily) lack creativity. As with the sales tactics that have barely changed over the years, the same tried-and-true categories continue to be successful: looking better, having more money, saving time. It is, very often, all about building a better mousetrap.

What all of these half-hour infomercials have in common, of course, is that they all offer some sort of cure. Late-night pitches aren't in the business of offering us dresses, trash cans, CD players, or cans of roach spray. They're in the business of presenting serious problems—and providing us with quick, easy, painless solutions. You have acne? Well, have we got just the product for you! Not only will it clear up your skin, it'll restore your confidence and allow you to venture into the world carefree. As you watch the infomercial unfold, you'll see a girl transformed from an ugly duckling into a beautiful princess. Once huddled under her sheets in horror, she now appears totally at ease with her friends. It's as if the product had just offered up the prospect of life itself. Tooth whiteners, makeup products, exercise machines: they don't just offer us the prospect of better health; they offer revolutionary change in a matter of minutes, hours, or days. Even more mundane devices offer us a good deal beyond the obvious. That blender isn't just designed to make smoothies. It's going to save you precious minutes every day and give you more time with your loved ones. Don't you *want* to be a decent human being and spend more time with your family?

There's a good reason products advertised on infomercials are tied to our emotional well-being, our self-image, and our relationships with others. It gives us a powerful reason to pick up the phone and place an order. It's hard to make the argument that having a CD player will change your life. I can suggest, though, that if you had white teeth, you'll be in a better position to find the man/woman of your dreams and find eternal happiness.

"Sex, vanity, religion, or greed," the late infomercial producer/ pitchman Mike Levey once said when he was asked about which categories succeed on TV.

This American quest for self-fulfillment dates back to colonial times. "It's not far-fetched to propose that Benjamin Franklin wrote the first American SHAM book—1732's *Poor Richard's Almanack,* with its bounty of homespun witticisms," writes Steve Salerno, the author of *SHAM: How the Self-Help Movement Made America Helpless.* (SHAM stands for the self-help and actualization movement.) During the early part of the twentieth century, a cottage industry was established with books like Dale Carnegie's *How to Win Friends and Influence People* and Napoleon Hill's *Think and Grow Rich,* titles that continue to sell decades after they were first published. (Indeed, Guthy-Renker's first infomercial in the late '80s was based on Hill's book.) The 1970s and '80s became very prosperous times for people pitching the notion we each possessed the power to effect personal change. The cultural shift of the '60s opened the door to countless new religious movements, cults, and self-improvement gurus.

Today we're inundated with people who tell us we can— and should—do better. Phil McGraw, John Gray, and Barbara DeAngelis offer hope for couples in trouble. Deepak Chopra and Andrew Weil instruct us on ways to live a more "harmonious" existence. Laura Schlessinger tells us how to adjust our moral compasses. Suze Orman promises us a cure for our financial crises. As for Tony Robbins, well, he says he can help us with just about anything.

Everywhere we turn there's a problem, and the problem is always accompanied by a cure. And when we don't have problems, we create them. Not long ago, GlaxoSmithKline started marketing Requip, a drug that treats "restless leg syndrome," a condition that precious few had even heard about before TV commercials blanketed the airwaves with a warning that the "consequences can be devastating." Not surprisingly, a study conducted at Dartmouth found that the ads sent thousands of people to their doctors seeking Requip prescriptions. Yet few of them actually suffered from a condition that required medical treatment.

It's this problem–solution dynamic that rests at the heart of almost every long-form infomercial. BareMinerals isn't just selling us makeup; the infomercial is also telling us that the makeup we currently use is full of chemicals and potentially harmful. (The infomercial quickly cuts to a woman's cheek brushing against the face of a newborn baby just to convey how important it is to wear "natural makeup.") That set of battery-operated light bulbs? It's not merely a question of convenience. They will protect our loved ones in darkened rooms where dangerous intruders may be lurking. OxiClean doesn't just keep your floors looking shiny and new; it will keep your whole family safe from dangerous spores that cover every surface in your home. Oh, and just in case you have any doubts, here are the lab results from a swap sample to prove it.

Of course, if you're going to actually sell the product, the solution to the problem needs to be relatively painless. No one wants to go to the gym for twenty-seven hours a week. No one wants to hear that he has to work sixteen hours a day to make his millions. So even when the products are legit, the work involved is usually vastly oversimplified. An exercise machine you buy at three o'clock in the morning will work, assuming you actually use it. (Of course, you could just as easily sit on the floor of your living room and do sit-ups and push-ups all day, too.) Is it remotely possible that you'll end up looking like the guy on the infomercial? Probably not, although it's not completely out of the realm of possibility provided you have six hours a day to dedicate to your Bowflex and you're prepared to make an investment in Lycra bodysuits and bottles of Hawaiian Tropic oil. The guy with the rippling muscles who looks like a runner-up in a Mr. Olympian contest didn't turn out that way because he used his home gym "twenty minutes a day, three days a week." Getting in shape requires motivation, and there are no shortcuts. Yet many of these exercise products make it look like they've taken all the pain and suffering out of working out, which explains why these shows occasionally feature a woman using an ab machine while happily chatting on her cell phone. Using this machine is plain ol' fun, the infomercials communicate to the audience, as if people will forgo a day at the beach to stay home and tone their abs.

The ab belts that were marketed on TV several years ago made precisely these sorts of claims: marketers suggested that the electrical stimulation could be used to tone muscles without doing any exercise altogether—you could set it and forget it, to borrow Ron Popeil's catchphrase. Although the fad prompted about a half dozen ab-stimulating infomercials to flood the air, it was never designed to give anyone an instant six-pack, a point that the Federal Trade Commission made on numerous occasions when it later cracked down on the product category and filed a series of lawsuits over unsubstantiated claims. Perhaps the only downside to the crackdown was that we're no longer treated to shows like the one that featured a suspicious man dressed in a tight blue jogging outfit named "Dr. Ho," who pitched an electrical stimulator that he marketed as a cure for pain. In his thick Chinese accent, Dr. Ho would attach the device to various bikini-clad babes reclining on lounge chairs in front of a whirlpool. "Come on, Jennifer, I promise it won't hurt," one girl tells another just before Ho straps her up and her muscles begin to twitch uncontrollably.

When there isn't any paranoia to capitalize on, there's always the tragic prospect of what will happen if you *don't* use the product. You can't find the time to use this exercise machine for ten minutes a day? Well, then, you're going to be fat and lonely. Many get-rich-quick infomercials make it seem that if you're a middle-aged man who *isn't* making millions buying real estate or trading currencies in your spare time, you're a lousy husband and father.

The messages that come at us in the middle of the night are powerful ones, and they're delivered at just the right moment. Just as Al Eicoff discovered decades ago, many infomercials perform best late at night when we're much more open to the power of suggestion. "People's defenses are down then; they're in what you might call the twilight zone," Greg Renker explains. It's at that late hour—minutes before our conscious minds head off into dreamland—that these entrancing images of white teeth, unblemished skin, extraordinary wealth, and perfectly toned bodies flutter in front of our eyes. For infomercial marketers, the effect is magic, perhaps less so for many consumers, who will soon find out that their brand-new treadmill has turned into an expensive clothes rack.

People occasionally confess to having purchased a product advertised on TV with a measure of shame or embarrassment, as if somehow they're admitting they were duped. Part of that, of course, has to do with the industry's reputation and the pervasive myth that the people who shop from home are reclusive shut-ins with nothing better to do. Perhaps another reason we're so resistant to admitting our TV purchases can be explained by why some people don't want to admit to buying lottery tickets. The act represents an elusive quest for fulfillment. Telling someone you purchased a Bowflex at three o'clock in the morning is almost like revealing one of your deepest insecurities.

. . . .

Not every infomercial has deeper psychological underpinnings, and these factors don't usually come into play with short-form spots, which often offer up cheaper novelties that are intended to be impulse buys. A short spot is akin to the sort of item that might tempt you while you're waiting at the grocery store checkout. What both long-form infomercials (which last twenty-eight minutes, thirty seconds in most markets) and short-form spots (two minutes or less) share is the call-to-action, an 800 number on the screen and an insistent voice urging you to "call now!" (and, at least in the old days, "Sorry, no CODs!"), often against the backdrop of the infamous "blue screen" with a mailing address that lists some random American city like Pueblo, Colorado, or Petaluma, California. A thirty-second commercial for Tide detergent doesn't ask you to do anything. You see the commercial, and hopefully it strikes a chord deep inside and you're motivated to buy Tide the next time you're picking up detergent at the grocery store. A short-form spot requires you to take action. One moment you're sitting on your couch thinking about whether you should take out the trash now or wait until morning; the next minute you've decided that there's really nothing you need in this world more than a Boogie Bass singing fish.

Short-form spots rely on novelty or, as in the case of the Boogie Bass, sheer idiocy. We've all had the experience of returning to our car on a hot summer day to find the interior unbearably hot. So someone clever comes along with the Solar Car Fan, which attaches to your car window and is powered by the sunlight and ventilates your car with air. An infomercial marketer must have taken notice when he saw his wife rooting around in her purse for her lipstick or cell phone, because then the PurseBright appeared, a little lighting system for the interior of a woman's handbag.

Half-hour programs usually offer you more. But that isn't always the case. Unlike physical stores, where a retailer carefully determines what inventory to carry, television has no such filter. Ultimately, the only test in the totally unfettered marketplace is whether someone buys the product or not. It's a question of supply and demand. If people are willing to fork over their hard-earned cash for an elaborate system that allows them to grow their own tomatoes in the back of their closet, there's a company that is more than willing to spend money advertising the product on TV.

It's supply and demand that also dictates when infomercials and short spots air. Half-hour shows don't just air late at night because our defenses are down; it also happens to be the only time when the networks sell off airtime. (The other popular time slot is on the weekend, particularly in the mornings.) Short-form spots often take advantage of remnant ad space, when the networks don't have glitzier, higher priced commercials to air. And both happily take advantage of networks that can't sell their airtime for whatever reason. When the gay/lesbian network LOGO debuted and traditional advertisers were skittish about buying time, direct response marketers happily filled the void. Fox Business has yet to attract more than a few brave souls to watch its programming, but infomercial producers have been more than happy to buy blocks of time late at night at a discount.

In the old days, airtime was relatively cheap, and infomercials represented one of the only channels available to smaller product manufacturers; direct response TV was one of the most reasonably priced ways to test out a kooky product to see if there's public demand. Television airtime isn't nearly as affordable as it once was, but late-night TV still functions as a giant entrepreneurial roulette wheel. And it continues to appeal to scrappy marketers with novel ideas. After all, a big multinational wasn't going to dream up the idea for a hose that hooks up to your vacuum cleaner and cuts your hair. Yet that's precisely what the Flowbee was when it debuted on late-night TV in the early '90s. Created by Rick Hunt, a San Diego carpenter who came up with the concept after he used a vacuum to remove the sawdust from his hair, Hunt first started selling his hair-cutting vacuum attachment at county fairs. A couple of years later, he took the Flowbee to TV and created a pop culture sensation thanks to what may very well go down as one of the most absurd products in TV history. But as silly as it was, it worked. Financially, at least. Sales shot through the roof and even prompted a rival, Robocut, to get in the act.

Equally nutty was the Aromatrim, which promised that if you put a little plastic device under your nose and inhaled a whiff, your appetite would instantly vanish. And just how did this happen? The disc inside the $49.95 apparatus contained a blend of aniseed, hickory, and fennel and delivered a horrific odor (it's been described as the smell of rotting food or vomit, at least by those who tried it) that would allegedly turn you off from eating for hours. The infomercial featured the host prowling the streets of LA with a plate of delicious cookies in hand. Tempting hungry passersby with her tasty morsels, she'd first place the Aromatrim under those noses. Sure enough, not a single person wanted to sample a cookie after that. The Aromatrim did what infomercials almost always try to do: come up with a clever, simple solution to an everyday problem. Ostensibly at least, the Flowbee offered people a way to break free from the chore of visiting the barber regularly; now you'd be able to tend to your mullet without leaving the trailer park.

But while infomercialers occasionally come up with nifty little gadgets that represent something new, they're just as likely to play off of a broader consumer trend, introducing a cheaper alternative to a mainstream product. When every teenage starlet in Hollywood started sporting a spray-on tan, along came Salon Bronze, a do-it-yourself home "airbrushing" tanning kit. Yes, indeed: for just $12.99 you, too, could possess Paris Hilton's healthy glow. It wasn't long after America became infatuated with impotency drugs like Viagra and Cialis that infomercial marketers started pitching over-the-counter remedies like Extenze, which featured porn star Ron Jeremy as the host of the show in the early days. (Memorably, in order to ensure that the show would be aired by the networks, everyone had to speak in euphemisms, referring to "enhanced confidence" and "that special part of the male anatomy.")

The difference between whether a product is advertised in a short spot or a longer, half-hour infomercial almost always boils down to economics. You're not going to be convinced to spent $800 on a piece of fancy gym equipment in sixty seconds. To sell you a $129.99 rotisserie oven is going to take some time, and someone charismatic is going to have to come on and show you how it works. A gimmicky novelty item that retails for $19.99 (plus S&H!) is perfect for short form. The price of the product could never justify paying for half-hour time slots—and it's unclear how anyone would be able to create twenty-eight minutes, thirty seconds of content based around the Owl, the magnifying glass with a little LCD light embedded in it, although I'm sure some creative infomercial marketer could find a way.

Some products rely on both formats. Proactiv, for example, features long-form infomercials when half-hour blocks become available late at night; during the day, the company targets acne-riddled teenagers on networks like MTV and Comedy Central.

The two formats complement each other. The sixteen-year-old high school student may have marveled at Jessica Simpson's crystal-clear skin on the extended Proactiv infomercial but forgotten to place her order. Then she sees the short spot come on while she's watching *TRL,* and it gives her just enough time to jot down the phone number. The thirty-second ad helps reinforce the brand.

Tuning In

Not surprisingly, one of the biggest problems with long-form shows is getting people to stop their channel changing long enough to tune in. A short spot comes and goes along with the millions of other commercials for mobile phones, SUVs, and the latest Hollywood blockbuster. A half-hour show requires you to bypass that episode of *Cops,* rerun of *Seinfeld,* or MSNBC documentary about prisons, and actively watch someone try to sell you something you probably don't need. That's why many infomercials have some sort of hook, something that momentarily distracts viewers and gets them to move their finger off the up/down dial on their remote control.

Sex usually works. What buying real estate has to do with women with big boobs is unclear, but moneymaking products have long featured cleavage-bearing babes. It isn't hard to see the psychology at work: it's late at night, the product is directed toward men, and there's no better way to make a white, middle-class, heterosexual man take action than to have a sexy chick insinuate he's never going to score with the opposite sex until he takes control of his financial future.

Elaborate demonstrations capture attention. Even though it's clear that the show is a sales pitch, people tune in much the way they stood around to watch demonstrations on the boardwalk. In the end, it's just amusing to watch Chef Tony toss a pineapple in the air and slice it in two with a Miracle Blade knife. People in Asbury Park gathered around to watch Arnold Morris cut into a cement block, too. We enjoy being sold to.

Yet another popular way infomercial marketers have gotten viewers to stop and tune in is to feature someone who appears so insane, you have absolutely no choice but to stop and stare. Tony Little, the hyperactive, buffed-up exercise coach, looked like he might collapse at any moment from a heart attack. Matthew Lesko looked like he might have an aneurysm on the steps of the Capitol as he bounced around in a suit with a giant yellow question mark painted on his back. Creating a show around an outrageous host, wild inventor, or inspirational guru has been one of the most tried-and-true ways to get attention—witness Don Lapre, Jay Kordich, Billy Blanks, and Susan Powter—although it's not unlike the pitches of a generation ago, when a frenzied pitchman could get a crowd to gather around thanks to his antics. (Although it's unlikely the men who appeared at fairs and carnivals a generation ago ever dressed up in skintight spandex bodysuits à la Tony Little.)

Many infomercials these days don't offer up such wildly enthusiastic pitches. As the wacky late-night pitchman routine played itself out in the late '90s, marketers turned to more sophisticated ways to reel in viewers. More upscale programs like Proactiv started using the allure of celebrity to hook viewers and keep them watching. Of course, not every marketer can afford to plunk down a few million for the pop star du jour, which is why some infomercial producers continue to believe that any familiar face—even, say, an actor who gained fame for his role on the *Love Boat* three decades ago—is an effective way to get channel surfers to pause for a second.

On the opposite end of the spectrum from an infomercial like Proactiv—and a longstanding industry staple—are the shows that blur the line between a paid advertisement and legitimate programming. Yes, I realize that it may seem nutty to many people that anyone would mistake Klee Irwin's pitch for Dual Action Cleanse with a real program about intestinal health, but that's what these marketers are counting on. And many viewers fall for the stunt, despite a disclaimer at the beginning and end of the program, which can also occasionally be seen in a nearly illegible font at the bottom of the screen.

One marketer who is particularly gifted at blurring the line is Donald Barrett, the founder of an infomercial production company called ITV. The infomercials, which Barrett hosts himself, resemble a talk show: He sits behind a Jay Leno–like desk with a giant microphone, the skyline of Boston glitters in the background, and Barrett appears to be conducting an interview with his "expert" guest about a vitamin supplement or "natural remedy" that the guest has developed. The product, naturally, is Barrett's own, although he comes off as the uninformed interviewer, feigning surprise as the guest details all of the extraordinary health benefits that go along with a supplement that you can find for about one-tenth the price at your local vitamin store.

Barrett's tactics are exceedingly crafty. To mimic a real talk show, Barrett will occasionally take "calls" from "viewers," which makes the program appear live and unscripted. Just as clever is the way Barrett weaves the sales pitch into the program. Before breaking for a "commercial," Barrett will tell the audience that as part of the guest's appearance on the show, a special offer has been graciously arranged for ITV viewers. "Fans of the show"—which slyly suggests the program is somehow episodic—are encouraged to pick up the phone "and mention ITV" to the operator to take advantage of their special discount. Every night, thousands of people are fooled into thinking the infomercial is some sort of low-budget chat show.

Almost everyone in the industry dabbles in deception of some sort. Ever notice that your program guide occasionally identifies a show as "Paid Programming" and at other times it may say something like "Real Estate Secrets!" or "Make Millions!"? Infomercial marketers know that you'll be much more likely to stop for a moment if you think you've landed on a real television show, not an infomercial, and have negotiated deals with the companies that operate the digital program guides accordingly.

The faux news show is only one of many formats that are regularly used on infomercials. And not every infomercial is actually selling something. Although most involve a "hard sell"— there's a product, price tag, and telephone number displayed on the bottom of the screen—some infomercials act as "lead generators," which means they're simply rustling up customers who will be asked to purchase something at a later date. The sponsors of a moneymaking infomercial that "invites" people to attend a local investing seminar in the basement of the Ramada Inn next to the airport aren't planning to dispense investment advice out of the kindness of their hearts. It's only when viewers sign up for the free seminar and show up at a rinky-dink hotel that they will be "encouraged" to plunk down hundreds or thousands for a longer course.

In addition to fake news shows, there are fake talk shows. Then there are semifake product demonstrations that occasionally involve a fake (and overly enthusiastic) studio audience. Fake game shows, you ask? It's been attempted but has never worked for whatever reason. Most "storymercials" or "sitcommercials" have been failures, too. During the '90s, several Fortune 500 companies were convinced that engaging in traditional infomercial tactics would cheapen their brands and inadvertently lump their expensive car/computer/phone service with the likes of Tony Little's Gazelle Freestyle or Tony Robbins's Personal Power series. So they rolled out expensive shows that didn't involve a pitch per se and hired pricey Madison Avenue ad agencies to create fake entertainment programming—with their products embedded in the storyline, naturally. In 1993 Bell Atlantic unveiled a faux sitcom featuring a family called the Ringers, who were thrust into a crisis until—surprise!—the call-waiting feature on their phone ended up saving the day. The spot generated a good deal of press (mainly because the phone giant was the first to test out the concept), but it didn't exactly send people running to Bell Atlantic to purchase such life-saving features as call waiting. A handful of other big companies learned precisely the same lesson over the course of the decade, as they launched nontraditional infomercials to middling success. Their mistake was abandoning what makes infomercials so successful in the first place: their singular focus on selling a product.

Ingenuity isn't rewarded on late-night television. The tired concepts of yesteryear continue to be the ones that perform well today, which is what leads marketers back to the same categories and products. The same images that impressed people twenty years ago—like a before-and-after photo of a woman who has lost fifty pounds—remain just as alluring today as they did back then. Glistening photos of men and women in perfect shape still get people to stop channel surfing at three o'clock in the morning. Every year a dozen new machines hit the air, designed to do precisely what similar products did years ago. And every year half a dozen new people take to the air with a colon-cleansing product, horrifying Americans everywhere with intimate stories of their large intestine.

Tactical Warfare

People are often surprised to hear that infomercials and home shopping networks are "sophisticated." How in the world can a commercial about garden shears or a half-hour program about a power drill be so complex? We're not talking about any sort of aesthetic sophistication, of course. What makes them so clever is that they've been carefully designed to get you to pick up the phone and order them. Dozens of strategies, many of which are relatively subtle, are employed to stimulate sales.

Many of them are not unique to the infomercial industry, to be sure. They're employed by all sorts of advertisers and marketers to move merchandise. But what sets infomercials apart is that they've been able to test the methods again and again to come up with what works. Whether it's the price, the number of freebies, the background music, or the graphics on the screen, every element on an infomercial can be deconstructed and tested; several different versions of the same infomercial can be aired to see which one does better. Along the way, infomercial marketers have picked up an amazing amount of knowledge about how we behave as shoppers and what motivates us to make a purchase. Unlike traditional marketers, who look at focus group results and examine psychographics, direct response marketers have a powerful testing apparatus to determine the effectiveness of their ads: either the phone rings or it doesn't.

It's a powerful medium. The Wes Anderson–directed American Express commercial may have been beautifully shot, and they may have spent millions producing it at a chateau in France with the fanciest equipment on planet Earth, but when you walked into the grocery store today, did it make you want to pull out your Amex instead of your Visa card? How many Coke drinkers switch to Pepsi every year thanks to the company's billion-dollar marketing budget? Madison Avenue agencies have never had to withstand the sort of accountability that comes along with an 800 number flashing on the screen, which will, in a matter of seconds, determine whether the spot was a success or not.

The amount of insight into consumer behavior possessed by direct response marketers versus traditional retailers is profound. For years, for example, major department stores knew next to nothing about why people came in to browse but didn't end up purchasing anything. They didn't understand why some people picked up an item from a sales rack and why some passed right by. Until the 1990s, retailers hadn't even grasped that the single most important factor in determining whether someone purchases a product once in a store is how long the line is. Paco Underhill, the founder of the retail consulting firm Envirosell, highlighted just how "woefully clueless" retailers can be in his bestselling book *Why We Buy*. During one consulting engagement, he visited a drugstore chain that had a large assortment of hair care products for blondes in a branch that was located in a neighborhood where ninety-five percent of the female shoppers were African American; at another location in Minneapolis, he noticed a wide assortment of suntan lotions on display in the middle of winter.

Needless to say, this doesn't happen with infomercial marketers, who have honed much of what they do down to a science. Media buyers target campaigns on specific networks to reach the right audiences—that's why you'll see a moneymaking show on Fox Business and a *Girls Gone Wild* pitch on E! And they know to flood the airwaves in January with exercise infomercials (so people can fulfill New Year's resolutions) and get-rich-quick infomercials in May (just after the pain of tax season). They've tested whether the host should emphasize the word *call* or *now.* They've researched whether the price should be structured as three payments of $33.33 or four payments of $24.99. They've turned it into a quasi-science.

There is no official handbook that industry players rely on— much of what they've learned they've picked up by trial and error—but they've certainly latched on to a few books that have helped guide much of their decision making. Social psychologist Robert Cialdini's best-selling book, *Influence: The Psychology of Persuasion,* which is now in its fourth edition, is a popular one. Cialdini's book outlines various "weapons of influence" and documents the tools that are used to hook consumers. While these tools of persuasion existed long before Cialdini first published the book in the mid-1980s (many of them were used by Ron Popeil when he was demonstrating knives outside the women's restroom), and while salespeople of all stripes have used them over the years, Cialdini rather neatly organized them in one volume, and he's since become a favorite in infomercial circles. He's spoken at a number of industry events. A glowing blurb by Greg Renker appears on the back of the fourth edition: "I read it three times in a row." (When I met with Renker, he told me he'd read the book "at least ten times over the years.")

Cialdini isn't the only expert on influence who has become a hit with direct response marketers. The noted political strategist Frank Luntz, who may be best known for changing the subtle ways many Republicans speak ("death tax" instead of "estate tax" and "climate control" instead of "global warming"), is also popular with the infomercial set. He gave the closing night speech at the industry's 2006 convention. When a man like Luntz is helping to shape the language used to sell acne products and electric blenders, you can be sure that those late-night shows aren't the unscripted cheese fests you may have thought they were.

WHILE SUPPLIES LAST

As a kid, I recall marveling that the infomercial hosts often told viewers that "supplies are running low!" and "this price is only available for the next fifteen minutes!" It was clear to me that the show wasn't live; it was the same taped program that was on every night. I remember once calling the 800 number on the screen and asking the operator what the price would be if I waited another fifteen minutes. "Oh, please," she said. "The price is always the same."

It was an early lesson in the scarcity principle, which is used over and over again on infomercials and home shopping programs. Hardly a minute goes by on Jewelry Television when there isn't a flashing number in the corner of the screen warning you about the network's rapidly declining inventory, as if they'd only bothered to purchase three hundred gold bracelets and don't have a million more collecting dust in a warehouse somewhere. And yet it works. Again and again. A limited time offer! While supplies last! This week only! False scarcity was a staple on the live pitchman circuit—"I'll only be here today with this special offer!"—and it's been a fixture on the infomercial scene since the very beginning.

This isn't limited to late-night television, obviously. Retailers of all stripes use it. And many companies intentionally limit inventories to keep up demand: DeBeers intentionally restricts the number of diamonds it distributes to keep prices high; toy manufacturers often release popular products in limited quantities to create a frenzy; Apple supplied its stores with limited numbers of iPhones to generate buzz; and luxury brands like Hermès create "waiting lists" for women who want to get their hands on $6,000 purses. Infomercials don't traffic in those sorts of practices. There are plenty of Swivel Sweepers sitting in the warehouse. Nothing will happen if you call to-morrow instead of in the next five minutes. But if they didn't warn you that you might miss out, would you be as likely to call? False scarcity "encourages us to buy sooner and perhaps to buy more than normal," writes John Quelch of Harvard Business School.

One notable exception, however, is the use of the infomercial staple "Not available in stores!" That may actually be true. You won't find Proactiv sitting on the shelf at CVS or Walgreen's. You will, however, find the Magic Bullet at Kmart, albeit wrapped up in different packaging and equipped with a different array of bonuses and extras, so as to explain why the retail version is about half the price of the unit sold on television.

FOLLOW THE LEADER

The scarcity principle may be at work when the counter on QVC shows you that their inventory of silver brooches is rap-idly declining or tells you that three minutes remain before your chance to buy the item will expire. But what about the counter that ticks upward? Just as ubiquitous on home shopping chan-nels is a small box in the corner of the screen that indicates the number of pieces that have been sold.

Obviously, unless you happen to be QVC's accountant, there is absolutely no reason in the world why you should care just how many $49.99 silver brooches the network has sold in the past fifteen minutes. What it does do, though, is offer social proof. It shows you that other folks—people just like you—are running to the phones to pick up the item. It tells you the item is popular. It communicates which direction the herd is head-ing. If everyone else thinks the brooch is the deal of the century, shouldn't you?

That we tend to follow other people's lead is nothing new. One of social psychologist Stanley Milgram's amusing experiments in the 1960s placed several researchers on the streets of New York looking up at the sky. When one researcher stood on the corner and gazed upward, not much happened. When a small group did it, many of the passersby stopped and followed suit, craning their necks to see what they were looking at.

We look to others for cues as to how to behave. We always have. It's an extraordinarily powerful force. Research has found that suicide rates increase in the aftermath of a highly publicized suicide: other troubled individuals, who read about the act in the newspaper or see it on TV, are inspired to follow suit. And it's used in countless everyday situations, although we rarely take notice of it. Clubs keep people waiting outside the velvet ropes to demonstrate it's a hot spot. Restaurants seat customers in the window to attract other diners.

For generations, pitchmen have recognized the importance of social proof. They knew very well that a crowd in front of their stall would attract others, which is why skilled pitchmen have long used a variety of tactics to rope people into watching and then preventing groups from dispersing after the pitch was complete. Social proof has been used on television for decades, too. The laugh track was implemented in the early 1950s to cue viewers when to laugh. Test after test demonstrated that viewers found shows "funnier" and gave programs higher ratings when they heard the sound of other people laughing. In fact, the laugh track continues to work, which is precisely why so many networks have been resistant to giving it up despite fierce opposition from many TV producers and writers.

Infomercials often structure shows around a studio audience to add an element of social proof. (Of course, it also helps disguise the infomercial as regular entertainment programming.)

A studio audience gives a marketer the power of the crowd: reaction shots of eager audience members nodding in agreement and demonstrating enthusiasm has been a perfect way to get the viewers at home to react much the same way.

Testimonials serve the same purpose. Almost every infomercial on the air features clips of exceedingly happy customers singing the product's praises on camera. The testimonials might come from people who have gathered in the studio to share their stories and maybe, à la Oprah, even shed a few tears as they talk about how the product changed their lives. They may come from people sitting on the couches in their living rooms, which can make the testimonial appear more intimate and honest. In other cases, the man-on-the-street approach is used, which conveys a different sort of false honesty—the perception of randomness, as if the person had been plucked from the masses on the street.

Testimonials work magnificently, not surprisingly, which is why few infomercials do without them. They work even better, research has indicated, when we see people on camera who remind us of ourselves. Numerous experiments have demonstrated that we're substantially more willing to perform an action when we're imitating our "peers." And so infomercials are carefully constructed to feature testimonials that match their target demographic, or at least show a range of different people from ethnic and socioeconomic backgrounds to appeal to as many people as possible. A get-rich-quick infomercial is going to show you a poor guy struggling to make ends meet one moment, a retiree looking to make a few extra dollars on the side the next. The hope, of course, is that you'll be able to relate to one of them.

Are the testimonials real? These days they usually are. Although some less ethical marketers have been known to pay for testimonials (or even feature friends and associates), most shows feature real customers. Obviously, they're not necessarily participating on the show because they've been so moved by their experience with the product that they *had* to speak up. In many cases, the people who appear on camera received the product free of charge, which makes it a bit difficult for people to say no when the marketer follows up a few weeks later and asks for fifteen minutes of their time to tell him or her about their experiences with the device. Taking part in a testimonial might come along with other perks, too. For one shoot, everyone who participated got picked up in a limo and treated to a weekend stay at a luxury hotel.

Social proof has its limitations. As James Surowiecki points out in his book *The Wisdom of Crowds,* Stanley Milgram did not, as far as we know, return to the street corner to see what happened the next time a passerby was walking down the street and saw a group of people gazing into the sky. He may have very well learned his lesson the first time and continued on. If you've been burned by one no-money-down program, all the cheery testimonials about another nearly identical product may not make a lick of difference.

RINSE AND REPEAT

In 2006 a short commercial for a headache product called HeadOn debuted on television. It was cheaply made, full of cheesy graphics, and featured a woman rubbing a topical analgesic on her head. What was most notable about the commercial, though, was that it repeated the product's catchphrase—"HeadOn, apply directly to the forehead"—again and again for ten straight seconds. It was, as you know if you had to sit through it more than once, exceptionally irritating. Yet it worked marvelously: millions of Americans were instantly familiar with the product. Describing the ad as "utterly genius," *Slate*'s Seth Stevenson mused that, "with this one 10-second spot, the makers of HeadOn have torn down all the pretenses that have gummed up the advertising industry for years." Many commercials don't even tell you what they're selling. HeadOn was like a two-by-four to the forehead.

Repetition lies at the heart of direct response TV, although the repetition isn't usually quite as obvious. Take an infomercial for a cleansing product. One minute the host is using it to show you how it can wipe out coffee stains on a bedroom carpet. A few minutes later he's demonstrating how the product can be used to clean your drapes. Next he's taken the magic formula to a grass stain on a pair of pants. Each scenario is different and no sentence will be repeated verbatim, but the central message— This product is revolutionary! It can remove anything! It won't damage fine fabrics!—will be incorporated in each, rephrased slightly so you don't even realize that you've just listened to the same spiel three times in a row. With HeadOn, the intent was to annoy you so you'd remember the spot. With infomercials, the repetition targets you subconsciously.

Research has demonstrated that this subtle repetition is highly effective. In fact, studies have shown that because infomercials expose viewers to the sales message for an extended period of time and do not repeat the same message but go back and rehash the same material while making small changes to the script, the repetition is actually much more powerful. When three marketing professors tested the effectiveness of infomercials as part of a research experiment in the mid-'90s, they determined that the influence exerted by an infomercial was more akin to a direct product experience (such as having a consumer try out a product at home) than it was to a standard thirty-second ad. In other words, when you sit and watch an infomercial for an

Oreck vacuum cleaner, the experience is nothing like watching a thirty-second ad for the same vacuum. It's as if you took the vacuum cleaner home with you and tested it out for a day.

Repetition serves another goal. Demonstrating multiple uses of the same product raises the "perceived value" of the product as you internalize all the ways you could possibly put the item to use. This blender doesn't just make frozen drinks; it also makes smoothies. You can prepare a delicious salsa. Do you like chicken salad? It can do that, too! And egg salad! Did we mention it can grind coffee? Every time you're shown a new use for the Magic Bullet blender, the likelihood that you'll purchase the product goes up.

Perceived value also comes into play when a demonstrator slices a knife through an old shoe or a cement block or uses a pair of shears to cut through a penny. Why would you need your steak knife to cut through a hammer, you ask? You wouldn't. But in addition to proving to you that the knife is indestructible, it's raising the perceived value of the product. Somewhere in the recesses of your subconscious, your brain is telling you that if for whatever reason you ever *wanted* to cut through a boot, you can rest assured that you have the knife that's up to the task.

AN IRRESISTIBLE OFFER!

Pitchmen have long had a saying: it's all about how you ask for the money. In other words, it often doesn't matter what the product is or even what price has been attached to it. Timing the offer—and phrasing it just right—can mean the difference between a sale and a viewer who simply meanders off to watch a rerun of *Will & Grace*.

As with a live pitch, infomercials are hoping to convince a viewer to buy the product even before the customer knows how much it's going to cost. Ideally, a viewer should be saying, "So how do I buy it!?" by the time the infomercial flashes the price and the 800 number on the screen. Building up enthusiasm is essential; creating momentum is the only way a marketer can get a viewer to rise up off the couch and head to the phone. It's a bit counterintuitive: one would expect that it would be in the best interest of the marketer to leave the toll-free number on the screen for the duration of the program. That's not the case. The information is handed over to viewers only after they've been hooked.

Pricing a product appropriately is a mix of art and science. Naturally, marketers need to make a profit and have to factor in their costs, which include both the costs associated with manufacturing the product and the airtime required to market it. The economics differ sector by sector, but typically an infomercial needs to factor in a six-to-one markup to make money, which means if you see a $60 toaster oven advertised on television, it probably didn't cost more than $10 to manufacture. But should the toaster retail for $59.99 or $69.99? Perhaps $79.99 is a reasonable price point.

Like other marketers, infomercial producers test different prices and run financial models to determine the effectiveness of each. But there are a slew of psychological factors involved as well. Unlike a retail store, where you can shop around and compare different models—or even head to the department store across the street to compare prices—an infomercial is only concerned with selling you in the moment. Perception is everything.

Most items you see on store shelves are usually priced one cent below a whole number, for example, $79.99 instead of $80.00. Research has long indicated that the use of "odd-even pricing" works because consumers do not process prices holistically; the public tends to read the numbers from left to right and place less emphasis—or "drop off"—the digits at the end of the sequence. Infomercials are no different. But that's only the beginning of the pricing game.

Let's return to the example of the toaster oven. For the sake of argument, let's assume that similar products retail at stores for $49.99. Does that mean I need to price the toaster oven that I plan to market on TV at the same price? Not necessarily. When you go to the store and plunk down your fifty bucks, all you're going to get is the toaster oven, wrapped in plastic and squeezed into a box.

I, on the other hand, am offering the toaster oven, plus a book of exclusive recipes, and a twenty-four-piece set of plastic containers so you can store all the tasty foods you make in your new oven. And I'm going to throw in—for people who call in the next fifteen minutes—a set of serving utensils. For the entire package—the toaster oven, recipes, plastic containers, and utensils—the price is $79.99. And because I'm feeling extra generous today, I'm also going to throw in three free marinades, which you can use when you're cooking foods in your new oven. So which is the better deal?

On the surface, my offer sounds pretty attractive. You'll get the toaster oven and all these goodies along with it. Of course, the deal will work out nicely for me, too: the recipe book might cost me a dollar to produce; the plastic containers and utensils cost me another three, and I'll pay another two bucks for the marinades at wholesale prices. All those extras that I just spent a few minutes describing in such alluring detail? They added a measly six bucks to my cost. And I priced my package for thirty dollars more than a comparable toaster oven at Kmart.

Infomercials thrive on complicating purchasing decisions for consumers by bundling items with free offers, bonuses, and rewards. A "but wait, there's more!" suddenly muddles our perceptions and makes it harder to judge the offer that's just been presented to us. The special offer also lends itself nicely to the drama of the pitch. The freebies are carefully revealed to the viewer, one after another, with each one making the overall offer increasingly irresistible. That cookbook? It's a $24.99 value! Those plastic containers? You'd pay another $19.99 if you bought them in a store! I'm no longer offering you a simple toaster oven. You're now focused on the fact that I'm offering you $189.99 worth of value for the low, low price of $79.99.

There are many varieties to this pitch. In the case of the Magic Bullet, they not only offer you the actual blender, they also throw in several blades, a collection of cups, a shaker, steamer tops, re-sealable lids, "party mugs with comfort lip rings," a "ten-second" recipe book, and a juice extractor. All told, it's twenty-one pieces. And then they go in for the coup de grâce and tell viewers that they'll double the offer—two sets of everything I just listed—for the same price of $99.99. "It's an $800 value!" the announcer proclaims. Considering the package cost them less than ten bucks, doubling your order is really the least they can do.

Of course, at no point does the announcer say the Magic Bullet is $99.99. In the case of my toaster oven, I may have decided to offer it at $79.99, but that's certainly not what I'm going to ask for when the infomercial hits the air. I'll tell you that you'll be able to enjoy this fantastic piece of machinery—and all these great goodies—for just four easy payments of $19.99. (Notice I didn't use the words *cost* and *sell*.) As is the case with odd-even pricing, consumers process the information differently when the price is divided into several smaller payments. I will incur some risks by offering you the opportunity to stretch out payments. While the first payment may go through now, a month from now, your credit card might be declined. (And you've already got my toaster oven.) Yet the difference in response rates is so significant that infomercial marketers almost always structure their offers using this "flex pay" format.

But wait, there's more! In the corner of the screen, you may have noticed that mysterious "+S&H" listed in small letters next to the price. Unlike a product you pick up in stores, the product you just purchased on an infomercial has to be sent to you. You're well aware of that, and you're also perfectly accustomed to paying for the service. The question now, though, is not how much the shipping costs; it's how much can I get away with charging you before you abandon the sale. Fortunately, by the time you learn the amount, you've already made the mental decision to buy the toaster oven, you called the 800 number, and you just spent five minutes on the phone placing your order. Are you going to hang up because the shipping was a few bucks more than you anticipated? You expected the shipping on my toaster oven to cost you ten or twelve bucks. You just found out it's an additional $29.99. But in your mind, you've already made plans to make tasty grilled cheese sandwiches.

Although in some cases there can be a significant expense involved in shipping an item (such as an exercise machine), S&H is often staggeringly overpriced and just another way to embed an additional profit—one that, in the consumer's mind, is separate and distinct from the price associated with the product. The Magic Bullet, which costs three payments of $33.33, tacks on another $39.95 for S&H, then charges an additional fee for shipping the second, "free" set that's offered as part of the package. And it's not going to show up on your door via Federal Express, in case you were wondering. Third-class mail all the way, my friend.

Cleverly, shipping and handling costs are often concealed from viewers until they call. It's also on the phone that viewers encounter a savvy telemarketer who has been trained in the art of the upsell. Would you like three more marinades for an additional $9.99? Normally, they're $19.99, but I can offer them to you today for half price. How about an extra set of cooking pans? Infomercial marketers carefully select and then test various upsells in the hopes that you'll tack on other products to your order. It's also on the phone that you may get to make certain decisions you didn't even know were available to you in the first place. Choice can invite paralysis. If I tell you on TV that the toaster comes in white, black, red, green, and chrome, you may—horror of horrors—decide to sleep on it. To prevent that from happening, I might just offer the item in black or white on the show and then give you the option on the phone. Why even bother to extend the option if the person has already decided to buy the item? It's a simple act of reciprocity. Consumers adore the idea of choice (witness the 182 varieties of mustard in the grocery store), and even though the person ordering the toaster may very well stick with one of the colors advertised on TV, I just generated a little goodwill by offering up a choice. Perhaps you'll pay me back by ordering that three-pack of marinades I mentioned a moment ago?

All of these clever strategies add up nicely. When you first called the 800 number to order the toaster, you were planning on spending $79.99. Now, thanks to shipping, handling, and that extra order of marinades, I'll be billing your credit card $117.97. Having second thoughts? There's no need! My toaster oven is backed by a thirty-day money-back guarantee. If for any reason you aren't completely satisfied, simply return the product to me, and I'll offer you a complete refund. There's nothing to lose.

The money-back guarantee is another exceedingly clever tactic in a direct response marketer's arsenal. It offers you a measure of comfort as you flip open your wallet and recite the sixteen-digit number embossed on your Visa card. The good news for me is that I know that even if you aren't entirely satisfied with the toaster oven, you probably won't return it. You'll be too lazy to bother. And unlike, say, a mail-order company, which may make the return process breathtakingly simple, that often isn't the case with infomercials. Returning a product purchased on television can be a complicated process. You'll have to find the address to ship the product back to, which may not be printed on the material in the package. You'll need to make a copy of your sales receipt. There may be all sorts of hoops to jump through before you can schlep to the post office and send back the toaster oven.

This discouragement tactic is now commonplace in corporate America. To discontinue your AOL subscription, for example, you'll have to call them since they don't let you cancel over the Internet, and you'll be dialing an unheard-of area code, by the way, not a toll-free number. You'll very likely remain on hold for a spell, and when you finally get through, you'll have to go head-to-head with a skillful customer service rep who will try to dissuade you from following through. It's worth noting, though, that infomercials have done it longer—and better—than anyone else.

Discouragement is also a key factor with so-called soft offers. Infomercial producers have long known that once the product lands on your doorstep, it's probably going to stay there, which is precisely why a number of the exercise machines advertised on late-night TV offer such astoundingly inexpensive free trials. A soft offer might allow you to test out a monster-sized treadmill in your living room for thirty days for $9.99. A bargain, right? What they know and many customers don't is that once you've unpacked the machine and set it up, it's unlikely you're going to disassemble it and drag the clunky thing to your local post office. And when the thirty-day trial is up, you'll see a charge on your Visa card for $399.95, the full value of the treadmill.

LET'S MEET OUR HOST

Given how much attention direct response marketers pay to the most minute details, it should come as no surprise that they think long and hard about the person—or people—they pick to host the program. They're the public face, the person entrusted with moving people to the phones. And while they're almost always reading a script that's displayed in front of them on a teleprompter, every body movement, every subtle signal they send out to the audience, can make a difference.

The ideal host for a show often depends on what's being sold. Certain products, like a self-help course or real estate program, rely on a guru of some sort, a person who can stand up and say that this product is the result of his or her extraordinary knowledge and experience. You wouldn't dream of buying Tony Robbins's CDs without Tony Robbins; viewers need to see and hear Dave Espino tell them how he made millions on eBay before they're convinced that they, too, can clear out their basements of junk they've collected over the years by pawning it all off on fellow eBay members.

Celebrities can certainly come in handy when marketing products like makeup lines and skin care programs. I can now wear the exact same shade of lipstick as Leeza Gibbons! How exciting! But paying Leeza Gibbons seven figures to appear on an infomercial for a power drill doesn't make nearly as much sense. Research has indicated that viewers make instant judgments about the authenticity of the celebrity endorsements they view on TV. When they sense that a celebrity is simply shilling a product and not likely to be a user of the product, they often turn off.

What's most important is that the host communicates authority. It doesn't have to be real authority, mind you. Just as TV doctors are used to pitch health-related products, it's merely the perception of authority that matters most. Clothes matter. The host of a get-rich-quick infomercial may be dressed in a suit or leisurely golf attire (which you'd be wearing all day, too, if you had millions in the bank); the shiny gold watch around his wrist is intended to convey affluence and success. A host with an accent isn't accidental: Americans perceive English accents as more authoritative, which is one reason why English pitchmen have been used so frequently over the years. And perhaps because Americans have difficulty telling the difference between Australian and English accents, a series of Aussies have become late-night fixtures over the past two decades. It's not just the host who is expected to convey authority. "Experts" regularly make appearances on late-night programs, although their credentials may be more than a little dubious. Never heard of the Clayton College of Natural Health? Neither have I.

Once you find a host for a show, the time-tested formula often requires the presence of a lackey, someone to play off against the pitchman. This is yet another form of social proof. Over the course of the infomercial, the clueless cohost—a proxy for the viewer sitting at home—will learn all the ways the product will change his or her life. If you've seen enough infomercials over the years, you're probably familiar with Nancy Nelson, a blonde, middle-aged Midwesterner who served as foil on countless programs in the 1980s and '90s, moving the show forward with absurdly naive questions like, "But how does it work, Jim?" and "Can it really do everything you say it does, Jack?"

OPERATORS ARE STANDING BY

Many people probably find the idea of an infomercial screenwriter a joke, much like the idea of an infomercial awards show.

(Yes, there really is one. It's held every fall in Las Vegas.) Yet the words that are used can be critically important to an infomercial's success. Good scripts can sell lousy products, but even an appealing product may have trouble finding customers if the sales pitch hasn't been formulated properly. And every word counts: Greg Renker pointed out that his infomercials always say "*when* you call," not "*if* you call." The nuance matters. It suggests the viewer will call—it's merely a matter of time.

When I meet Colleen Szot, I'm instantly reminded of Frances McDormand's character in the 1996 movie *Fargo*. There's the accent: Colleen is from Minnesota. And she's unfailingly polite and cheerful. But just like McDormand's Marge Gunderson, don't let the kindly exterior fool you into thinking she's a pushover—she's a shark. One of the most popular infomercial screenwriters, Colleen knows just what to say to manipulate drowsy, impressionable Americans to get off the couch and head to the phone.

Ever hear the line "If the lines are busy, please call back"? Then you're familiar with Colleen's work. Amusingly, she didn't come up with the line because, in fact, the lines were actually busy. She just knew that the mere suggestion of a rush of callers would send people scurrying to the phone. But she also can play with the heartstrings, too. One of her other famous TV phrases is "Make the call that can make the difference," which has stirred the guilty conscious of more than a few Americans.

Colleen has a big grin on her face when we meet, although I'd soon discover she's incapable of not smiling. That's just the sort of cheery person she is. She looks like a mom you'd find in any small town in America: she's in her fifties and dressed in a colorful embroidered shirt, and when we meet, she takes a moment to introduce me to her husband, a high school teacher.

So how does one become an infomercial screenwriter, I ask as we sit down to chat. Colleen spent her early career as an ad copy-writer in Chicago before moving back to the Twin Cities. It was in the late 1970s when she started writing direct response pitches, penning ads for Oral Roberts's evangelical ministry, which was a surprisingly good place to learn the ropes. Before 1984, televangelists were exempt from the restrictions on paid programming and had developed savvy tactics to solicit contributions. After infomercials reemerged from their twenty-year hiatus, Colleen cut her teeth penning infomercials for the NordicTrack exercise machine in the 1990s, which remains one of the most successful campaigns of all time. Since then, she's crafted the scripts for the George Foreman Grill, Tony Little's Gazelle Glider, Turtle Wax, Hooked on Phonics, and many, many more.

As Colleen explains it, an infomercial has to build momentum right up to the "call to action" (or CTA), the moment when viewers are directed to the phone. Much like the live pitch of a generation ago, it has to build to a crescendo. Unlike a county fair, though, Colleen is fighting inertia. It's two o'clock in the morning. People are tired. She has to generate the sort of language that will inspire a person to leap off the couch and head to the phone. It's no easy task.

Colleen's first step, though, is familiarizing herself with the product. "I write for me," she tells me, explaining that if she can't really understand or relate to the product, she turns down the work. She's avoided working on infomercials for stock trading programs and real estate courses. And she steers clear of products that seem suspicious. When a company asked her to write the script for a powder that you were supposed to sprinkle over your food to reduce the food's caloric content, she told them the product was "bullshit."

When she does take on a project, she crafts the all-important call to action first. She then works on the rest of the script, fine tuning it to eliminate any language that might invite doubt or suspicion, and eliminating what she calls "ear stumblers," phrases that might encourage a viewer to stop for a moment and think. She's reeling a customer into a dreamlike world. Pick the wrong word or phrase and it's tantamount to a shockingly loud noise when you're sleeping peacefully. It can instantly turn a viewer off.

Glamorous work it is not, but Colleen earns satisfaction from knowing precisely how she performed. When Colleen worked for an ad agency, she had no idea how she did. Someone who writes a thirty-second Pepsi commercial has no idea if the ad he or she created influenced anyone to pick up one soft drink or another. Colleen can tell almost instantly if her work paid off. "It feels really good when the phones ring and the orders come rushing in," she says. Of course, the tidy paychecks don't hurt either. Colleen charges a cool $15,000 to write up a half-hour infomercial. And if you want her to make revisions or stand on the set during the shoot and help the hosts deliver their lines, you'll pay thousands more. But she's quick to point out that she's worth every penny. She takes credit for honing Tony Little's sales pitch for HSN in the late 1990s when he ended up breaking the network's record at the time, ringing up $50,000 a minute in sales.

OPTICAL ILLUSIONS

If you've ever seen a get-rich-quick infomercial, you've probably also seen a parade of gleaming homes and oversized, cardboard checks. It was a staple in the early days: the millionaire guru with a private jet, Rolls-Royce, and yacht, and perhaps even a few babes in bathing suits thrown in for good measure. Although much of the over-the-top imagery has been toned down in recent years, infomercial producers carefully examine the messages that each image and backdrop deliver to the viewer at home. Once again, manipulating the imagery isn't unique to direct response programming. But some of it is extraordinarily subtle.

When you watch an infomercial for a knife set, you probably don't notice that the tomato used in the demonstration of the "old" knife was a bit overripe, while the tomato used in the demo of the "new" knife—the product they want you to buy—is actually a bit underripe. Cutting the mushier tomato doesn't create the same crisp, satisfying cut, and while the difference is hardly noticeable, you can be sure that some far-off corner of your brain has noticed it. Less subtle is the use of black-and-white for a "before" sequence, which is then contrasted against colorized "after" footage, as if somehow you were living in the Middle Ages before that snazzy power drill came along. This is a tactic we confront routinely, of course: nearly every diet ad shows "before" photos that are hardly comparable to the ones taken after the weight loss. Not only has the woman lost a few pounds, she may very well have a new haircut, highlights, fake tan, and professional makeup job.

Infomercial producers do much of the same, but they have thirty minutes in which to operate and dozens of opportunities to communicate messages. From the houses in which infomercials are filmed to the body language of the people delivering testimonials, every element is under control. In one self-help program, a couple can be seen sitting next to each other on a couch as they explain how their relationship was on the brink of collapse. It wasn't a coincidence that when they started talking about the cure, they moved six inches closer to each other, and the wife moved her hand to rest it on her husband's knee. The "healing" process was unfolding before viewers' very eyes.

Marketers can insert all sorts of visual cues that aren't obvious on the surface. Bill Guthy and Greg Renker once suggested that the reason Proactiv was often displayed against the background of running water was because people expect acne products to dry out their skin. The image of the bottles of Proactiv covered in condensation and with a luxurious waterfall as a backdrop stimulated "the idea of hydration," according to Guthy. "We want the feeling of water. It works," he explained. Cosmetics manufacturers use water imagery, too. And beverage manufacturers use condensation to convey refreshment. But the effect of these tactics in the span of a half hour is far more powerful if you're a viewer sitting at home.

The cues are particularly obvious on exercise infomercials. The models using the machine are perfect specimens, their skin glowing from sweat and the seventeen gallons of oil that has been meticulously applied to every square inch of their bodies. When a handful of average people come on to share their stories of personal transformation, they haven't just lost weight and traded in their size 28 dresses for a tight, extra-small miniskirt. Their kids look happier, the unappetizing gruel on the dining room table has been replaced with a bountiful plate of fresh fruit and veggies, and sunlight streams into the family room for what seems to be the first time in their lives.

Many of these tactics are perfectly legal and are used by all sorts of marketers. Every food company on the planet hires a team of stylists to make sure that everything looks scrumptious. To be sure, there are limits to how far they can go: in the '70s, the Federal Trade Commission ordered Campbell's to stop putting marbles in its vegetable soup in commercials to make it look like it contained more vegetables than it really did.

Plenty of trickery takes place in the infomercial world. Several veterans said that their competitors sped up footage when demonstrating certain household appliances like power drills or electric knives to make the devices appear more powerful; some said they knew of marketers who cooked various foods in a conventional oven before they transferred it to the thimble-sized steak grill that was made for $3 in a sweatshop in Indonesia. But it's hardly all that different from the ads you'll see in magazines or newspapers. You won't find a drop of milk on the set of a cereal commercial. What's all that white stuff in the bowl? It's often Elmer's glue.

CHAPTER 3

The Kingpins of Paid Programming

Thousands of people are responsible for keeping the airwaves inundated with pitches: entrepreneurs and inventors who come up with the gadgets; directors, writers, and assorted production personnel who put the shows together; media buyers who coordinate the purchase of airtime and network employees who accept their orders; manufacturers who turn out the $6 blenders that sell for $129; and telemarketing people who pick up calls to 800 numbers on the second ring 24 hours a day, 365 days a year.

Few of the industry's top dogs earn public attention, which isn't entirely accidental. Keeping a low profile makes business sense. With the millions being made every year and scant regulatory oversight, the best tack often seems to be to hover in the background. Those who do become well known are often the ones who are doing things they shouldn't be doing. No one wants to turn into the next Joe Francis or Kevin Trudeau or enter into the crosshairs of a *Dateline NBC* or *20/20*. As an infomercial company spokesperson once neatly summed up to a reporter, "The spouting whale gets harpooned."

Most of the companies active in the industry are relatively

small; many that have had success have come and gone. Like the music and film industries, direct response is a hit-driven business. A company might come along and have a big earner or two, then turn out a handful of duds before filing for bankruptcy and disappearing from the late-night landscape. The infomercial graveyard is littered with companies that earned millions but went bust, like Twinstar, National Media, Quantum Marketing, and Synchronal Corp.

Two of the companies that have managed to stick around since the very beginning are Guthy-Renker and Telebrands. Both have managed to succeed—amid ups and downs, of course—since paid programming inundated cable TV in the mid-'80s. Yet they have very little in common. Guthy-Renker is famous for their lavish, half-hour productions, which cost a million or more and are jam-packed with celebrities. Telebrands relies on short-forms spots that are cheap to produce. Guthy-Renker hires Cindy Crawford to sell a line of skin-care products. Telebrands sells the Doggy Steps. Telebrands is presided over by A. J. Khubani, an Indian-American entrepreneur in New Jersey with a taste for expensive suits and starched shirts. Guthy-Renker is based in an affluent community near Palm Springs and operated by Bill Guthy and Greg Renker, who look like they spent a fair share of their teenage years surfing the waves off the coast of California. They share at least one thing in common, though: they're three of the richest men in the business.

You've probably seen the infomercials for Guthy-Renker's most successful product, Proactiv. Over the years, P. Diddy, Jessica Simpson, Kelly Clarkson, and Lindsay Lohan, among many others, have appeared on the program to discuss, in embarrassing detail, their struggles with acne. You may have even been taken aback to see big-name celebrities hawking skin care products on a late-night infomercial. What you probably didn't know is that Proactiv generates $750 million in revenue every year, which makes it the single most popular acne product on the planet, vastly more popular than competing products manufactured by blue-chip companies like Johnson & Johnson and Procter & Gamble. With sales of that magnitude, it wasn't such a stretch for the company to pay Combs $3 million to show up and describe how Proactiv "moisturizes my situation and preserves my sexy."

The offices of Guthy-Renker are headquartered in a modest, low-rise office building in the sleepy town of Palm Desert, California. The first thing you notice when you walk in are the smiling faces of all the ladies who keep the lights turned on. Leeza Gibbons, Cindy Crawford, Daisy Fuentes: giant posters of the women hang on the walls, and their bright, white smiles radiate across the room. They have good reason to be happy. Although most of them saw their careers peak more than a decade ago, each has earned millions in recent years thanks to their products with Guthy-Renker on late-night television.

After I'm provided with a security pass, I'm led to the second floor, where Renker's office is located. (Guthy spends most of his time at the company's Los Angeles office.) Renker, who is nearly fifty, is tall and trim. His hair is flecked with gray. He doesn't look anything like some of his colleagues in the industry, men who seemed to be fond of Hawaiian shirts and gaudy, gold watches. When I walk into Renker's office, the television is tuned to CNBC, and the *Wall Street Journal* is open on the coffee table. Dressed in a designer shirt and expensive Italian loafers with no socks, Renker reminds me of the sort of Hollywood überproducer you might find lunching at The Ivy.

Over the past two decades, Guthy-Renker has established itself as the most successful company in the direct response industry. The privately held firm generated $1.5 billion in sales in 2006 and has been profitable since it was founded in 1988. Although it's hard to estimate the value of the company, it's safe to say that each owner is likely worth several hundred million dollars. Although the headquarters of the company give off few signs of their extraordinary success, it's quite clear all those bottles of acne medication have added up nicely for the duo. They own two private jets. In the last two years, Guthy has purchased a $17 million home in Beverly Hills and a $12 million pied-à-terre on the Upper East Side of Manhattan.

Although both men have a majority stake in the company, they've had several outside investors over the years. In 1993 they sold a third of the company to billionaire financier Ron Perelman for $25 million. Perelman later sold his stake to Rupert Murdoch's News Corp., and Guthy and Renker eventually reacquired Murdoch's stake. In the late 1990s, they sold shares in their Asian subsidiary to one of Japan's largest trading companies as part of an effort to expand the company's global operations.

A global operation it most certainly is. Guthy-Renker's programs air in fifty countries around the world. Each year, the company spends tens of millions to create infomercials in dozens of languages. While you're watching a Proactiv testimonial by someone named Brooke or Britney in the United States, someone in Slovakia is watching Eva Skovajoskovà, a *studentka,* talk about how much the acne product boosts her self-confidence.

Renker has lived in the California desert for much of his life. Born in Phoenix, he went off to college at San Diego State, paying his tuition selling advertising space on bus benches. He then moved to the Palm Springs area, where his father ran the local racquet club. Guthy was born in New York and moved with his mother to Pasadena as a teenager, later enrolling in Ambassador College, a religious school affiliated with the Radio

Church of God and the controversial radio evangelist Herbert Armstrong. When the two men met in the early '80s, Renker was selling real estate and working for his dad at the tennis club. Guthy was running a company he'd founded, Cassette Productions Unlimited, which duplicated audiotapes, primarily for people who sold self-help packages, real estate courses, and subliminal programs.

It's easy to see why the two became fast friends. Both played tennis and golf, and they both shared a fascination with the burgeoning self-help moment. They were both regular attendees at real estate seminars and motivational courses. Indeed their fondness for the self-empowerment movement remains part of their corporate philosophy to this day. The company has a rather new-agey list of "commandments of management" that they circulate to employees and clients:

1. **Thou shalt not be afraid to take risks.**
2. **Thou shalt make thy competitor thy friend.**
3. **Thou shalt pick great partners.**
4. **Thou shalt build thy Rolodex and use it.**
5. **Thou shalt test, test, and test again.**
6. **Thou shalt cultivate the mini-media universe.**
7. **Thou shalt join and lead thy association and trade group.**
8. **Thou shalt cultivate the press and build thy company's brand name at all times.**
9. **Thou shalt not limit thy upside.**
10. **Thou shalt be prepared to eliminate all these commandments and start over.**

The idea that the infomercial business might be a money-maker came to Guthy when one of his audio duplication clients, real estate pitchman Paul Simon, started placing increasingly larger orders. Simon aired his first infomercial in 1984, and demand for the product was so overwhelming, Guthy says he had trouble keeping up with Simons's orders. After studying one of the early companies to exploit the infomercial marketplace, American Telecast, which had found success with a show called *A Millionaire's Notebook,* Guthy and Renker decided to base their first program on Napoleon Hill's book, *Think and Grow Rich,* which Hill originally wrote in 1937 and revised in 1960. Long-time fans of Hill's volume, the duo acquired the rights to the book and produced their first infomercial in 1988 using former NFL quarterback Fran Tarkenton as the host of the show. They grossed $10 million.

It was their first product that led them to their first mega-hit. One of the testimonials on *Think and Grow Rich* had been delivered by a dynamic, young self-help coach named Tony Robbins. When Guthy and Renker realized he had star potential, they signed Robbins to do a show of his own a year later. Robbins generated Guthy-Renker's first home run. Intensely charismatic and full of self-confidence, Robbins took the country by storm when he invaded the late-night airwaves in the late '80s. His first product, Personal Power, generated $50 million in sales in its first year. Guthy-Renker soon had the wherewithal to start rolling out new products and expanding to new markets.

In the early '90s, Guthy-Renker moved into the women's market with a line of skin care products by *Dallas* star Victoria Principal. They followed up with a teeth whitening system pitched by Vanna White and first introduced Proactiv in 1994 with Judith Light of *Who's the Boss?* fame as host. In the infomercial mania of the mid-'90s, they jumped into the fitness sector with an array of new products like Power Rider, Perfect Abs, Turbo Glider, and Fitness Flyer. In more recent years, though, they've focused on a smaller set of higher-end products, almost all of which feature a celebrity as the face of the brand. There's Meaningful Beauty, which is hosted by supermodel Cindy Crawford; Youthful Essence with soap star Susan Lucci; Natural Advantage, hosted by Jane Seymour; and Sheer Cover with Leeza Gibbons.

Not all have been successes, but in an industry where more products fail than succeed, they've had a better run than virtually all of their competitors. And they've built a reputation for offering decent merchancdise and dealing with customers honestly. That isn't to say they haven't been involved with a few products of questionable taste. In the mid-1990s, they aired a psychic program starring the flamboyant, androgynous Latin American TV staple Walter Mercado, a product they weren't particularly proud of. "It was great that we were making the phones ring. But why? Do we really want to be here?" Renker asked as we chatted about Mercado in his office. The company eventually dropped the product. "The universe will reward you if you put something out that's going to benefit people. Like Tony Robbins. We definitely got rewarded for *Think and Grow Rich,* the first show we did with Tony, and we're still getting rewarded for it. We did that from our heart and soul."

There were a number of things that Guthy and Renker did differently in the early days compared to many of their late-night peers. They typically spent much more money creating their infomercials, which resulted in higher production values, a sharp contrast from many of the other infomercials on the air at the time. They often relied on famous faces to promote their products. And, Walter Mercado aside, they generally stuck to more reputable products that wouldn't attract controversy. Both were active in founding the trade group in an effort to clean up the industry, and it was Renker who testified in front of Congress in 1990 when Washington lawmakers investigated the direct response industry in the wake of several scandals over illegitimate products.

It's been Proactiv, though, that has turned into their big money maker in recent years. Perhaps their wisest business decision was to offer it on a "continuity" basis, a model that has emerged as one of the most successful formats used by direct response marketers. Continuity programs get customers to agree to receive future shipments of the product on an ongoing basis. It's a subscription plan: when you call the 800 number to buy Proactiv, you're billed every sixty days and receive a new supply in the mail automatically. Like the mail-order record clubs that were popular in the 1980s and '90s, they take full advantage of customer inertia. Many people stick with Proactiv because it shows up on their doorstep every two months. For Guthy-Renker and its peers, the continuity program offered a solution to one of the industry's greatest challenges, namely, that even if you have a hit, it's extremely hard to turn them out one after another. A continuity program guaranteed a predicable revenue stream, not to mention that it allowed them to use their relationships with customers to offer other products and programs. They have since changed the business landscape for direct marketers. Nowadays most infomercials rely on the "back-end" to make money. Given the cost of the product and the airtime, a company may only break even on the initial sale. It's only by repeatedly selling you the same product that they make their money back.

To be sure, there was nothing especially unique about the Proactiv formula. Originally crafted by two dermatologists, Katie Rodan and Kathy Fields, the product features many of the same ingredients as other acne treatments on the market: benzoyl peroxide and salicyclic acid. What explains the reason Proactiv overtook brands like Clearasil, Clean & Clear, and Noxzema has almost everything to do with how Guthy-Renker marketed it.

Acne represents one of those problems that is almost per-fectly addressed by an infomercial. It's an emotional topic; it's deeply connected to issues of self-image. And as teenagers and young consumers in their twenties know all too well, not treat-ing acne can have far-reaching social consequences. The Pro-activ infomercial adroitly capitalized on the "trauma" angle. If you'd started watching the infomercial thinking a few pimples were harmless, you might have very well walked away thinking acne was akin to leprosy. Having acne is described as a "taboo." Teenagers talk about how miserable they were when they ar-rived at school with blemished skin and how their lives were to-tally transformed when their acne cleared up. The celebrities on the show pulled on heartstrings as well. P. Diddy explains that "the way you take care of your face I think reflects who you are." Host Vanessa Williams humbly suggests that she and Proactiv are changing the world. It's heavy stuff.

Today Proactiv remains the most expensive infomercial on the air. Not including the price of the talent, the thirty-minute production costs more than a million dollars. It also happens to be one of the only infomercials on the air that is shot on 35 mm film instead of video. The show is the handiwork of Lenny Lieberman, who Renker occasionally describes as the company's "Steven Spielberg." Lieberman has been working with Guthy-Renker since the days of Tony Robbins. The Proactiv program is only one of a handful of glossy productions that Lieberman has created for G-R. (In 2007 his company, Lieberman Productions, was acquired by Guthy-Renker, and he's since joined the infomercial powerhouse on a full-time basis.) All of them are a world away from the cheap productions that many people associate with the late-night infomercial circus. The soft-spoken Lieberman tells me that the huge costs that go into recording the show on film are well worth it.

The close-ups on people's faces don't look nearly as impressive when they're shot on video, he explains.

I suppose it only makes sense to spend the extra dollars, considering how much Guthy-Renker paid to get those faces to promote an acne solution in the first place. Although the program didn't launch with a pool of A-list talent, the program has since featured a long list of celebrities, most of whom would have never been caught dead appearing in an infomercial. Kelly Clarkson, Lindsay Lohan, Jessica Simpson, Serena Williams, Jennifer Love Hewitt, Brooke Shields, and Alicia Keys, among others, have all appeared on the show to discuss their ignoble battles with blemished skin.

That so many infomercials have featured celebs on the downward slope of their careers hasn't made it easy for direct response marketers to recruit top Hollywood talent. But while an infomercial may not be as glamorous as, say, a L'Oreal cosmetics contract, money talks. "If you take a supermodel that can get paid $2 million per year by a New York–based cosmetics company, they look at the cachet associated with that, and that's very exciting. What we basically say is, we can guarantee the $2 million a year, plus you're going to get a royalty," Renker explains to me. "I tell them: 'If we're super successful, you can ride this to the moon. And this could go on for a long time. You have the potential for a lot of upside.'" The royalty can go as high as three percent, depending on the star, which may means millions of dollars for years.

So do the celebrities on the show even use the stuff? Renker insists they do. And since the money is so significant, Guthy-Renker claims it can verify a celebrity's interest in the product before deciding to sign him or her to an endorsement deal. "Proactiv is really unique in that for the last two to four years, agents have been calling *us* to say, 'My client is a Proactiv user. Let's talk.' We're always appreciative because it's exciting, but our first reaction is 'Tell us the story exactly about how your client got involved with Proactiv and how they've used it and how they still use it.' And you'd be amazed how many of them fall out as a result of our drive to get that story." P. Diddy, Renker says, was using Proactiv for six years before he appeared on the show.

Success has brought out competition. There are now a handful of similar products on the air, including Murad, which was on the market before Proactiv's debut but has since started airing suspiciously similar programs on late-night TV. Counterfeiting has become a major issue, too. These days many of the bottles of Proactiv you'll find on sites like eBay were manufactured in China and packaged in almost identical-looking bottles. Their celebrity endorsements can backfire, too. In 2006 Guthy-Renker hired Lindsay Lohan to join the Proactiv cast, just months before she was arrested for drunk driving and drug possession and later landed in rehab, which is why you won't see Lohan touting the miracle powers of the acne-fighting formula on television anymore nor find her glowing testimonials on the Proactiv Web site.

One infomercial marketer who will never have to worry about a celebrity endorsement disaster is Ajit (A. J.) Khubani, the founder of Telebrands. He's never paid a celebrity a dime to appear in any of his short-form spots.

Unlike the majority of the late-night infomercial impresarios who live in sunny climes like south Florida, Arizona, and California, Khubani works from a low-slung office building located off the interstate in Fairfield, New Jersey. A glam building it is not, but it bears an impressive address: One Telebrands Plaza, although the "plaza" in question is really just an expansive parking lot. It's fitting that Khubani is geographically removed from his colleagues in the industry. Although he's one of the most powerful men in the business and the reigning king of novelty items sold in thirty-second spots on cable television, the hard-charging Khubani isn't at all like his peers. Khubani isn't the cheerful, back-slapping sort who finds any humor in his profession. He's serious and intense and rarely cracks a smile. And while his counterparts in the industry affect the sort of jeans-and-blazer casualness popular with West Coast execs, when I meet Khubani, he's dressed in a crisp gray suit, starched shirt, and perfectly fashioned tie.

Telebrands rules over the low end of the direct response industry. Khubani doesn't pay for expensive shoots or hand over millions of dollars to A-list stars (or even thousands of dollars to C-listers). His products could never be described as high end. If Bill Guthy and Greg Renker represent the Tiffany & Co. of the infomercial industry, Khubani is the Piercing Pagoda: he's looking to move product and make money.

Khubani's company has been responsible for dozens of products over the years. Typically, the company inundates the airwaves for a few months with its short-form spots, which then disappear almost as quickly as they arrived, fading into our collective memories of the junk that's been proffered on TV over the years. His products are impulse buys; almost all cost less than twenty or thirty bucks, which means they're cheap enough to get someone to run to the phone without deliberating for very long. They're intended to hit a nerve and generate a response, at which point Khubani floods discount stores with the product, using the spots to drive both TV and retail sales—and dropping the price along the way as he runs through his inventory. By that point, Khubani is on to the next gimmicky product. It's a process he repeats a dozen times a year.

Khubani tells me he was inspired to create Doggy Steps when he noticed his aged dog was having trouble climbing up on the sofa. But the product wasn't new, nor is anything else that Telebrands sells. Similar products had been sold in catalogs and pet stores for years. But Khubani did what he does best: he manufactured the product in Asia extraordinarily cheaply, made the steps lightweight and collapsible (which would both save Telebrands on shipping and allow him to boast about the product's "space-saving" features), and relied on his oversized presence in the market to move millions of units. Whereas similar products retailed for $50 or $100, Khubani made the Doggy Steps available for a third of that. And he managed to make a killing in the process: He estimates the Doggy Steps have made Telebrands more than $30 million.

He's done much the same thing with countless other products. Telebrands is responsible for the Flat Fold Colander, the Better Pasta Pot, and the Owl. He's the man behind the Grease Bullet and the PianoMan Roll Up Piano. He also produced the OneSweep, which is pitched on TV by Anthony Sullivan, who also handled the on-air honors for Khubani's Stick-Up bulb. It's quite an empire: the company grosses more than a quarter-billion dollars a year.

Khubani is a first-generation American—his parents emigrated to the United States from India and settled in New Jersey. In 1982, after graduating from Montclair State University, Khubani joined his father's import business in New York City. His first experience with print direct response came a year later when he purchased a $7,500 ad in the *National Enquirer* and advertised an AM/FM radio, which he purchased through his father's company for $6 and retailed for $10. This first venture only ended up breaking even, but after that, he says, he was "hooked." He spent the next few years advertising a handful of products he came across, like a pair of massage slippers with bumps on the bottom, which massaged your feet as you walked.

It was in 1987 that Khubani first moved into TV, with short spots for Easy Cycle, an ultrasonic flea collar, and AmberVision sunglasses. It was the latter that earned him his first big hit. His father's suppliers in Taiwan manufactured them for a dollar a pair. Khubani, in turn, sold them on TV for $10. Fifteen million pairs later he'd racked up a small fortune, and the product was later picked up by major retail chains, a channel he'd use widely and aggressively to sell his products over the coming years.

Khubani's greatest distinction, though, is that in an industry where almost every new product is a rehash of a previous product and there are precious few true inventions, he has carved out a reputation as one of the most shameless copycats in the business. Khubani's taste for appropriation dates back to his very first success, AmberVision. It only appeared on the market after an entrepreneur named Joe Sugarman had found success with a similarly cheesy pair of glasses called BluBlockers. The big difference: whereas Sugarman had been offering the glasses on TV for $59.95, Khubani's ads featured a similar looking item for one-sixth the price.

Creating cheaper versions of other people's products has since become firmly embedded in Telebrands' business plan. It's a strategy that often results in a generous—if occasionally somewhat messy—payday. A successful product in the marketplace means there's demand for the item, and Khubani can usually figure out how to manufacture it (and then sell it) for less. He can also take advantage of the free publicity—his competitors' ads on TV, which tout a more expensive product—and use that to drive sales of his product. Thanks to his deep relationships with discount stores, by the time a smaller entrepreneur approaches a retailer with his $20 gizmo, Khubani has often already negotiated to stock the chain with millions of his knockoffs for $10.

To be sure, it's a path that involves some risks, although Khubani says he doesn't infringe on existing patents. But he's learned that potential litigation isn't such a bad thing. The threat of an extended lawsuit and millions in legal bills often deters many smaller entrepreneurs from going up against him; Khubani knows full well that if it does turn into a legal brawl, he can probably settle the matter by offering a miniscule royalty to the inventor. In other cases, he's gone on the offensive by finding similar patents to the same product. He then acquires the rights and goes after the company offering the product that predated his own. When Khubani noticed that Guthy-Renker was offering a teeth whitening product in the 1990s, he hunted down a patent that Guthy-Renker hadn't bothered to secure, purchased it from the inventor, then threatened litigation. The end result? Khubani negotiated a settlement that resulted in Guthy-Renker paying *him* a royalty rate for every product *they* sold.

His most brazen knockoff, though, came when he launched the ThighShaper, which Khubani started selling after the ThighMaster became a TV sensation. Developed by an entrepreneur named Peter Bieler, the ThighMaster show, hosted by Suzanne Somers, quickly became a hit. (By Bieler's account, it grossed more than $100 million in its first few years.) Not long after, Bieler learned Khubani had a similar product in the works. Bieler had an idea of what was in store. "He was a legend in his own time, a knockoff artist par excellence," Bieler recounts in his memoir, *This Business Has Legs*. "He had a reputation in the infomercial business as someone who'd kill your direct response campaign by selling his copies to the retailers, who'd sell them for half the price. Your phones stopped ringing."

Sure enough, Bieler soon got a call from one of Khubani's deputies. "So are you going to sue me?" he asked Bieler, knowing full well that Telebrands could crush his upstart under a legal avalanche. Bieler did sue and entered a tortuous legal battle that lasted for years. Bieler ended up winning, but it was a bruising battle that cost him a fortune.

The ThighMaster defeat set in motion a precipitous fall for Khubani's Telebrands. During the boom years, the mid-1990s, Khubani expanded rapidly, plunging millions into rolling out new products. But a few setbacks upended the company. In addition to the ThighMaster suit he also lost a fortune on two other abdominal products, the AbFlex and the EZ-Krunch, both of which failed to take off. The losses and the messy litigation forced Telebrands to file for Chapter 11 protection in 2000. He's since rebounded nicely, though. These days Telebrands is as big as it was before its tumble, and it continues to pump out the same sort of cheap junk it always has.

Coming up with these novelties isn't quite as easy as it may appear. Like many in the business, most of Khubani's products don't see the light of day. He says one in ten items that the company tests on TV eventually turns into a serious ad campaign. One in five, he claims, makes him serious money. (He doesn't even count a product a success, he says, unless it makes him $10 million or more.) Once he has what he thinks is a hit item, it receives Telebrands' standard ad treatment. If all those short commercials you see during the day seem exceptionally repetitive (they all usually begin with the question "Have you ever . . . ," which highlights a problem that will be solved ten seconds later), that's because they're all created by the same group of people inside an ugly white office building in New Jersey.

He occasionally has failures (he lost millions on his AirPress Massagers, bizarre-looking plastic "space boots" that were supposed to stimulate muscles when inflated), and he's had ongoing patent issues to contend with (his best-selling Owl is now the subject of a lawsuit). But Khubani continues to hunt for new products, looking for inspiration, of course, in what already works. And it's not just his fellow infomercial entrepreneurs in the United States who have to worry about Khubani encroaching on their turf. Occasionally he'll find an item that's successful abroad and simply introduce the product to the American market. While his tactics haven't earned him much respect among his peers, due to his oversized presence in the market, even his competitors fear speaking out about him.

The government hasn't been quite as timid. In 1990 the Federal Trade Commission took action against Khubani, accusing the company of failing to ship on time, make refunds, and cancel orders, all violations of the FTC's Mail-Order Rule. Telebrands and Khubani paid a $35,000 civil penalty, but he was back on the FTC's radar screen in 1996, when he was accused of violating the Mail-Order Rule once again and paid a $95,000 fine. The same year the FTC took action against Telebrands for airing misleading ads for two products, a television antenna and a hearing aid. In 2003 Khubani paid his biggest fine when the FTC went after Telebrands for its Ab Force electronic stimulation belt. Arguing that the company participated in "unsubstantiated and false advertising," Khubani and his company were fined $800,000. According to the government, Khubani sold more than 700,000 Ab Force belts and accessories and earned approximately $16 million; the agency also accused Khubani of transferring some of the earnings to his wife to hide just how much he made.

Khubani has nothing to say about the charges, nor does he profess any interest in money. "Money isn't the driver anymore. It's the passion," he says to me without any hint of irony. I suppose that's not completely off the mark. He could have sold the business for a small fortune by now or passed it on to one of the various family members who work with him. He does seem to genuinely get a thrill out of unleashing yet another silly novelty product on half of America.

That money doesn't concern him much is a bit less credible considering he and his wife occupy a 27,000-square-foot mansion in Saddle River, New Jersey, that features nine bedrooms, seventeen bathrooms, and a six-car garage. Russell Simmons and his ex-wife, Kimora Lee Simmons, used to live down the street. In an interview with an Indian-American publication, his second wife, Poonam, a pop star in her native India, bragged about the NSX, Hummer, Mercedes S55, BMW 745, and green Lamborghini in their driveway, not to mention her husband's yacht.

"And that brings us to the closets!" the publication breathlessly reported as Poonam gave the writer a tour of the manse. "Khubani has such a huge shoe closet loaded with footwear that her friends tease her, 'This is worse than Imelda Marcos!' She has one huge walk-in closet just for her Indian outfits, another for her western outfits, yet another closet for her winter clothes, and a cedar closet for her furs." The couple spends weekends at a luxe beach house in Long Branch, New Jersey. Those mops and Doggie Steps add up.

"I love what I do," Khubani tells me, which I don't doubt for a moment, considering the riches he's acquired. Naturally, he's focused on the new products he has coming to market, new solutions to old problems. Recently, Telebrands debuted the Ear-Lift. "Do your favorite earrings pull on your earlobes, making them sag? Have they become stretched, unattractive, even torn? Now there's an amazing new solution called EarLift!" the spot starts off.

The glorified adhesive tape will run you $16.

CHAPTER 4

Crooks and Liars

Have you ever noticed that when a movie features a serial killer or some other evil monster holed up in a cheap motel room, he's often watching an infomercial as he sharpens his knife/cleans his gun/weaves a dress out of human skin? That's no accident. Based on the premise that any exposure is good for the bottom line, infomercial producers are the only content owners willing to grant broadcast rights to moviemakers under such less-than-desirable circumstances.

Few infomercial tycoons have ever been implicated in anything quite as horrific as murder, of course, but late-night television has become a haven for shady characters peddling products of little or no value with dubious claims.

The industry's ties to questionable business practices date back to the beginning of the medium. Some of the very first people who marketed products on TV later found themselves in legal hot water after their products were revealed to be frauds. While the industry has matured and cleaned up a good deal since then, without controls in place to keep the bad guys out, it still remains a popular business for people looking to make a quick buck. The infomercial's guiding principle—give people solutions to their everyday problems—has brought out dozens who have peddled products that promise the world and rarely deliver. Despite suggestions to the contrary, there is no product marketed on late-night television that really cures cancer and diabetes. And there isn't a no-money-down course in the world that will make you a millionaire overnight.

It's hardly surprising that scamsters have come along to prey on the most desperate Americans, people looking for a ray of hope on a TV screen in the middle of the night. Infomercials can be fantastically lucrative. Remember Miss Cleo, that kindly Jamaican woman with a headscarf who spent years promoting a psychic hotline? She had quite a good run in the 1990s, until, that is, the company behind the show and its founders, Steven Feder and Peter Stolz, were busted as part of an investigation into fraudulent business practices and it was revealed that Miss Cleo, better known as Youree Dell Harris, wasn't even Jamaican. (Nor was she psychic, but you probably already knew that.) The ensuing investigation uncovered a litany of devious ways that gullible callers had been scammed out of their money. Phone operators had put people on hold for twenty minutes and assured them they wouldn't be charged during that time, which wasn't true, of course. Representatives would even try to get previous customers to call back, leaving enticing messages on their answering machines when they weren't at home: "Miss Cleo had a dream about you last night!" But what was most remarkable was the sheer size of the scheme. When the case was eventually settled, Feder and Stolz agreed to pay a $5 million fine and forgive $500 million in outstanding charges. Yes, indeed, the company had racked up a half billion bucks in phone fees by the time it was shuttered.

The sheer number of legal actions taken by the government over the years is sobering, considering how rarely the authorities even take action. Since deregulation in 1984, the attorneys general in almost every state have commenced investigations and filed lawsuits; the Federal Trade Commission has filed hundreds of suits against scores of companies and individuals; there have been wide-ranging investigations conducted by the Securities and Exchange Commission, U.S. Postal Service, and Federal Bureau of Investigation; and more than 100,000 Americans have filed grievances with various Better Business Bureaus, their local police, and assorted government agencies.

It's hard to judge what percentage of the business dabbles in unethical behavior—and there's no question that the bad apples tend to dominate the coverage of the industry. But it's also quite clear that the infomercial attracts a higher proportion of disreputable entrepreneurs than other industries. Given the lack of measures in place to keep out the crooks, that isn't altogether surprising. As tainted as Wall Street may appear to the average citizen, you can't get a job as a broker at Merrill Lynch or Morgan Stanley if you're a convicted felon: brokerage firms are required to run FBI background checks on their employees. There's no background check when someone comes along with a supposed cure for cancer. As long as you have a program on tape and you can cover the cost of the airtime, you're good to go.

Of course, not every misdeed is the same; there are most assuredly shades of gray. There are products that are outright scams; there are items that don't live up to the claims described on television; there are sleazy tactics used to charge people for additional products and services; and there are customer service abuses that charge people for things they didn't sign up for and prevent people from returning items for a refund. Not all are equally pernicious. Someone who sells a consumer a worthless product or someone who manages to drain someone's bank account of every last cent isn't on par with someone who has a misleading money-back guarantee. And it's worth noting that these aren't problems confined to the infomercial trade. You can check your newspaper or turn on your computer and find the same sorts of tactics used by scamsters everywhere.

But collectively, the list of offenses is so long and the number of products that have generated legal action so numerous that it makes your head spin. Just a few of the products that have resulted in FTC and/or Food and Drug Administration (FDA) action over the years: vitamin supplements like CalMax, Carti-let, Coral Calcium, EnerX, Lifeway Vitamin Sprays, Seasilver, Smoke-Less Nutrient Spray, Supreme Greens with MSM, and Mountain-High Bee Pollen; various hair potions and formulas, including Copa Hair System, Folliplexx, Hair Farmer, Helsinki Formula, InVisions Process, Omexin System, and the Sable Hair Farming System; pain relief remedies, like Bio-Tape, Blue Stuff, Eze-Away Relief, and Therapy Plus; products that promise to improve memory, such as Mega Memory System and Focus Factor; purported cures for addictions, including Doctor Callahan's Addiction Breaking System and Smoke Away; countless diet products, like Exercise in a Bottle, Fat Trapper, HGH–3X, Hydro-Gel Slim Patch, Nu-Day Diet, Peel Away the Pounds, Slenderstrip, Slimdown, ThermoSlim, and Cholestaway; various skin care products, including Acne-Statin, Anushka Bio-Response Body Contouring Program, and the California Facial Skin Rejuvenating System; ionic bracelets, such as the Balance Bracelet and Q-Ray Bracelet; and snoring remedies, such as D-Snore and SNORenz. And who can forget those ubiquitous ab devices, including the Ab Isolator, Abs Only Machine, Abtronic, Ab Energizer, Airofit, and the Fast Abs Exercise Belt?

This is by no means a complete list, and it doesn't cover the people who have proffered moneymaking schemes over the years (we'll get to them later) or some of the worst offenders in the genre, like Joe Francis of *Girls Gone Wild*. The reasons these products have spurred legal action often vary. Some are downright nonsense, of course, like hair growth formulas that contain no special ingredient, or those ionized bracelets that are marketed for their healing properties despite plenty of research to the contrary. (A Mayo Clinic study published in 2002 determined that the bracelets didn't do anything to relieve pain, but that the placebo effect often made people think they worked.)

In other cases, products have generated heat for their misleading claims. There's nothing wrong with a device that helps you tone your abs or a supplement containing calcium or vitamin D. Using one of those ab devices that mimics a sit-up might help you firm up your abdomen. But using it for five minutes a day won't compensate for the six cheeseburgers you ate for dinner last night. And while calcium might be good for your bones, it won't help a paraplegic leap out of his wheelchair. In countless other cases, the product isn't really the issue at all. It's simply what happens once the transaction begins and a variety of unsavory and illegal tactics are used to inflate the price or sign consumers up for additional products.

Just as it's impossible to lump every misdeed together, there are degrees of ethical responsibility along the food chain. There are the people who hatch these schemes. But then there are countless people involved in bringing the product to market— from production companies to media-buying agencies—who may or may not be aware of the profound problems associated with the products. Some of this is clearly a case of people choosing to ignore the truth that is staring them in the face. A number of people in the industry who worked with disreputable people in the past told me that they had no idea the product was fraudulent, although it was occasionally hard for me to see how that could have been possible. These were exceedingly smart, savvy businesspeople. Did they not have their doubts that a two-time convicted felon pitching a real estate course might just not be the real deal?

You can't blame them for turning a blind eye any more than you can blame network executives for allowing these programs to air on their channels. I'd venture to guess that Philippe Dauman, the chief executive of Viacom, is aware that Joe Francis isn't a church-going philanthropist. But that won't stop Viacom's Spike channel from happily taking Francis's dollars tonight when *Girls Gone Wild* comes on at 2:30 a.m.

It's easy to paint the industry with a broad brush and assume that all infomercial marketers are crooks and intent on defrauding America, or that every personality hawking a product on late-night TV is a con artist. In reality, it's a lot more complicated than that. Tony Robbins has made a fortune selling hope via a series of DVDs, CDs, and assorted books and manuals, but he's never claimed he can cure you of your cancer or make you instantly rich. What he promises is that he can motivate you and pump you up, which will, he suggests, put you in a better position to take control of your health and finances. Yes, he profits off the hopes and dreams of average Americans sitting at home worrying about their credit card bills and lack of health insurance coverage. But Dr. Phil, who offers much the same sort of hope on his syndicated TV show, isn't in it for charity either.

It's not hard to see how a man like Robbins operates. He's an electrifying presence. Due to a congenital endocrinologic disorder that resulted in higher-than-normal levels of the growth hormone somatotropin, he is, quite literally, larger than life: he's six foot five and possesses the largest head and teeth I think I've ever seen attached to a human body. His staggeringly high energy levels could rouse someone in a coma. Can I see how he might get a room full of computer salespeople pumped up so that they go out and do better than the day before? Absolutely. Will buying his DVDs magically give someone the willpower to give up their long-standing addiction to alcohol? Perhaps not. Ultimately, whatever impact Robbins has is purely mental—and that isn't an easy thing to calculate. There's no way to measure the benefit of a Robbins seminar or DVD series any more than there's a way to measure the progress seeing a psychotherapist once a week.

What is offensive to so many is that Robbins has created such a mega-brand around his numerous courses and seminars, many of which don't seem to quite deliver on the incredible hope that he offers at the outset. That he's also made such a fortune in the process also sticks in the craw of critics. Robbins can pack stadiums and get people to pay thousands just to watch him via teleconference; he can organize a weekend retreat at a five-star hotel and get three dozen couples to pay $20,000 each to spend a total of a few hours in his presence; companies routinely pay him a quarter of a million bucks for an hour of his time. The silly stunts he pulls at lectures and seminars, like having people walk on a bed of coals, a trick that's been trotted out by magicians for years, don't bolster his image. Add in a very generous helping of braggadocio—including frequent references to his many homes, his helicopter, and his private island on Fiji—and his tendency to go after anyone who dares to criticize him, and he doesn't come off as the sort of guy interested in much beyond padding his own bank account.

But is this really all that different from what happens on daytime television? Phil McGraw probably earns just as much money every year lecturing couples on healthy relationships, notwithstanding the fact he (allegedly) cheated on his first wife, (allegedly) subjected her to mental abuse, was sanctioned by the state of Texas in 1989 for (allegedly) having an inappropriate relationship with a nineteen-year-old patient, and wasn't even licensed to practice psychology for nearly two decades.

As distasteful as Robbins (or Dr. Phil) might be, at the end of the day, it's important to make the distinction between those who peddle false hope and those who flagrantly violate the law, such as Kevin Trudeau, who has suggested he has the cure for everything from cancer to AIDS to diabetes. Neither Robbins nor McGraw, of course, has been sent to prison. Then again, there are plenty of people lurking in the infomercial business who probably should be behind bars, although it's unlikely they'll ever see the inside of a courtroom during their lifetimes.

No Money Down?

When I first saw Donald Trump on an infomercial, I was taken aback. Okay, fine, he'd stamped his name on bottled water, vodka, and a line of steaks, but did the self-described billionaire really need to stoop to this? Late-night TV infomercials were the province of men who *hoped* to get rich, not people who'd already made it. What made the show even more bizarre were the absurdly low production values. The interviewer was not a glamorous celeb; it was a woman named Anne Howard, who'd hosted a number of infomercials over the years and looked a lot like the sort of person who might have anchored a local news broadcast in Tulsa around 1986. To add insult to injury, the set was atrocious, and not because Trump had insisted on painting the entire room gold. It looked like the infomercial had been filmed in the A/V lab of a junior college. Naturally, my first reaction was to immediately call the 800 number on the screen and reserve a seat for an upcoming Trump Institute seminar.

The following Monday afternoon, I headed to a rather un-impressive Holiday Inn in Midtown Manhattan. On my way over, I wondered why Trump didn't simply schedule the event at one of the hotels he owned. Why not save a few thousand bucks? As soon I saw the assembled crowd, I understood why. Here was one of the most depressing, downtrodden audiences I'd ever seen, a room of people who embodied the very margins of American society. Many of the people were elderly and infirm. More than a few looked emotionally troubled. This was a group of people who either desperately needed a solution to their financial troubles or had nothing better to do than to spend their afternoon in a poorly ventilated basement ballroom for the promise of a free paperback book written by none other than Donald J. Trump. I found a seat toward the back of the room just as the show got under way.

The Web site had made it clear that The Donald himself was not going to be attending the seminar in person. Not everyone in the audience seemed to know that, though, and when Trump's proxy, Saen (pronounced "Sean") Higgins, stepped on the stage, there were more than a few disappointed faces in the crowd. Higgins was aware that there might be some confusion about whether Trump would be present, but he elegantly segued into a video of "introductory remarks" by Trump that seemed designed to soothe the audience as well as suggest to the crowd that this program was, in fact, connected to the billionaire real estate mogul. The video was just a couple of minutes long— Trump complimented us on taking our "first step" to financial freedom. When it was done, the audience inexplicably started clapping. Then Higgins launched into his act.

Dressed in a suit and bright pink tie ("Do you mind if I loosen my tie?" he asked the audience within minutes of taking the stage, as if the disheveled crowd could care less), Higgins was every bit the slick pitchman you might see at a state fair. He was full of energy and occasionally bounded down the aisle to try to coax more enthusiasm into the crowd. He trotted out all the clichéd devices that they must teach at public speaking school: he memorized the names of a handful of people in the first couple of rows and went back to them again and again so he could personalize each "lesson." He complimented the audience repeatedly—for our foresight, our wisdom, our desire to make better lives for ourselves. The lecture itself was like an extended infomercial. Higgins started to run through homes he'd purchased for pennies on the dollar and later flipped for a profit. It sounded exactly like what I'd seen on countless no-money-down real estate shows in the middle of the night.

During the first break in the proceedings, I struck up a conversation with the elderly Korean man sitting next to me. What brought him here, I asked. He confessed that he often attended free real estate seminars for fun. He was retired and had nothing better to do. He explained that he'd purchased a couple of real estate programs in the late 1980s and early '90s. "They never work," he explained in broken English. "But you never know. Might pick up tip," he said. Plus there was the free book they'd be giving out, he added. That alone was a $7.50 value. What was most remarkable, though, was what he said next. "I seen this guy before. He's okay," he said, then proceeded to explain that he recognized Higgins from another real estate seminar for another infomercial.

He was absolutely right, of course. The billionaire mogul had merely licensed his name and collected a fee—a Donald Trump trademark. The man who spent his career building skyscrapers in Manhattan had no part in what was unfolding in front of us. We'd been handed off to a bunch of get-rich-quick pros. Higgins, it turned out, was a regular pitchman for National Grants Conferences, which holds similar events at hotels and sells a $999 course on how to get "free government money." NGC had partnered with Trump to create the Trump Institute. Higgins's job was simply to lure people into buying real estate courses—it really didn't matter which one.

NGC has a checkered legal past. A handful of investigations failed to find a single NGC customer who had managed to make any money with the program. The attorneys general from no fewer than twenty-four states condemned the company and its business practices in a letter to the FTC in 2007. The year before, Vermont's attorney general, William H. Sorrell, filed suit against the company for consumer fraud; NGC settled by handing over $300,000 in restitutions and paying a $65,000 fine. But the company's sordid record goes back further than that. Michael Milin, who founded the company with his wife, Irene, and appears on camera in the infomercials for NGC, started his path of deception back in the 1980s as a seminar salesman for get-rich-quick guru Tony Hoffman, who'd been one of the infomercial industry's first scammers to appear on the scene. Hoffman's first infomercial company went bankrupt in the late '80s, but he resurfaced again in the '90s. He's been in and out of trouble since then. Most recently, in 2003, Hoffman was sued by the FTC over his breast enlargement and male virility pills, and he and his partners were forced to pay $3.2 million. Perhaps the classiest footnote to Hoffman's career was his ill-fated attempt in 1996 to produce a video in partnership with O. J. Simpson about the former football star's whereabouts on the night Nicole Brown Simpson and Ron Goldman were murdered.

Milin's companies have since racked up a lousy track record. Dozens of complaints have been registered over the years with the Better Business Bureau and the BBB of Southeast Florida gives Milin's current company its lowest rating, an F. While the long list of angry customers might have discouraged lesser entrepreneurs, the Milins have simply moved on. Their persistence has paid off in a new business partner: Donald Trump.

As the seminar continued, Higgins recounted tantalizing stories of people who purchased homes for nothing and then resold them for big bucks. These "case studies" were almost identical to the scenes from countless infomercials: stories of people who found homes in foreclosure, applied a fresh coat of paint, cleaned up the weeds in the front lawn, then sold them for a fortune. I later found out that Higgins used the very same material—and the very same photos—for his NGC presentations.

"Don't have the money for a down payment?" Higgins asked. "That's what credit cards are for," he said and walked us through the concept of credit. Every once in a while he'd toss in a fancy phrase that he thought might impress the crowd. When he told the audience that they needed to "think outside the box," he uttered the words as though he'd coined the phrase.

It was clear from the outset that Higgins had no plans to give any useful information away. This was a sales pitch, designed to get us to sign up for a weekend course that would take place the following month at another hotel, two full days of instruction for $1,499. And just why did Higgins suggest that Donald Trump needed to charge this much to impart his real estate wisdom when he was already a billionaire? Higgins actually asked this question aloud as if he knew that would present an obstacle for members of the audience. You need "skin in the game," Higgins said, suggesting that we needed to demonstrate we were serious about "change" by coughing up our own cash before we'd be able to reap the rewards. Paying the fee would prove we weren't lazy losers. Trump, Higgins explained, needed to see that we were totally committed before he'd hand over his precious knowledge.

Higgins then pointed our attention to fancy black attaché cases that would be handed out to people who signed up. There wasn't anything very valuable in them—they were filled with brochures, pamphlets, and a spiral notebook—but they were emblazoned with the Trump name on the front, which I'm guessing was intended to carry some cachet. He then proceeded to explain to us that the price of $1,499 was a limited time offer and available only today. "If you wait a few days and think about it, the classes will fill up, and you'll miss your chance to be a millionaire," he warned.

As disturbing as all this was, what followed was even more troubling. Sensing that some of the gathered welfare recipients might have trouble scraping together $1,499 on the spot, Higgins suggested that if attendees needed to make arrangements—like, say, contact family members for assistance or borrow from a friend—now would be a good time to step out of the room to do so. He then mentioned that if people needed to spread the purchase across several credit cards, it could easily be arranged.

When I first walked into the room, I noticed that there were probably two dozen Trump Institute employees on hand, including a handful of burly fellows in suits. As the course wound down, I realized why the company had so many people present. Like a scene from a movie where police officers swarm to the exits to foil an escape plan, the men quickly blocked the exits, enrollment forms in hand. This was a carefully choreographed act. Sure, you could walk past them—we weren't hostages—but these intimidating sales reps weren't going to let you walk out before they had a chance to convince you otherwise. After concluding his pitch, Higgins paused to give those who had already decided to shell out their cash a chance to head to the back of the room to hand over their credit card numbers. It was hard to tell how many people signed up on the spot; judging by the number of people who were clutching black attaché cases several minutes later, I'd guess that thirty people had just surrendered $1,499. The Trump Institute had just collected $45,000. And another demo would take place at the hotel in three hours.

Higgins had no intention of giving away the free book until he tried to sell us one more time. This was the freebie, the only card he was holding in his hands; he was going to squeeze it dry. After the wave of new customers started to file out of the room, he resumed his shtick. This time, though, his enthusiasm and excitement gave way to an extraordinarily hard sell as he mocked us for showing up for a free book but not having the guts to take our destinies in our hands and make the next move. When he was done, I got up out of my chair and headed to the exit. Before I got to the door, though, I was approached by a sales rep who asked me if she could talk to me for a moment. I had seen her stopping people the first time around; I knew full well she planned to make a last-ditch effort to turn me into a customer.

Dressed in a black pantsuit, she started off by telling me about herself. "I'm twenty-four. I made $151,000 last year. Almost $152,000, actually," she added, which sounded like the kind of line she'd been practicing for weeks. She explained that she'd purchased another real estate course that had cost her $4,000, but that "this one is much, much better." I should have kept quiet, but I couldn't resist speaking up. If she were making all the money she wanted in real estate, I inquired, why was she spending her days in a Holiday Inn ballroom selling the course? "For my resume," she said. "When Mr. Trump offers you a job, you don't say no," she sneered, as if The Donald had called her personally from his Boeing 737 to implore her to join the "Trump team."

"So, are you ready to enroll?" she asked me. I told her I wasn't. I'd have to give it some thought. Then she turned nasty. She told me my indecision was "lame." "When are you going to take control of your life and be a man?" she asked. If nothing else was going to work, perhaps shaming me and questioning my manhood might force me into submission. "Don't you want to have money? Don't you want women to be attracted to you?" she asked as I felt my face flush with embarrassment. I was so shocked by her approach, I couldn't muster a reply. After wishing me the least sincere "good luck in life" I have ever heard, she walked away in search of more vulnerable prey. Slightly sickened by the encounter, I made my way to the door, accepted my copy of Trump's paperback book, and bounded up the stairs to the hotel lobby. As I exited the building, I noticed the kindly Korean man a few steps ahead of me. He gave me a cheerful little wave as he walked off in the other direction.

My encounter with the Trump Institute was a sobering one, but it's hardly unique. Turn on your television tonight and you'll encounter a dozen similar-sounding, no-money-down programs. Suffice it to say that if land ever does become available for pennies on the dollar, you won't hear about it on late-night television courtesy of Gary Collins, whose most noteworthy accomplishments over the past decade include a guest appearance on *Baywatch Nights* and two drunk driving arrests in two different states.

Almost every get-rich-quick infomercial on television is a sham. Yet they continue to flood the airwaves year after year, taking money from gullible Americans who think the answer to all their problems is contained within a ten-CD, four-workbook set that looks like it was designed by a six-year-old. It isn't hard to see why some people might be fooled. We're inundated with messages that tell us it's possible. This is the land of opportunity! If we only try, we'll succeed! With great risks come great rewards! Business magazines breathlessly detail tech wunderkinds who achieved billions almost instantly. We pick up a celebrity weekly and read about the hot young actor who was discovered on line at Starbucks, then we head off to the newly minted millionaire's house in Beverly Hills and see all of his new material possessions on MTV's *Cribs*.

Success, we're told, can happen in the blink of an eye and without much work on our part. The prospect of making money the old way—working for three decades and building up a pension—seems as out of date as ever. Who wants to work for The Man for a lifetime, only to walk away with a six-figure pension and a gold watch? Didn't you see what happened to those poor people who worked at Enron? Their 401(k) accounts were wiped out overnight! In the day of instant rebates and instant fame, the idea we can make a million dollars in two weeks flat is as appealing as ever.

While the themes of infomercials vary, nothing has endured quite like the prospect of making money through real estate, buying land for nothing, then selling the property for a hefty profit. Owning a home, we're told, is the American dream; it represents safety and security. You can never go wrong buying land, we hear time and time again. And outside of finding a massive oil deposit under your home, it's often framed as one of the few ways you can get disgustingly rich in America without an education or any professional training. Wall Street or Silicon Valley may seem like a world away to the average American, but there are real estate opportunities in every town. Plenty of shows on television attest to the opportunity and help further the mythology. Shows like *Flip That House* on TLC show us people buying a home, fixing it up, and selling it at a profit, all in the course of a tidy half-hour episode.

The premise with most infomercials is that there are homes in every community that are undervalued. They may have gone into foreclosure. They may be homes owned by people who can no longer afford their monthly mortgage payments and who are willing to part with their residences for a fraction of their worth. For whatever reason, you, the late-night viewer, are told that you can buy these properties for very little money down and flip them for a profit—or, if you feel like it, you can simply rent them out to generate "cash flow."

It sounds like a simple enough plan. You buy a house for a few thousand dollars in back taxes, throw on a new coat of paint, and—voilà!—two weeks later you sell it for its full market value. You then take your winnings and do it again and again until you're such a success story, you're invited back on the infomercial, where you can hold up your six-figure deposit slips for all to see.

Of course, it has never been quite so straightforward. Contrary to what you may have heard in a glowing testimonial on TV last night, there are no three-bedroom ranch houses in Orange County that can be purchased for $953.80. If that were the case, there'd be a very long line of people standing outside with their checkbooks in hand, myself included. Sure, there's money to be made buying homes in foreclosure. It's not impossible. But it takes time and experience—not to mention a hell of a lot of hard work—none of which a course advertised on TV will provide you with. And while there are ways to purchase real estate without putting a great deal of cash down, rest assured that banks aren't handing out million-dollar loans to burger flippers at McDonald's.

But the idea is a tantalizing one—so tantalizing, in fact, that this pitch has endured for more than twenty years now, through countless cycles of booms and busts. When the real estate market was booming in the late '90s, viewers were told to get in now while the market was still on the up. Think the recent mortgage meltdown took the wind out of marketers' sails? Hardly. Rising foreclosures just mean tons of super-cheap properties are now on the market. With the possible exception of a nuclear meltdown (or a government crackdown of some sort), it promises to be a moneymaker for infomercial marketers for years to come.

For the people who sell these programs on television, the get-rich-quick scheme has been a perennial moneymaker. There's precious little work for them to do. Most of the programs offer a "formula" that has been repackaged time and time again: it's no coincidence that many give phone numbers that haven't been in service for years or reference laws and regulations that became outdated a decade ago. Not a single one has information you couldn't pick up for free at your local library or for twenty bucks at a bookstore.

To see just how little the pitch has changed over the years, all you have to do is turn to the Internet, where old infomercials live on in perpetuity. One of the most amusing early real estate shows appeared on the scene in the late 1980s, a no-money-down program pitched by a man named Tom Vu. If you spent any time watching TV back then, you probably came across Vu; he was hard to miss. Standing on the deck of a luxurious yacht and surrounded by a half dozen bikini-clad babes, the Vietnamese immigrant and professed real estate tycoon (real name Tuan Anh Vu) would look at the camera and taunt the audience. "Look at the choices I have today!" he would shout as the camera focused on the girls standing by his side. "Wouldn't you like to have choices like this?" For about five years, Vu was a bizarre fixture on late-night television, promoting his "Tom Vu Real Estate Seminar," as he tooled around in his convertible Rolls-Royce, showed off his mansion, and took us aboard the aforementioned chick-magnet yacht. To this day, Vu's program is probably the silliest infomercial that has ever graced cable at two o'clock in the morning. Its ridiculousness, though, explains why I must have watched it fifty times from start to finish. In the annals of campy television programming from the late '80s and early '90s, Tom Vu's would rank in the top five.

Like many of his colleagues, Vu would start off the show with a depressing tale of pain and suffering, which for Vu meant an impoverished upbringing as one of ten brothers and sisters in war-torn Vietnam. After moving to America, Vu described how he landed a busboy job at a ritzy country club full of millionaires and captains of industry. One day, while filling up glasses of ice water, the young Vu summoned up the courage to approach a particularly wealthy old man. "Would you please tell me how to be rich like you, sir?" Vu supposedly asked him. The millionaire obliged and uttered three words, three magical words that turned everything around for Vu and set him on a path to extraordinary wealth. What were those words, you ask? Vu's answer: "Come to my seminah, and I'll tell you!" (It was a seminar, of course, but since Vu couldn't really pronounce the word, it came out as "seminah.")

The structure of Vu's show wasn't that different from the one that's used today to hawk real estate business opportunities. There's always a proprietary secret that's mentioned, one that sets *this* program apart from the rest. There's a constant parade of average people who appear on camera to describe what life was like before the windfall: angry phone calls from collection agencies, towering piles of credit card bills, bread and water for dinner, and so on. Then the show cuts to what these people's lives look like today. There are photocopied checks that seem to offer irrefutable proof that they're telling the God's honest truth—and plenty of footage of their current existences, which invariably feature big backyards, shiny cars in the driveway, and smiling, doting wives.

At this point, the host of the show aims to clear up any last-minute doubts while injecting a little guilt into the equation. Don't you want to stop living paycheck to paycheck? Don't you want to be your own boss? Haven't you dreamed about making more money than you ever imagined—and in your spare time? This is freedom we're talking about! Don't you want to be able to spend more time with your kids? It isn't enough, apparently, to tell a guy sitting in his dingy apartment that you're going to make him filthy rich. You also have to tell him that if he doesn't fork over $49 to buy the product, he probably doesn't love his wife or kids very much.

Like most infomercials of this kind—and like the Trump infomercial I watched—Vu wasn't selling a product. Vu was just asking people to attend his free ninety-minute seminar, where, much like what happened at the Trump event, Vu and his team of "sales associates" would try to convince attendees to part with thousands on a real estate "boot camp." Despite the show's extraordinary cheesiness, it worked. Vu racked up millions in sales before he ran into legal trouble in the early '90s with Florida's attorney general.

Vu's trajectory from obscurity to national TV fame, then back to near-total obscurity, isn't unique. It's the same path dozens of crooked infomercial pitchmen have taken over the years. They come from nowhere (it's unclear what Vu was doing before he turned to TV) and scurry off to calmer waters when the authorities come calling. One of the early get-rich-quick pitchmen, Dave Del Dotto, was laying sheetrock in Modesto, California, before he took to the air and promised he had "secrets" worth millions. After he was the target of a 1995 FTC suit, which he settled in 1996 by paying a measly $200,000 fine, he moved to Northern California and used the ample fortune that remained to start a new career. Today he oversees Del Dotto Vineyards,

400 lush, organic acres in the heart of Napa Valley that produce bottles of Merlot selling for $60 a pop.

Del Dotto's path is typical. Someone appears on the scene with a suspicious product and promotes it for as long as possible, until the complaints pile up and the authorities finally take action. In most cases, the marketer settles with the feds (generally for a sum that's substantially less than what was earned through the swindle) and either returns a few years later with another equally dubious product or, like Del Dotto, takes his or her earnings and moves on to something less risky. Only the exceptionally unlucky end up in prison. As for Vu, he continues to take big risks, although it's not because he's still making infomercials. He moved to Las Vegas a few years ago and now spends his days playing high-stakes poker. He's doing pretty well for himself. He took home $364,761 for second place at the World Series of Poker in 2007.

Of all the crazy real estate schemes promoted on late-night TV, perhaps the most outrageous scam was carried out by a man named William J. McCorkle. This isn't because McCorkle did anything that different from anyone else. In fact, he probably made a lot less money than many of the men who plied the airwaves at the same time. The difference was that McCorkle was busted and sent to prison, and every tawdry detail from his scam was exposed for the world to see.

William McCorkle, it should be mentioned, wasn't the name the get-rich-quick pitchman was born with. Raised in Lake Mary, Florida, he was known throughout his younger years as William Gonzalez; he adopted his stepfather's less ethnic-sounding name before plunging into the infomercial business. A former $4-an-hour busboy, male stripper, and unsuccessful real estate agent, McCorkle first appeared on the air in the early '90s, with a product called "William McCorkle's Fortunes in Foreclosures." The program wasn't that different from what other real estate gurus were offering, but he did manage to up the ante a bit. Not only did McCorkle promise he'd help you find these undervalued homes, but he also promised he'd invest his own money to help you buy it. "You find the property," McCorkle would say, "and I'll put my money down, and we'll split the profits fifty–fifty." What a deal! Viewers wouldn't even have to take on any risk. All they had to do was find the property, and McCorkle would whip out his own checkbook and take care of the rest.

As you can probably guess, McCorkle wasn't planning to give anyone the cash to buy as much as a taco. All he wanted you to do was spend $69.95 on thirteen flimsy, black-and-white booklets and two VHS cassettes. Once you'd received the materials in the mail, his sales associates would try to convince you to invest in an "advanced level" course for another $1,000. Between McCorkle's outrageous claims and his gift for gab on camera, he turned "William McCorkle's Fortunes in Foreclosures" into a profitable little business. In lieu of Vu's bathrobe-and-track suit look, McCorkle opted for a conservative business suit and red salesman's tie. Instead of T&A, he focused the camera on his Rolls-Royce, private jet, helicopter, and luxurious yacht, each emblazoned with the name McCorkle. It was a compelling show: at its peak, in early 1996, McCorkle's company employed 400 people and was grossing $50,000 a day. According to several of his former employees, his toll-free number was ringing every six seconds on average.

Unfortunately for McCorkle, it all came to an end on May 9, 1996, when the million-dollar Seminole County home that McCorkle occupied with his wife, Chantal, was raided by agents from the Florida attorney general's office, the IRS, the FBI, and the U.S. Postal Service. They'd been investigating him for months following a flood of complaints from people who hadn't managed to make the program work. Not a single one had gotten McCorkle to fund their real estate deals; when dissatisfied customers had tried to return the booklets and cassettes, they'd been turned away. When angry customers started contacting local news organizations (and when a disgruntled former McCorkle employee materialized), the authorities started looking into the matter. It wasn't hard to see something was amiss right off the bat: the man who claimed to be worth millions had paid just $10,000 in taxes the year before.

It was after accessing McCorkle's home and office that the fun began—at least as far as the investigators were concerned. McCorkle had kept meticulous records that detailed every aspect of the scheme. The authorities discovered invoices for the planes, boats, and helicopters; it turned out that he didn't actually own the luxe assets he bragged about on the show, but had simply rented them on an hourly basis, arriving with "McCorkle" decals in hand. In a desk drawer, investigators found a copy of one of Tom Vu's old scripts with a word changed here and there. (At least that explains why their impoverished upbringings sounded so familiar.) The get-rich-quick guru had also been kind enough to save all of the outtakes and unused footage from his infomercial shoots. Not only did it quickly become clear that the testimonials had been delivered by McCorkle's close friends and business associates, but McCorkle himself could be heard off camera telling them what to say.

The scheme had paid off nicely. When government investigators finally tallied things up, they determined that McCorkle had made $28 million from "Fortunes in Foreclosures." It was a substantial sum, obviously. But it wasn't because he and his wife, Chantal, ripped off thousands of gullible Americans that they went to prison. (His wife was accused of taking part in the scheme and charged accordingly; she later denied she had any knowledge of what he was up to.) It turned out that the money McCorkle had collected had been stashed in secret accounts in the Cayman Islands. Thanks to money laundering laws that were intended to punish drug dealers who moved their cash offshore, the McCorkles were collectively charged with more than a hundred counts as part of the indictment. The 1998 trial lasted just under two months. After a defense by F. Lee Bailey (of O. J. Simpson "Dream Team" fame), husband and wife were both convicted on dozens of counts of fraud and money laundering. The consummate actor, William McCorkle passed out in court as the verdict was delivered and had to be rushed to the hospital. At their sentencing the following year, each was handed twenty-four years in a federal penitentiary. (The couple has since divorced, and their sentences were reduced to eighteen years in 2006.)

As one of the few who have ended up doing time in prison, McCorkle is one of the great anomalies in the infomercial business. His sentence represents one of the stiffest penalties that has ever been handed out in connection with an infomercial-related scam. But as fake as his show was—and as brazen as McCorkle appeared on camera—the actual material he offered to the public wasn't that different from what is marketed on TV today. Set aside the fact that he claimed he'd help finance the deals and he was touting yet another method to buy foreclosed real estate for no money down. You can find precisely the same sort of course if you flip on the TV tonight and tune into Carleton Sheets or John Beck. Or Russ Whitney. Or Jeff Paul. Or Dean Graziosi. Presumably they've learned the most valuable lesson from the McCorkle case and invested in a decent paper shredder.

But not every real estate pitch is the same these days; there have been new incarnations, too. Russ Dalbey, for example, offers up "Winning in the Cash Flow Business," a program that involves purchasing real estate loans at a discount. Once again, this is a real market—banks buy and sell notes every day, roll them up into complex securities, and sell them on Wall Street. (It's also one of the reasons why so many banks have announced multibillion-dollar write-offs and why some firms, such as Bear Stearns, have gone under.) But the odds that some naive auto mechanic in Wichita is going to be able to find these note holders, convince them to sell, then arrange to sell them to a third party? Not too great. Despite what Dalbey says on the infomercial, you won't make a fortune in twenty-four hours or, like "Don B.," make $712,860 on your first deal.

Of course, the ever-smooth Dalbey doesn't see it that way. When I reach him on the phone from his office in Colorado, where he operates the very impressive-sounding Dalbey Education Institute, he's full of boundless optimism. "I think it comes down to hope," he says. "People want hope. And that's what infomercials provide. The hope they can change their lives for the better." He pauses. "The only way you can get their attention is appealing to their hopes and dreams."

I have no doubt about that. Dalbey doesn't seem to have any trouble in the hope department. It's the will-people-actually-make-a-dime department I'm more concerned about. But it's quickly apparent that Dalbey is much more interested in luring customers in, not figuring out how to help them. He explains how meticulous he is about scripting his infomercials to generate the highest response rate. He talks about how he tests his show again and again to make sure it's sufficiently alluring. And because he knows full well that you don't make any money selling them on the "frontend," he tells me about how once a customer is in his "database," he "loads them up with additional products and services."

He has a fine set of role models. "Back in the 1980s when all of these infomercials were going on—Don Lapre, Carleton Sheets, Ron Popeil—I used to actually record 'em, and I would watch them and study them over and over and over. It would give me ideas on how I could work certain verbiage into my direct mail programs. I loved it. Sometimes I'd use the same phrases."

Dalbey's personal history is hard to piece together or confirm. He says he was a champion cyclist in his younger years and was once a member of the U.S. Cycling Development team; he says he later gained a spot in the Guinness World Records for his one-mile speed record. (I didn't find anything to confirm these details.) He later turned to a career as a stockbroker (he won't say where) but moved into real estate when he quickly grew disillusioned with the stock market. Dalbey says he learned the ropes from an LA-based real estate guru named Carl Abe, at which point he was making more money than he ever dreamed of. "By twenty-six, I was a millionaire! I could have retired!" After Abe's "passing," Dalbey says, he took over his real estate educational seminar business, which, in turn, led him to what he's doing today with the Dalbey Education Institute.

Indeed, there was a man named Carl Abe who was a real estate promoter in Los Angeles in the 1980s and early '90s and billed himself in his ads as "Mr. Mortgage." Until, that is, he shot and killed his wife and then turned the gun on himself—in front of their six-year-old daughter—in 1994.

Dalbey says he first started delivering his courses in 1995. Yet in 1997 he filed for bankruptcy in Colorado. And it wasn't the first time. Back in 1989, right around the time he was supposedly a "millionaire," he'd done the same thing in the state of California, too. There are plenty of other questionable details when I pull up Dalbey's records. He's been subject to numerous tax liens over the years. And he's had nasty encounters with other unsavory characters in the business. In 2003 Don Lapre filed suit against Dalbey in federal court for $100,000 over a contract dispute. The matter was later settled out of court.

Dalbey has been rising fast the last few years. "We started with $4 million [in revenues] in 2001. Then $40 million, $50 million, $80 million. It's now $100-plus million," he says, rattling off his successes. The infomercial world has paid off handsomely for him: in late 2006 local papers in Boulder, Colorado, reported that he'd purchased a 5.8-acre parcel of land worth more than $5 million; he now plans to tear down the 24,000-square-foot school on the site to construct an elaborate home, pool, and orchard.

Dalbey concludes our chat by pointing out that his product actually works and that all the testimonials are real—but that I shouldn't be fooled by his competition in the business opportunity sector. "There's a lot of crap out there," he says.

I've noticed, Russ, thanks. Indeed, there's crap in every direction you turn. In addition to real estate courses and "note networks," the TV airwaves are now used to sell actual real estate. Erik Estrada of *CHiPs* fame can be seen offering property in places like Arkansas and Texas. Promising monthly payments as low as $220 a month (with "E-Z financing!"), it's easy to see how the program works. A quarter-acre plot in rural Arkansas will cost you some $40,000 after the payments are made and you account for interest. A quick check of the Century 21 affiliate in the area turns up a listing for twenty-five times the amount of the land for exactly the same price. Of course if you call Century 21, you won't get a free weekend vacation for two (no sales pressure!). Nor will your purchase have the imprimatur of the ever-savvy real estate expert Erik Estrada. But it's turned into a profitable model for the company that markets the "homesites," National Recreational Properties. They now have two all-star celebrity endorsers on the roster—former *Love Connection* host Chuck Woolery has joined the effort—and they're now pitching property in rural parts of New Mexico, California, and Washington State.

But real estate won't be the only item on the menu if you tune in this evening. When the stock market took off in the late 1990s and day trading became a popular phenomenon, a series of trading infomercials popped up, each offering a surefire way to make money in the stock, currency, or commodities markets. Since most of them were targeted to people who normally spent their days handing out Denny's Grand Slam specials, the marketers had kindly simplified things for total novices. Little green lights on your computer, several of them promised, would indicate when to sell; red lights would tell you when to hold. They'd reduced the most complex financial markets in the world into something about as complicated as playing Minesweeper on your computer. Naturally, there were plenty of testimonials from customers who professed to having known nothing about the stock market beforehand but were now generating eye-wateringly large daily returns.

Many infomercials merely identify their testimonial givers by their first name, or their first name and last initial. In the case of "4X Made Easy," they were kind enough to post each person's full name on the screen. I quickly jotted down the first name I saw—"Willie Guevara"—and made a plan to find out if he was for real.

Turns out he was. I eventually found Willie living in California. I was, however, a bit taken aback to hear he had an MBA from Wharton—not the typical path for most people who pick up infomercials late at night—and that he had a decade of experience trading foreign currencies. (Forex—or "4X"—is Wall Street jargon for "foreign exchange.")

So does the average person have a fair chance at success? "No, I don't think so," he says. "Most people don't want to do the work, number one. They think just because they paid a lot of money—which is $3,000—they're entitled to make money. They look at this as a hobby."

It's hard to totally blame people for thinking that, I suggest, considering the show repeatedly describes trading as a great way to make lots of money in minutes with no experience. "That's true. It's promoted as something you can do in your spare time. That's totally incorrect. They make it appear easy. That's the biggest misconception. The company sucks people in, and that's unfortunate. But people don't do their due diligence," he explains. Guevara assigns blame to everyone involved: the company for serving as "a slick marketing and sales organization" and consumers who should know better. Guevara has a good point. The people who buy these products bear some responsibility. Then again, it's hard to think straight when someone is waving a check in your face.

There are other new routes to take if you're a sleazy infomercial marketer intent on promising a quick path to profit. When the Internet bubble expanded and the papers were filled with stories about overnight tech billionaires, Dave Espino came along with the "Internet Treasure Chest." For $49.95, Espino promises he can teach you how to make millions buying and selling merchandise on eBay. (Needless to say, people who buy the product soon find out that the only ones who make millions on eBay are eBay employees when they cash in their stock options.) But the old tactics endure. There are a handful of multilevel marketing programs that continue to sell online, some of which haven't changed all that much over the years.

Multilevel marketing (or MLM) programs turn the purchasers of the products into salespeople themselves, and they're often totally legal: Amway and Mary Kay turn the women who join their organizations into independent retailers. When the format is abused, though, it can quickly devolve into a pyramid scheme where the only money being made is from signing up more members, not actually selling products or services.

For an MLM program to work, the people have to be selling products that other people want to buy, which is most certainly not the case with SMC, a multilevel marketing product that's been marketed on television for years. You may have seen the SMC infomercial. It stars Tom Bosley of *Happy Days* fame, who promises that if you sign up as an SMC member, you'll have access to a vast warehouse of inventory that you can then purchase at wholesale prices and sell to your friends and neighbors. If you've ever watched for more than a minute or two, you may have realized that the best salesperson in the world wouldn't be able to unload SMC's junky collection of ceramic figurines or woodcarvings, even if each piece cost a dime. You're certainly not going to be collecting $10,000 for your efforts. And if you can sell an $11 porcelain fountain shaped like an angel, well, then, you should probably give some thought to selling condos, cars, or infomercials, where the real money is.

One man who has managed to dabble in just about every shady sector of the infomercial trade over the past decade and a half is Don Lapre. I first noticed him on the air in the early '90s when he hosted a program called *The Making Money Show.* Dressed in a yellow polo shirt—and speaking in an exceedingly whiny and insistent voice—Lapre would promise you that he could make you a fortune thanks to "tiny classified ads."

Needless to say, the product was a scam, of course, but Lapre had been in trouble even before he debuted on late-night TV. A high school dropout, his first company, a dating service, went bankrupt in 1988; he and his wife later set up a credit repair business that was shut down by the Arizona attorney general's office for violating the state's consumer fraud act. With two big failures under his belt, he turned to TV and debuted *The Making Money Show,* explaining how from his "tiny one-bedroom apartment" he managed to become a millionaire thanks to those "tiny little ads."

Lapre's spiel was as distinctive as Vu's boat-and-babes routine. (He later earned himself a David Spade imitation on *Saturday Night Live* for his contributions to pop culture history.) His program, however, quickly ran into trouble. In 1994 the state of Arizona moved against Lapre for failing to pay taxes; in 1995 Michigan's attorney general took action against him for failing to register his business in the state; in 1997 the Internal Revenue Service issued a lien against the Lapres for close to a million dollars for failing to pay delinquent taxes. Finally, in 1999, Lapre filed for Chapter 11 bankruptcy on behalf of himself and the many companies he'd used to sell his products, including New Strategies, Tropical Beaches, Dolphin Media, Don's Making Money, and National Reminder Service. Trouble followed him even after the businesses were sold off. The man who took ownership of his program—and simply ran the same infomercials that had featured Lapre—was shut down by Arizona's attorney general in 2002.

Lapre represents a common paradigm in the world of scam infomercials. He wasn't forced out of business because he ripped off everyone who ever gave him a penny. Like William McCorkle, who was sent away for money laundering, it was Lapre's tax violations, not his fraudulent consumer violations, that ultimately drove him out of business.

Of course, he wasn't out of business for very long. Within months, Lapre had moved on to a new scheme, teaming up with an "herbalist" named Doug Grant to sell vitamins. Lapre's product, however, had a twist. Instead of actually selling the vitamins, which they'd humbly named "The Greatest Vitamin in the World," they'd use the infomercials to hire salespeople to sell the vitamins for them. Now Lapre would be able to tell you he'd make you healthy and make you rich, all at the same time. The airwaves were quickly blanketed with ads promising the public

that they could earn "$200 a month for life!" by signing up as
sales reps. "If a billionaire wanted to create the most amazing
nutrition supplement for the human body and money was no
object, he or she would end up creating a product just like The
Greatest Vitamin in the World! It's that simple!" Lapre intoned
on the half-hour infomercials.

There were a few problems, the least of which was that the
bottles of vitamins looked like they'd been designed by Lapre's
daughter. The vitamin had not, in fact, been the product of "over
one hundred studies from the *New England Journal of Medicine*."
Nor was Doug Grant, Lapre's partner, the official nutritionist for
the Miami Heat, as they both had claimed. The story took a turn
for the even tawdrier when Grant was charged with first-degree
murder, after his wife ended up dead in their bathtub in 2005.
Poor Mrs. Grant had been drowned in her bathtub, pumped full
of Ambien.

In July 2005 the FDA warned Lapre to stop claiming that
his vitamin product could cure a long list of diseases. But Lapre
wasn't about to let a murder allegation or an FDA warning letter
get in the way. By 2006 he'd created a new infomercial, one
without any mention of Grant's involvement, and perhaps because he was worried his name had been tarnished by his numerous legal run-ins, he didn't even appear on the program
himself: he had a buxom brunette named Tylene Megley, who
once worked for Grant, stand in for him instead.

Lapre is now facing more trouble. In 2007 the U.S. Postal
Service raided Lapre's home and office as part of an investigation into what the search warrant described as "deceptive and
aggressive" telemarketing tactics. The IRS later joined the case,
and although Lapre has yet to be charged as of September 2008,
both agencies have active and ongoing investigations under way.
It's unlikely that they'll make anything stick, though. Lapre is

one of the savviest scamsters in the business. Very few assets are held in his name; his home is owned by "The Lapre Children's Trust." He operates his business empire from a cell phone and Yahoo! e-mail address. (Lapre refused to talk to me.) And even if he is brought down, there are plenty of people—including his own protégés—who will be happy to fill the void. One night I noticed a real estate pitchman named Dean Graziosi deliver a spiel that sounded suspiciously like something out of a Lapre production. Just a coincidence? Not so much. When I looked up the incorporation records for Graziosi's company, Think a Little Different LLC, the company's return address listed Lapre's home in suburban Phoenix.

When Chantal McCorkle appealed her lengthy sentence, her lawyers and supporters described her actions as a "victimless" crime. "Had she been convicted of second-degree murder, child rape, child pornography, or smuggling thirty-three tons of marijuana into the United States, she would have received a lighter sentence," one of her friends later argued. Fair enough. Even her reduced sentence of eighteen years was an awfully long time considering she was a first-time offender. "Victimless," though, it was not. Infomercial scams don't just rob people of the $59.99 they spend to purchase the product; they occasionally defraud people of every dime they have to their name. Get-rich-quick guru John Beck nearly ruined Gabriel Ruiz's life.

Beck has been a staple on late-night TV for years. He offers a product called "John Beck's Free & Clear Real Estate System," which promises viewers that his methods can help consumers "purchase homes all over the United States and Canada for as little as two or three cents on the dollar." He isn't that different from the other people hawking real estate late at night. But it happened to be Beck who piqued Gabriel's attention, and he spent $39.95 to buy the course over the phone.

"When I got it in the mail, I reviewed the material, and what I realized was that the CD-ROMs were basically just other infomercials," he tells me. Apparently, he'd expected to find the key to making millions in the flimsy package that had arrived on his doorstep: "I started looking through things, and there weren't any step-by-step instructions. I didn't have any understanding of what I needed to do next."

Like other products of this kind, Beck's $39.95 system doesn't make him any money. The fee just about covers the airtime to market the product. But it gives Beck an easy mark, someone who can be squeezed for more cash at a later date. "A couple of months went by, and all of a sudden I get a call from someone from the offices of John Beck," Gabriel says, describing a call he received one afternoon from someone who spoke fluent Spanish. (Gabriel is Mexican American.) The caller introduced himself as Jaydar Salazar. "I told him I didn't really know what I needed to do exactly. He explained I needed a coaching program to make it work."

Coaching programs are the dirty little secret behind many of these courses. People who purchase the product are told by company reps that they can't take full advantage of it unless they sign up for a coaching service, a personal adviser who will guide them to real estate riches. The coaches can tack on thousands in additional fees.

Gabriel's story isn't unique: thousands every year buy a get-rich-quick product, then get scammed into signing up for a personal coach. What was so disturbing were the circumstances that led to his fateful phone call in 2004. When he picked up the phone to dial the 800 number late one evening, he was home in bed and heavily medicated. A twenty-three-year-old Marine,

Gabriel had recently returned home from the war in Iraq. He'd been injured fighting in one of the bloodiest, most dangerous places on the planet. He was now at home, on full disability, and confined to bed. He was unable to sleep and recovering from severe burns and posttraumatic stress. He was on a regimen of meds that made it difficult for him to think clearly. He was, clearly, a perfect target.

Gabriel had been a member of the Second Assault Amphibious Battalion, Second Marine Division, based out of Camp Lejeune in North Carolina. In the run-up to the war in 2003, his unit had been transported to Kuwait. He was deployed into the war zone within days of the U.S. invasion and spent months fighting in some of Iraq's most hostile areas. His unit participated in the Battle of Nasiriyah, the exceptionally bloody encounter in March 2003 that left eighteen Marines dead and more than sixty others wounded. It was while on patrol in late 2003 that Gabriel was injured. A machine gunner aboard a tank, Gabriel's finger was on the trigger when the long barrel of the gun accidentally made contact with a downed power line. Gabriel was instantly electrocuted. The ensuing fire left him with second- and third-degree burns all over his body.

By the time he called John Beck's 800 number more than a year later, he was back at home in California with his family, figuring out what to do with the rest of his life. "I didn't want to make millions from the John Beck course," he tells me. "I just wanted to learn how I could buy a house for myself to live in."

Jaydar Salazar didn't tell Gabriel how much this "coaching program" would cost when he first called him. Salazar did what many of these sales reps do—he made nice. "He befriended me, he invited me to come visit him sometime and hang out," Gabriel recalls. Over the course of several lengthy calls, Salazar also got a handle on Gabriel's financial situation: "Eventually he started asking me how much money I had, how many credit cards I have, how much I have in the bank." At the time, Gabriel didn't have a credit card. Salazar explained to him how to fill out an application. But what the eager salesman was most interested to hear was that Gabriel had recently received payments totaling $8,000 from the U.S. government. It was for back pay that he was owed and for the reimbursement of medical expenses. It was, Gabriel explained, all the money he had in the world. Not long after, Salazar told Gabriel how much the coaching plan would cost him: $7,000.

This is the way it usually works. It's only after the sales rep ascertains just how much the person can afford that a price for the coaching program is established. If the person on the other end of the line thinks he can only squeeze out a few thousand bucks, then that's the price that he comes up with. Others have reported paying more than $15,000 in connection with these mentoring products. Developing a rapport with the mark is part of the process.

It isn't hard to understand why Gabriel agreed to go along with the plan. Salazar had assured him repeatedly that he couldn't go wrong. He also promised him that there was an iron-clad, money-back guarantee. "If it doesn't work for you and if you don't make millions, you'll get your money back," he assured the disabled veteran. Gabriel was twenty-three years old. He was homebound, depressed, and on medication. Here was Salazar promising him a way out—a big, bright future.

Naturally, these coaching programs aren't any more informative than the booklets that come in the mail when you pay the initial $39.95. Gabriel's $7,000 entitled him to a fresh batch of CD-ROMs and ten half-hour sessions with an "expert" on the phone. But he quickly discovered that the experts hadn't actually used Beck's product. They were glorified customer service reps, taking calls from naive would-be millionaires from home. "I could hear her kids crying in the background," Gabriel says, describing his first encounter with the mentor who had been assigned to him. "She'd put me on hold to go and shut the kids up and come back. And I was on a timer, too, which meant every time she put me on hold for five minutes, I was losing money." The woman didn't strike Gabriel as very knowledgeable. On their second call, she didn't remember anything they'd discussed the week prior. Who could blame her? She was probably juggling dozens of customers.

After their second session, Gabriel requested a new coach, and he was handed over to someone who was described as "much more experienced." It didn't help matters much. It was after his fourth call that Gabriel decided to start tape recording the sessions. It wasn't because he thought he was being cheated; he was just concerned that he wasn't keeping track of the information that Dave, his coach, was giving him. Keeping a recording would allow him to refer back to the sessions as he set out to find foreclosed properties in his area.

Listening to the tapes of Gabriel struggling for answers while talking to Dave was depressing, to say the least. He was having trouble performing the tasks that the materials and Dave outlined, not because it was especially complicated, but because much of the advice was totally inaccurate and incomplete. Dave told him he could simply buy land in other cities and states and then "flip them" on eBay. But purchasing these distant properties first required Gabriel to conduct a title search. To do that, he had to find a company that would conduct the title searches on his behalf. Each would cost hundreds of dollars, and Dave had suggested running dozens of searches. When Dave suggested he could just buy cheap property at real estate auctions around the country, Gabriel found out that many of the auctions required bidders to appear in person.

Everything was infinitely more complicated than Gabriel had expected, and Dave had few solutions. At one point, he suggested that Gabriel make some easy money by setting up an investment club in the area and renting a hotel conference room for $100. Then you charge each person $10 and get twenty people to attend, Dave advised. It was the blind leading the blind. To keep the momentum going, Dave regularly mentioned to Gabriel that plenty of his other "clients" were generating fantastic returns. "Someone two years younger than you just bought land for $500 and resold it instantly for $10,000," Dave tells Gabriel at one point.

By the time he'd run through his ten calls, Gabriel realized that he wasn't going to be making the millions he dreamed about. And so he did what Salazar had told him to do: he called up John Beck's company and asked for his $7,000 back. "Salazar had disappeared by that point," Gabriel says. "The company acted like they didn't know who the guy was. When I told them about the money-back guarantee that I'd been promised, they told me that I didn't have any proof of that and that those guarantees weren't corporate policy." Best of luck, kid.

Gabriel's options were limited. He contacted a couple of local attorneys; each told him that taking legal action would be costly—money he didn't have. They both suggested that he file a complaint with the Better Business Bureau or the attorney general's office. He soon spiraled into depression. "Every time I would think of what happened, I'd get really upset," he recalls. "I didn't tell my family—I was too embarrassed to tell anyone. This was $7,000 that almost cost me my life. What's so sickening is that guy knew that."

For months, Gabriel says he was consumed by thoughts of revenge. He went through the phone book looking up people with the last name of Salazar, calling them one by one, searching for the man who'd befriended him by the sound of his voice. When he found a "J. Salazar" in the phone book who lived twenty miles from Beck's offices near Los Angeles, he thought he'd gotten lucky. He called the number again and again until he finally got the guy on the phone. It wasn't him. "I couldn't stop thinking about finding this guy. I became obsessed with him." He combed message boards looking for other people who'd been victims of similar scams.

Fortunately, Gabriel's story has a happy ending. Information he located on the Internet led him to file a complaint with Utah's attorney general—Beck's coaching program, Mentoring of America, is based there—and he got a letter in the mail one day informing him that he'd be receiving a refund. In July 2006, two years after the ordeal began, he received a check for $7,000. It came just three months after Utah's Division of Consumer Protection filed a lawsuit against the company, which resulted in restitutions of close to $400,000. He was one of the lucky ones. Most people never end up seeing a dime.

Notwithstanding Gabriel's ordeal and the experiences of countless others, Beck's show continues to air nightly across the country. He spends millions of dollars every year to promote his course. And he's only one piece of a larger con. The company that bears his name, John Beck's Amazing Profits, LLC, is controlled by a Van Nuys, California–based firm called Family Products, LLC. Family Products is a tidy, little conglomerate of late-night real estate scams: in addition to Beck, it promotes two other "gurus," John Alexander and Jeff Paul. But it goes even deeper. Family Products, in turn, is controlled by the LandBank Group, Inc., a firm that was founded in 2005 and became a publicly traded company a year later after it merged with a struggling technology company called iStorage Networks. And just who is behind Land-Bank? Meet Doug Gravink and Gary Hewitt.

In 2002 the duo—along with several others—were sued by the Federal Trade Commission over AB Energizer, yet another product that promised it would help people lose weight thanks to electrical stimulation. As part of the settlement, both men agreed they wouldn't sell abdominal muscle stimulators. (Apparently, they turned to real estate instead.) But they've had other legal run-ins. In 1990 Gravink, who worked at an infomercial production company called Twin Star, was party to an FTC settlement over three controversial products: EuroTrym Diet Patch, a weight loss product; Foliplexx, a baldness product; and Y-Bron, an impotence product. All three products, the FTC argued, made claims that were "false, misleading, and deceptive."

As for the Utah-based coaching program that ripped Gabriel off, Mentoring of America, not surprisingly, it's part of this same tangled mess, too. Although it's not part of LandBank, the privately held corporation is controlled by Gravink and Hewitt, who are both majority shareholders. In 2005 Utah's *Deseret Morning News* reported that five employees were rushed to the hospital for drug-related reasons, and the police conducted an investigation. (You'd probably swallow drugs by the handful, too, if you had to spend your days stealing money from wounded veterans.) Then there was the company's run-in with Utah's attorney general that led to a $400,000 settlement.

What's truly astounding is how so many of these scams are interconnected. Take John Beck's infomercial, for example. Just who was responsible for setting up the shoot? A company called DirectFX, based in Phoenix, Arizona; the same company that has filmed infomercials in the past for none other than Don Lapre, Dean Graziosi, and Guinness World Records cycling champ Russ Dalbey.

Cure in a Can

When—and if—the cure for cancer is eventually discovered, you can be sure the first place you hear about it will not be on a late-night infomercial courtesy of a quack who claims to have cured herself of cancer and also happens to run a Holocaust denial Web site in her spare time. And you can be sure Kevin Trudeau will have nothing to do with it.

The miracle pill/cream/potion remains one of the other dark corners of the infomercial industry: remedies for AIDS, cancer, diabetes, multiple sclerosis, and heart disease have all been marketed on TV over the years. It's almost always the same story: some run-of-the-mill vitamin or nutritional supplement is heralded for its rare healing powers. Of course, there's no scientific research to support the claims, which is why little disclaimers that read "This product is not intended to cure or treat any disease" appear with regularity. But it's awfully hard to remember that when the disclaimer is barely visible to the human eye, flashes by at about ninety miles an hour, and is immediately followed by tearful testimonial from a woman who says that a $19.95 bottle of calcium instantly cured her of a malignant breast tumor.

These health-related infomercials that appear late at night and on weekend mornings may be the worst of the lot. John Beck might take every dime you have in the bank, but you'll live to see another day. Miracle diets might not help you lose weight, but if and when you die, it will probably be because you were eating six pounds of greasy bacon for breakfast, not because you purchased NutriSystem. When people like Lorraine Day, Kevin Trudeau, and Donald Barrett convince people that they can bypass traditional therapies and rely on these "all natural" remedies, people can end up dead. Stories about people who forgo legitimate treatment for some potion they purchased after

seeing an ad appear in the press regularly. One recent news account concerned a man with a very treatable basal cell carcinoma
of the mouth. For a decade, he used a holistic remedy he'd seen
advertised on TV, even as the tumor started to expand. What
could have probably been treated in its early stages ended up
killing him.

Yet thousands of Americans every year get caught up with
these products and their ridiculous claims. In the late 1990s, a
company called Enforma got into trouble with the FTC for promoting two nutritional supplements, Exercise in a Bottle and
Fat Trapper. Exercise in a bottle, you ask? Yes, the makers of
the product claimed that they'd invented a pill that would allow
people to eat all the fried chicken, hamburgers, and pizza they
wanted and still lose weight. The FTC took action against the
company (as well as one of the show's hosts, former baseball star
Steve Garvey), and Enforma's founder, Andrew Grey, paid a $10
million fine. He returned to the scene in 2005 with yet another
weight loss scheme. He's since been banned by the FTC from advertising weight loss products, but that just means he's probably
working on a get-rich-quick infomercial these days.

The fines hardly prevent someone from discontinuing a controversial product and starting a new line of business. What's a
few million in fines when you rake that in every week? In 2005
a man by the name of Stephan Karian paid the largest settlement in infomercial history in connection with Ultimate HGH,
which Karian's company had promised could reverse the aging
process. "Unfortunately, no pill or spray can turn back the hands
of time," the FTC waxed poetically, announcing that Karian
and his associate, Dr. Michael Teplitsky (who had his license to
practice medicine suspended after he sexually assaulted a patient
in 1995, among other grievances), had agreed to pay $20 mil-
lion to settle claims associated with Ultimate HGH. The settle-

ment also covered claims the duo had made about several other products, including their Super Wild Oregano Oil, which had been touted as a way to "prevent colds and flu and, when taken orally, treat and relieve bacterial and viral infections and their symptoms." But while a $20 million fine might sound like a good chunk of change to you or me, consider this: Karian made nearly $80 million from sales of the product before the FTC intervened. Which probably explains why when I reached him at his home in Destin, Florida, he was surprisingly relaxed about the ordeal.

"I would have never believed eleven years ago when I was working out of my room in my mother's apartment that I'd ever get to his point," he says, laughing. A New York City native, Karian tells me he was a "perpetual failure" in his younger years. He dabbled with a few multilevel marketing programs, including one for the Cambridge Diet. It was while living at home that he launched a vitamin sales company, which eventually turned into a $50,000-a-month business. He moved to Florida and launched his first infomercial a few years later.

If there's anything refreshing about Karian, it's that he freely admits he did wrong. "I screwed up," he says matter-of-factly. As for what it is exactly that he did wrong, Karian doesn't quite see eye to eye with the government. He places the blame on the company that he hired to perform a double-blind study: "The company I hired took shortcuts. I had no idea whatsoever." It's a little hard to imagine how, even if the company had followed every protocol—or if Karian had hired every Nobel Prize– winning scientist on the planet—he would have ever been able to claim he had the fountain of youth in a plastic bottle. But I don't press the subject. I ask him about the settlement.

"The first offer was to put me out of business," Karian says as he explains the negotiation process with the FTC. "When they saw my assets, they thought they'd hit the jackpot. Their first deal? It was crazy! Something like $59 million or $67 million. We finally came up with $20 million." While Karian could have elected to fight the FTC in court, he decided against it. "I didn't want to take the risk, he says. "Okay, fine, here's your $20 million."

Amazingly, the fine hasn't dissuaded him from returning to the industry. Karian's company is still in business—and he has plans to return to the air, too, although he says now he will have "experts review the work" before making any claims. Why not just move on to something else? I ask. Karian is just forty years old. "My wife wanted me to walk away," he tells me. '"Why don't we just travel?' she asked. Okay, so I never have to work again. My kids don't have to work again. But I'm in it for the long haul."

It's a delicate balancing act. In order to get the phones to ring, people like Karian have no choice but to feature outrageous claims. Tone down the rhetoric by just a bit, and the sales vanish. Marketers like Karian have to get as close to the line as possible, without going over. But even when they do go over, they can always chalk up the fines to the cost of doing business.

Karian isn't, by any means, the most famous person to have sold supplements with dubious claims. When it comes to shady vitamins and fictitious miracle cures, no one has managed to stir up as much controversy as Kevin Trudeau, who has spent more than a decade appearing on infomercial after infomercial.

Born in Boston, Trudeau was given up by his birth mother and handed over to a Catholic charity group when he was just a few weeks old. He was later adopted by Mary and Robert Trudeau of Lynn, Massachusetts, although the couple did not disclose this information to Kevin until he found out by accident when he was twelve, a factor to which his adoptive parents would later attribute his behavioral problems as a teenager. Trudeau's own record of his childhood is decidedly cheerier: in his official bio, he says he made his first $1 million in direct mail marketing at the age of fourteen. What is known is that at some point after high school, he took a job at a car dealership, and it was there that he met the owner of a company called Memory Masters Institute, who offered him a job selling seminars, books, and tapes on how to sharpen your thinking and improve your memory.

Trudeau's first brush with the law came in October 1988 when he was twenty-five. A grand jury in Massachusetts' Middlesex County indicted him on seven counts of larceny for writing bogus checks. (In a strange bit of foreshadowing, he had posed as a doctor when he showed up at the bank to deposit the checks.) In 1990 Trudeau pleaded guilty to the charges and spent twenty days in jail. He didn't seem to learn his lesson. The same year he was indicted by a federal grand jury in Boston on charges he'd stolen names and Social Security numbers and had applied for credit cards using these stolen identities. He was accused of bilking credit card companies out of more than $100,000. By the time his second plea came to pass, it was clear Trudeau was headed in the wrong direction, and Mary Trudeau knew it. In a letter to the court in 1991 in which she and her husband begged the judge to be lenient, Mary Trudeau described him as "a young man with a problem" who was desperately "trying to prove himself." A report submitted by a psychiatrist hired by the defense also turned up emotional issues, diagnosing Trudeau with "mixed personality disorder" and "adjustment disorder with mixed disturbance of emotions and conduct." The doctor concluded that Trudeau was "driven by a subconscious urge to succeed, to the point where he may have shown poor judgment."

The judge sentenced Trudeau to two years in prison. He spent twenty-one months behind bars before being released on

August 20, 1993, with two years of probation. Alas, Trudeau's
stint as federal inmate No. 18046–036 did not, in fact, turn him
in a more constructive direction. He did, however, gain a business partner who would go on to help him carry out his schemes.
It was while in the clink that he teamed up with Jules Lieb, who
had been sent to jail for conspiracy to distribute cocaine. Following their release, Trudeau and Lieb partnered with a company
called Nutrition for Life International and set out to market vitamin distributorships. The multilevel pyramid scheme was shut
down in 1996 by the Illinois attorney general; Trudeau eventually paid a $185,000 fine as part of a settlement with Illinois and
seven other states.

It was at that point that Trudeau turned to television to continue his career as a con, and a series of dubious products soon
followed. In an infomercial for Doctor Callahan's Addiction
Breaking System, Trudeau promised that the formula, which had
been developed thanks to "quantum physics," could cure any addiction: "Dr. Callahan came up with the breakthrough that in
sixty seconds can eliminate your addictive urge to overeat, to
smoke cigarettes, to do any compulsion, any type of addicted
behavior, whether it be alcohol, drugs, cigarettes, food. Now
this technique will take sixty seconds to apply and works virtually one hundred percent of the time." What was Dr. Callahan's
magical technique, you ask? "A series of gestures, including tapping the face, chest and hand, rolling the eyes and humming,"
according to the complaint later lodged against him.

For the Sable Hair Farming System, Trudeau claimed that
the product would "finally end baldness in the human race"
and that his groundbreaking research would soon be lauded
by the world's most prestigious medical journals. (Needless to
say, the *New England Journal of Medicine* never had much to say
about Trudeau's topical lotion.) For *Howard Berg's Mega Reading,*

Trudeau promised that his home study program "could improve anyone's reading speed and comprehension by as much as ten times," and even claimed that the system could teach the severely disabled and brain damaged to read. A "partially brain dead" woman had been taught to read "more than 600 words a minute!" the infomercial claimed. For another infomercial that marketed Trudeau's own Mega Memory System, he asserted that everyone had a photographic memory—and he would show you how to develop yours, too.

In 1998 Trudeau was fined $500,000 by the FTC for his involvement with six different infomercials, and officials at the commission thought this might be the end of him. But in an industry where some successful producers can pocket $500,000 over the course of a weekend, Trudeau did what many do: he took his drubbing and moved on to a new set of products. He teamed up with "Dr." Robert "Bob" Barefoot, a quack who describes himself as a doctor despite the fact he never even graduated college, and debuted Coral Calcium Supreme. The duo claimed the pills could cure a long list of diseases, including cancer, diabetes, and multiple sclerosis, on what was an especially bizarre show. At one point Barefoot claimed that residents of Okinawa, Japan, lived healthy lives because the water there contained higher calcium levels. "They don't *have* children until they're in their *seventies,* when they're mature enough to handle kids," Barefoot told Trudeau. "But they have the body of thirty-year-olds!" The magic fountain of youth—discovered again. Of course, the product was similar to the bottles of calcium you'd find at an ordinary drugstore except they cost thirty times more and, according to one scientific review, contained considerably higher levels of lead.

It didn't take long for the authorities to step in. This time the FTC planned to shut Trudeau down for good. In 2003 it fined

Trudeau $2 million and banned him for life from "appearing in, producing, or disseminating" any infomercial that advertised "any type of product, service, or program to the public." The only thing he would be permitted to sell on air was "informational publications," which was covered under his right to free speech.

Ah, yes, the big loophole: free speech. Together with his lawyers, Trudeau hatched his most ingenious strategy yet. Instead of selling the promise of eternal health as a pill, he put the information in a book. Like any smart infomercial marketer, he realized that once people purchased the book, he'd make money on the back-end with supplements, memberships, and the like.

In 2004 Trudeau returned to the air to promote *Natural Cures "They" Don't Want You to Know About*, which he self-published and sold for $29.95. Given his tangles with the authorities over the previous few years, his return to the airwaves also gave him an opportunity to advance his new conspiracy theory, namely, that he was the victim of a witch hunt. So every few minutes, Trudeau reminded the audience that this groundbreaking research on natural cures was such a grave threat to drug companies that the government, at the beck and call of the pharmaceutical lobby, was determined to silence him.

Alas, those who purchased the book hoping for answers were almost always disappointed—the volume is filled with dozens of wacko theories. In *Natural Cures,* he claims all disease in the world is caused by the pharmaceuticals we ingest (wild animals apparently never get sick) and argues that the sun doesn't cause skin cancer—it's sunscreen that does. Trudeau claims he knows a doctor who found a cure for AIDS, and that another doctor friend of his "discovered a serum that virtually made cancer tumors vanish in ninety minutes." Who are these people? He doesn't say. But he does mention that he knows a researcher who has figured out how to use "thought" to "change a person's DNA."

His rhetoric was extraordinarily well timed. Trudeau's pitch about the drug lobby coincided with a growing sense of mistrust about the nation's troubled health care system. As Trudeau railed against pharma companies, newspaper headlines carried news of harmful drugs like Vioxx; as Americans were talking about the influence of the pharmaceutical industry in Washington, Trudeau suddenly materialized and claimed that all of his legal ordeals were attempts by the drug lobby to silence him. He was being targeted for standing up to the big boys! For daring to speak up! He was Martin Luther King Jr., Mohandas Gandhi, and Louis Pasteur rolled into one! It was a brilliant act. To add fuel to the fire, Trudeau even filed suit against the U.S. government, claiming *they* had defamed *him*. A complete crook he may be, but it's hard to argue with his talents as a showman.

Trudeau's business has expanded in recent years. In 2006, he linked up with a new partner, Donald Barrett, and unveiled a series of shows including The Weight Loss Cure "They" Don't Want You to Know About and Debt Cures "They" Don't Want You to Know About, in which Trudeau goes after banks and credit card companies. In Trudeau's world, there are lots of "theys"— and Trudeau has been determined to go after every one. (In late 2008, a federal judge fined Trudeau $5 million and banned him from infomercials for three years; Trudeau is appealing the verdict and his shows continue to appear on the air.)

And while Trudeau's business ventures have earned him a fortune, don't expect much to be netted from the legal proceedings against him. When he settled his last case for $2 million, he paid the fine by surrendering his home in Ojai, California, worth $1.5 million and by handing over the keys to his $180,000 Mercedes-Benz SL55. So where's all the other money? Good question. In the past, Trudeau's companies have been incorporated offshore, in places like the Isle of Man in the

British Channel Islands, a well-known tax haven. God only knows how much Trudeau has accumulated over the years and where it's located.

Trudeau doesn't have much interest in talking to reporters these days (a bruising interview with *20/20* in 2006 seems to have put him off the media), but Barrett is willing to sit down for a chat. When I meet him at the guest villa he's renting in Las Vegas, it's immediately clear that whereas I might have found his infomercials amusing and hokey, plenty of Americans were taking him—and his products—very seriously.

"Oh, yes, Mr. Stern. We've been waiting for you," the elegantly dressed concierge says as he notes my arrival in an old-fashioned ledger sitting on top of an antique desk. A butler is summoned to personally escort me to Barrett's Mediterranean-style villa, which features a private pool and priceless art—including a Picasso—on the wall. It's a thoroughly impressive affair. Many millions of vitamins had been sold to pay for this $15,000-a-night suite.

Barrett is Trudeau's doppelgänger. Both were raised in middle-class circumstances in the vicinity of Boston. Both got involved in multilevel marketing as young men. Both have pursued vast wealth with a single-minded focus. And both are comfortable bending the law to make a buck.

Although Barrett has a lower profile, he, too, has been in hot water with the Federal Trade Commission. In 2004 Barrett and his company, ITV, were sued over a product called Supreme Greens with MSM. The FTC argued that Barrett had promised the supplement could cure cancer, diabetes, and heart disease; in addition to making "numerous false and unsubstantiated claims," the agency alleged that ITV had made unauthorized charges to consumers' credit and debit cards. (A federal judge ruled in favor of the FTC in July of 2008.) So it came as little surprise to hear that Barrett had decided to team up with Trudeau. Rather ominously, though, the announcement of their joint venture was released to the press on September 11, 2006.

When I walk into the spacious living quarters, I'm greeted by Barrett and no less than three lawyers. Christopher Robertson, his outside legal counsel from Seyfarth Shaw LLP, is present, as is Barrett's general counsel and another member of his internal legal team. Given the heat on him and his partnership with Trudeau, he's anticipating a barrage of tough questions.

Barrett looks nervous. He's dressed in a deep blue suit, starched white shirt, and bright red tie. A thick gold Rolex is strapped to his wrist. There's a thin layer of sweat on his forehead. I'm sweating a bit, too. I hadn't expected to have three lawyers facing me down. But they're friendly, and we sit down at the dining room table. Everyone takes a moment to introduce himself, including a handful of ITV executives who have gathered in the room. Each hands me a gray business card and briefly tells me what he or she does at ITV. It's a very impressive show, but Barrett is fond of shows. On his company's Web site, there's an article about his return to Saugus High, where he graduated in 1993. He delivered an inspirational speech to a math class, handed out copies of motivational speaker/author Earl Nightingale's book, and later gave rides to the impressionable youngsters in the company's limousine.

"I started my direct marketing business out of my mother's house in 2001," he begins, giving me a bit of backstory. "The first product I ever ran was a program called *Dr. Morter's Dynamic Health.*" This was while he was moonlighting as a pizza maker in the suburbs of Boston. The nutritional field caught his attention, he says, after both his brother and father were diagnosed with cancer. "So I started reading books like crazy on marketing," he says. He tells me he was particularly influenced by *Seven Steps to Freedom* by Benjamin Suarez. I'm a little confused as to how he transitioned from worrying about his ill family members to obsessing about marketing strategies; from the sound of it, raking in the big bucks was his primary concern. So how is your family doing? I inquire. "My brother passed away, but my father is doing very well," he says before diving right back into the conversation about how to make money using infomercials.

Barrett has come a long way since 2001. ITV now grosses more than $100 million a year and employs 500 people at the company's headquarters in Beverly, Massachusetts, and smaller offices in New Hampshire, Chicago, and California. It's all thanks to infomercials that market products like Almighty Cleanse, a colon-cleansing product pitched by a Christian evangelical minister and avowed vegan named Danny Vierra; Flex Protex, a "cutting-edge, natural joint support supplement"; and Rice 'n Shine, another rice-based nutritional supplement that supposedly boosts energy levels and helps people lose weight.

His most notorious product, though, may be *Cancer Doesn't Scare Me Anymore,* a DVD that was pitched by a former physician named Lorraine Day. Once a practicing surgeon, she quit medicine, she says, after she was diagnosed with breast cancer and healed herself with a natural cure. Day has never proven she was ever sick or was ever healed. What is for sure is that at some point in the early 1990s, she gave up her medical career and had a religious awakening. She's now a devout Christian. More troubling, though, is that she also happens to be a rabid anti-Semite. Through a company she controls, Spencer Publishing, Day operates GoodNewsAboutGod.com, a site that denies the Holocaust and accuses Jews of controlling world affairs, championing communism, and dominating the media. In 2006 she testified on behalf of Ernst Zündel, a Holocaust revisionist who Canada was trying to deport to Germany to face charges of inciting racial hatred. Day, who describes Zündel as "a friend," later explained that he was being persecuted by "the media, which is controlled by the Zionist Jews." Of course, Barrett probably doesn't care about any of that: she moved product, which is the only thing that matters.

Barrett hosts his shows himself using a faux news format: they feature Barrett and his guest chatting about the product—and all of its magical properties—over the course of a half hour. His shows are soft sells: Barrett doesn't mention the price and only barely hints that he's selling anything. Viewers are asked to call the 800 number for more info. I ask Barrett about his pitch, and he delights in delivering one for me in person: "If you'd like some more *free* information on Patty McPeak or on Flex Protex, *call* the number on the screen. We have *trained* representatives standing by who can answer *all* of your questions. So pick up the phone and give us a call," he says. I'd seen precisely the same display on TV; it was eerie to hear it in person. "That's pretty much how we do it," Barrett explains. "We generate more phone calls—a soft offer show always generates more phone calls—but you need talented people to answer the phones."

Indeed. Unlike many companies that outsource the call taking to a third party, Barrett has his own staff to take the calls. Since viewers may not even realize that they're getting looped into a purchase when they call, it's entirely up to the phone reps to make a sale happen, add as many products as possible, and—most importantly—get them to agree to an auto-ship program, which will ensure that Barrett can keep billing the customer again and again, month after month. It's rough work: sales reps are commission-based and have to do whatever it takes to convert callers into customers. A breezy encounter it is not. When I called one day to ask a simple question about the product, I had to actually hang up on the phone rep who took the call. He wasn't about to let me go.

"We have a three-phase hiring process when we bring in our salespeople," Barrett says, describing how he recruits phone reps. "The first phase is when they come in and we tell them the good, the bad, and the ugly: what they'll love about the job, what they won't like about the job, and all the perks and benefits that they'll get." He then has new recruits run through calls with other staff members. "We see if they have natural ability, good tonalities, and good inflection on the phone." If they pass the test, they get two weeks of training. It's a methodical process, instilling the tools and tactics to make bleary-eyed callers fork over their credit card numbers. With motivated, aggressive salespeople, Barrett says ITV can close on the offer thirty to forty percent of the time. "We have very low turnover because we pay our salespeople tremendously well. I think ten percent of our sales staff is making over $100,000." Barrett runs a tight ship: he mentions that all of his salesmen are required to wear white shirts with their suits when they're on the sales floor. "White shirts?" I ask. "They sell better when they wear white shirts," he explains.

Hooking up with Trudeau was Barrett's masterstroke. Trudeau's 2004 infomercial "ban" prohibited him from selling products and services with the exception of information. But just selling books on the air wasn't going to make Trudeau the kind of money he'd make if he had a juicy back-end. A marriage between Barrett and Trudeau made perfect sense: ITV had all the facilities to shoot and edit an infomercial; it had the staff to purchase airtime and rooms full of sales reps to take calls; and Barrett could help develop the back-end of supplements and memberships. Viewers who paid for the book would be encouraged to sign up for $9.95 a month if they wanted a steady stream of "natural cures," or $499 for a lifetime membership.

In 2006 their first infomercial hit the air. They've since shot a handful of new iterations of the show, all of which rail against drug companies and the FDA. Barrett explains how they can use any bit of bad news—such as a recall or lawsuit—to their advantage. "If something happens today on the news with a pharmaceutical drug and there's a natural alternative, I can do a show and have it up in thirty days."

As our chat winds down, Barrett and I step into a lush courtyard outside. He inhales deeply. "Do you smell the lemon trees?" he asks. I do. There's a lovely citrus scent in the air as we stand outside the villa. It's a spectacular setting—and a world away from naive callers desperately looking for a cure for cancer or diabetes or sales reps barking into the phones.

"You know, if you ever want to do a book, you should talk to me," he says. I'm confused as to what he's talking about, but I nod my head and smile. It occurs to me that he might be signaling to me that there could be some money down the line if I play my cards right. "We'll have to discuss," I say.

Moments later, Barrett's very prim assistant, Kristen, comes over. "Do you have a driver who will be picking you up?" she asks, as if most Americans avail themselves of a chauffeur-driven limo at all times. I tell her I'll just catch a cab. "Very well then," she says. "I presume the concierge will be able to assist you." . With that, Barrett and his right hand slip back into the villa.

The Not-So-Long Arm of the Law

The problems with get-rich-quick and health-related infomercials are especially clear, but even some of the more reputable products advertised on TV cross legal lines. Marketers have used the credit cards they have on file to charge consumers for services and products that the customer never asked for. They've automatically enrolled customers in continuity programs without asking for consent since they know very well that many people won't even notice the charges at first, and by the time they do, months may have passed. Other marketers have run into trouble after failing to honor money-back guarantees or for refusing to accept returns. Still other companies may charge your credit card immediately, then take weeks to ship you the product, despite the fact that by law they have thirty days to mail the item to you or must otherwise inform you of the delay and give you the chance to cancel the transaction. There's still room to play games: if you get a product shipped to you on day 29, and you have a thirty-day money-back guarantee, that means you have to decide the same day you receive the product if you want to keep it. Companies also occasionally intentionally fail to enclose return instructions because they know plenty of people will simply give up and keep the product. To be sure, these are smaller offenses compared to promising someone a cure for cancer or stealing someone's life savings, and the penalties for these misdeeds are relatively minor.

But even in cases where the fraud is truly outrageous, there's little true enforcement on the part of the government. If Stephan Karian paid $20 million and that barely made a dent in his business, how much of a deterrent is a $1.6 million fine against Joe Francis? By one account, the *Girls Gone Wild* impresario was earning that in a single week.

There's little reason to believe that things will change anytime soon. The Federal Trade Commission is perpetually underfunded and understaffed. Its purview is vast. The FTC is charged with tracking everything, from credit card rip-offs to identity theft to used car scams—not to mention having to keep tabs on the millions of products sold in stores all over the United States. There's no way it can keep track of every misdeed on the nearly three thousand new shows that appear on TV every month.

When the FTC does find someone breaking the law, the agency isn't in much of a position to play hardball. The prospect of a years-long lawsuit is daunting on both sides, so overworked government lawyers typically settle the cases, and their targets are only more than happy to oblige. The FTC gets to claim it "nabbed" a bad guy and issue a press release that it extracted some seemingly large sum of money. In doing so, the FTC reassures the American public that it's looking out for the consumer. Then the agency can close the case and move on. The infomercial marketer moves on, too—to the next scheme.

The FTC and FDA seem to take a harder line when it comes to ingestibles, which has led some conspiracy theorists to suggest the government's distaste for nutritional supplements has to do with the influence of the drug lobby. Rest assured the CEO of Pfizer isn't sitting up at night worried about Coral Calcium. But the government does seem more concerned about products you actually have to swallow since they pose broad public health implications. The claims made on health-related infomercials also happen to be a lot easier to discount. It doesn't take a year-long undercover investigation to determine that calcium doesn't cure cancer. The understaffed FTC doesn't have the resources to send agents to a real estate seminar to try to figure out whether or not it's possible to earn $100,000 in a week.

Infomercial marketers point out—and rightly so—that this isn't a problem restricted to direct response television. Similar schemes are carried out on the Internet every minute of the day, and there are equally misleading ads in newspapers and magazines all over the country. But what often gets left out of the discussion about fraudulent infomercials—and this is no accident—is the role of the networks. Infomercials don't just magically appear in your living room. They're transmitted into your living room by the largest media companies in the world. These companies generate billions every year from those half-hour blocks in the middle of the night. Men like Kevin Trudeau and Donald Barrett help keep television networks in business.

In 2006 *Dateline NBC* aired an hour-long exposé in which the show's producers demonstrated just how easy it is to market anything on television. They came up with a fictitious product, Moisturol, which they said would hydrate your skin "from the inside." (In reality, the capsules were filled with Nestle's Quik.) The next step as part of the hidden camera investigation was to find an infomercial producer willing to assemble a Moisturol infomercial. They soon found someone to take the bait, a respected industry vet with a long list of credits to his name who put the show together from A to Z. He hired a doctor to appear on camera to give the product a glowing recommendation and found ordinary citizens to deliver positive testimonials.

Naturally, *Dateline*'s John Larsen was aghast that the producer had taken such a phony product and made an entirely believable program out of it. But was it really that outrageous? For the producer, this was a simple contract assignment: *Dateline* told them what they wanted, and the producer made it happen. He didn't come up with the scam. He took money from his supposed client and just followed along. Sort of like what happens when Kevin Trudeau delivers a Betacam tape of his latest infomercial to NBC's offices. They do the job they're paid to do. That might explain why the complicity of the networks in these scams was only briefly addressed in the last few minutes of the show. The infomercial producer was an easy target. Presumably turning the camera on NBC executives, and asking them why their company profits from fraudulent cancer cures wasn't quite as attractive a proposition.

An infomercial is worthless unless a national network or local station agrees to air the program. Unless CNBC or Lifetime or KXGN-TV in Glendive, Montana, agrees to air your show for a fee, all you have is a slick program filled with dubious promises. Of course, the networks and stations don't have any incentive to turn anyone away; in fact, quite the opposite. Infomercials represent a major profit center. At local stations, unless a show is going to cause embarrassment or deeply offend the community, station personnel are generally inclined to let it air. At national cable networks, there are standards departments that are responsible for "clearing" shows. But the guidelines are fairly loose. Local stations and major networks bear no legal responsibility or have any obligation to vet the claims made in infomercials. Nor are they thrilled with the prospect of losing income if stricter standards were ever imposed. So they carry on and collect the cash. And just in case there's any doubt, they run brief disclaimers both before and after every half-hour block of paid programming to make that clear.

As attention is focused on the shady characters who create the phony infomercials, what tends to get lost in the discussion is that the largest media conglomerates in the world—companies like General Electric (the parent company of NBC Universal), Viacom (MTV, VH1, Spike), Disney (ABC), News Corp. (Fox News, FX, Speed), Tribune, and Hearst—are the grand enablers. The government has never taken action against a station for airing a fraudulent infomercial.

"The FCC has never been inclined to take anyone's licenses away because the industry they nominally regulate actually regulates them," says Todd Gitlin, a professor of journalism and sociology at Columbia University. "The industry is too powerful to contend with, and regulation is largely farcical."

This is why it's a tad ironic when self-righteous news personalities like *20/20*'s John Stossel launch "investigations" into an industry that is "victimizing America," then fail to mention who and what allows the shows to air in the first place. People like Kevin Trudeau help pay Stossel's outsized salary. Three hours after Stossel reported on the cure-all purveyor, one of ABC's sister stations was broadcasting the very garbage he just railed against.

Let's say I invented a small, junky electric blender. Let's also assume that my product is a wee bit defective, and every once in a while it malfunctions and slices off fingers. If I managed to get Wal-Mart to carry my blender on its shelves, you can be sure that after the first fingerless moms called up corporate headquarters in Bentonville, Arkansas, to complain, Wal-Mart would immediately pull the product. It wouldn't be acting out of any deep sense of altruism. (This is Wal-Mart, after all.) Corporate lawyers would know full well that they had a potential legal liability and public relations crisis on their hands.

No such thing happens with TV networks. The networks disavow all responsibility for the claims made on these shows. Just imagine for a moment if every time you walked into Costco, you had to review a legal form that indicated that the store was not, in fact, responsible for selling you fresh food. It might sound like a silly analogy, but this is precisely what's happening. ABC and NBC happily stand behind their regular programming, except late at night and on Saturday and Sunday mornings when they flash a legal notice across the screen, in which case they have nothing to do with it. At 11:00 p.m., you are supposed to believe what you're seeing on the local news. At 1:00 a.m.? All bets are off.

For most of us, this is a no-brainer. We'd never take anything we saw on an infomercial especially seriously. But a great many viewers don't quite realize the difference. To my surprise, many of the victims of scams told me that they assumed that if a show was appearing on a major network, someone at the channel had ensured that the product was legit.

"Since the shows are carried on major networks, they're under the impression that the network would never air a product that was scamming people," explains Justin Leonard, who runs the infomercial watchdog site InfomercialScams.com. And the line between regular programming and the paid variety is only getting blurrier. A few years ago, the words "paid programming" almost always appeared in *TV Guide* and on set-top boxes. Now that infomercial marketers have cut deals with the data providers that create the listings, you might think there's actually a show called *Winning in the Cash Flow Business*.

The only people with an interest in keeping out the bad guys are reputable infomercial producers. It's a matter of self-preservation. Honest brokers know full well that the industry has long had a seamy reputation. More than a couple producers joked that they didn't always tell strangers what they did for a living since a suspicious glance invariably followed. They know that if too many Kevin Trudeaus come along—and there's a public outcry—legislators in Washington might get some funny ideas. That's precisely what happened in 1990. After the airwaves were flooded by crooks in the late '80s, Congress launched an investigation into direct response television. Infomercial veteran Greg Renker, who has one of the best reputations in the business, testified on behalf of the industry and announced the formation of a trade group, now known as the Electronic Retailing Association. It's the ERA that coordinates the industry's annual convention in Las Vegas. The group has also established a set of guidelines it expects its paying members to follow. Virtually all of the legitimate companies in the direct response television industry are affiliated with the group; the more brazen producers like Trudeau and Barrett stay far away.

The ERA oversees a committee called the Electronic Retailing Self-Regulation Program (ERSP), which reviews suspicious infomercials and turns over unscrupulous producers to the authorities when committee members see evidence of wrongdoing. The program has had an impact: more than a hundred shows have been modified following investigations by the ERA. In cases where infomercial producers fail to comply with the trade group's findings, the group has turned over evidence to the authorities, and several highly publicized lawsuits have resulted. Agencies like the FTC are grateful for the service the ERA provides. Since they don't have the resources to review the thousands of infomercials that air every year, the ERA can do some of the leg work and bring the most egregious offenders to their attention. For example, the ERA has been a very vocal critic of Kevin Trudeau. When the president of the group said that Trudeau was a fraud and had "tarnished the infomercial industry," Trudeau responded by filing a $10 million defamation suit.

The ERSP has made direct response marketers a bit more careful. In the old days, a disclaimer might appear once during a show. Nowadays, disclaimers that read "your results may vary" and "results not typical" now flash across the screen every few minutes, although when the disclaimer is in a 0.1-point font, you'd be hard pressed to notice it unless you watch TV with a microscope attached to your head. But the ERSP has its limits. Clearly, it's hard for any industry to police itself. As one veteran infomercial producer pointed out, several seemingly upstanding members of the ERA are also people who have been involved with questionable products in the past. Some have suggested that paying members of the ERA, who may fork over hundreds of thousands of dollars a year to fund the group, generally receive less scrutiny than those who don't join.

Other critics say that the group does just enough to convey the impression they're cracking down on the bad apples, when everyone knows that there are plenty of scammers who slip through. Don Lapre and Donald Barrett aren't exactly losing sleep waiting for the ERA to burst through the doors of their multimillion-dollar mansions.

Of course, it's clear that the TV networks could do more to stem the tide. The networks have no legal obligation to sell their airtime to con artists. Kevin Trudeau may have a legal right to disseminate information, but the networks get to pick and choose who they accept money from. They can— and do—discriminate. Only a small handful, for example, accepted infomercials for *Girls Gone Wild*. Since the sexual content made network executives skittish, for years only E!, Spike, and Comedy Central would carry the show. Yet when it comes to an alleged cure for cancer or a get-rich-quick scheme, virtually every network is happy to accept the programming and collect the checks.

Cleaning up late-night television wouldn't require much effort on the networks' part. One relatively painless solution would involve partnering with various industry groups and federal agencies to establish a list of habitual offenders, much like the "no-fly" list that the federal government maintains in cooperation with the airlines. It would be simple to come up with the dozen or so people who have systematically abused the public over the years and who have been subject to repeated legal proceedings. These people would then be blocked from buying time on major networks. Sure, a few crooks would get by. And, yes, the networks would lose revenue. But the networks could take some pride in having done the right thing. Money isn't everything: if revenues were the only thing that mattered in this world, CBS would have hired a handful of chicks in bikinis to

deliver the nightly news instead of paying Katie Couric $15 mil-
lion a year. They'd be in first place right now.

It's thanks to the Internet, though, that consumers have started to
fight back. There are now several popular sites where victims of
infomercial-related schemes share their stories of deception and
coordinate letter-writing campaigns to the authorities. True, by
the time people make their way to an online message board to
complain, it's too late—they've already paid for an infomercial
scam artist to take a weeklong vacation to Hawaii. But the sites
help prevent people from falling for the scheme in the first place.
A Google search for John Beck or Russ Dalbey invariably references results from sites like Justin Leonard's InfomercialScams
.com, where dozens or hundreds of customers have listed their
grievances in detail. For people who do a quick search online
before calling the 800 number to purchase the product, the information they find on the Net might just save them a good deal
of time, money, and agony.

Justin Leonard, the founder of InfomercialScams.com, is an
unlikely interloper in the multibillion-dollar world of direct response television. A former bodybuilder and now fitness coach
in Arizona, he's never worked in the industry, nor has he been
a victim of an infomercial-related ploy. But he's one of the few
people who has infomercial scammers quaking in their boots.

Leonard put up his first site in 2000, and he initially focused on posting reviews of various fitness regimens. He soon
found that people were writing in to inquire about the merits
of various fitness products they'd seen advertised on TV and a
year later he launched FitnessInfomercialReview.com to serve,
as he puts it, as the *Consumer Reports* of exercise products. When
he realized that people had lots to say about countless other

products marketed on TV (and when he noticed that many of the complaints sounded all too familiar), he branched out with InfomercialScams.com.

"There were consistencies in every review," Leonard said, explaining the moment when he realized that there was public demand for a clearinghouse of information. Many people flocked to the site with suspiciously similar tales to tell, stories of shipping scams, auto-bill trickery, and packages with no return shipping addresses. Today the site is home to thousands of descriptions of infomercial-related schemes, organized by product name. Hundreds of different items advertised on TV have received reviews from members of the public.

The well-spoken online watchdog runs the site on his own dime. Although there are ads on the site, the income doesn't cover his costs or the time he puts into managing it. (A site dedicated to exposing faulty products doesn't hold enormous appeal with advertisers.) But he takes satisfaction in the knowledge he's providing an invaluable service.

One of the most interesting aspects to the site is that it's provided a venue for former industry insiders—people who worked as salespeople, for example—to describe the operation from within. The posts from disgruntled former employees shed a good deal of light on how such companies conduct business day to day:

> You're right, if you buy into the SMC scam you will
> get screwed. We are not out to help you guys at all. It's
> all about how much money the "business consultants"
> can make for themselves and the company. The custom-
> ers don't stand a chance in hell. . . . Think of SMC
> as a mini casino. The only people who make money
> in a casino are the owners. The coaches are told by the

supervisors to upsell you guys as much bullshit as pos-
sible. Web sites, books, gift cards—the whole shebang.
The more you buy, the more commission we make
because we only get a base pay of about $500 a week
before taxes. It's our job to pump and dump. We pump
up your dreams of owning your own business and then
dump a load of merchandise in your lap. . . . Some of
us make $1,500 to $2,000 a week selling you crap
that you'll never be able to sell . . . anywhere. I have
so many stories I could share with you. It would make
your blood boil. . . . Want a better idea of what the
environment is like? Rent the movie Boiler Room.
Here's a better idea, instead of getting screwed by SMC,
save your money, go back to school and get a degree in
business. Then you'll be prepared to enter the world and
make some money.

It's worth noting that Leonard isn't uniformly critical of infomercials. He recognizes that some are better than others. Not surprisingly, it's the get-rich-quick category that he finds the most fault with. He says he regularly receives e-mails from people who lost everything they had. "They're really the most vulnerable group. They're gullible," he says. "And they get taken in by these mentoring programs. It's truly the worst." He's a bit more forgiving when it comes to some of the fitness products: "Many of them will work—if you use them. It's the claims that are often totally ridiculous."

Shady infomercial marketers have taken note of Leonard now that their schemes are laid bare online. Over the past couple of years, he's been on the receiving end of several cease-and-desists and at least one full-fledged lawsuit. Direct Buy, a company that operates a discount furnishings membership club, has threatened

Leonard with suits on several occasions; more recently, Video Professor, the company that offers up "free" computer learning courses and then charges you an arm and a leg for future installments from its "library of learning," filed suit against Leonard claiming defamation. Video Professor's lawyers are now seeking to compel Leonard to turn over his computer records so they can unmask the names of the site's anonymous commenters—and then sue them, too. Leonard would have probably had to shut down the site had he not found a nonprofit legal rights group to take on the cases pro bono.

InfomercialScams.com is just one of several sites that take on the scam artists. Another is Quackwatch.org, which is operated by Dr. Stephen Barrett (no relation to Donald), a retired psychiatrist from Pennsylvania who now resides in North Carolina. Quackwatch.org is an umbrella for a collection of twenty-two sites that Barrett operates. Each is dedicated to sniffing out faulty medical claims. His sites aren't specifically focused on infomercials. But given their oversized presence in the quack market, many of his detailed reports involved products that have been marketed on television.

Barrett started pursuing people purveying dubious medicinal remedies in the 1970s as a part-time hobby back when he practiced psychiatry. It became a full-time job in 1993, when he gave up his private practice and retired. He's since assembled a comprehensive database of information on hundreds of shady characters throughout the United States and Canada, and he's written critiques of just about every zany healing regimen that's been marketed in the last three decades, including such obscurities as light energy implantations, crude herb moxibustion, physio-spiritual etheric body healing, and holographic replaning. He also closely follows the movements of infomercial pitchmen like Kevin Trudeau.

Quackwatch has gained momentum in the last few years.

Barrett now has an advisory board of close to a hundred doctors, scientists, and researchers who help him review products and their ridiculous claims. He's been called on to assist with several government investigations. The media has relied on his expertise as well. Barrett spent several months advising the *Dateline NBC* producers with their Moisturol segment. It's an extraordinary effort—and like Leonard, he funds the site out of his own pocket, accepting contributions from people who support his work.

Barrett, too, has had to deal with blowback from the people he targets. A couple of years ago, he filed a defamation suit after a fringe nutritionist set up several Web sites to besmirch Barrett's name. Lorraine Day has an entire section on her site dedicated to discrediting Barrett, and she even posted photos of his (now former) home in rural Pennsylvania. Day and other targets of Barrett often accuse him of being a shill for drug companies and the American Medical Association. Some of his more prominent targets simply consider him close-minded and old-fashioned. After he published a particularly biting critique of Deepak Chopra, Chopra dismissed Barrett in the pages of *Time* as "a self-appointed vigilante for the suppression of curiosity."

Barrett has been supportive of the infomercial industry's efforts to crack down on its own. "I think it [the ERSP] is a very significant thing. The FTC doesn't have the capacity—if they did nothing else—to take down all the bad infomercials. They like the idea that the ERA gives them suggestions," he says. "But if the infomercial industry really wanted to do more about it, there's a hell of a lot of other things they could do. If the media wanted to do something, they could do a hell of a lot, too. The fact that the networks don't have any standards should be front-page news."

That's unlikely to happen any time soon. The victims of these frauds aren't wealthy or political insiders. The average infomercial shopper earns $51,000 a year; one in three has attended college. Clearly, if the victims of these frauds lived in Brentwood or the Upper East Side of Manhattan, much more would have been done by now.

It comes as little surprise that in a culture obsessed with sexual prurience, the infomercial entrepreneur who has raised the biggest furor in recent years is Joe Francis. That isn't just because he's selling sex on TV. He also happens to be an extraordinarily odious and unsavory character. Yet even as he sat in prison for much of 2007, his shows continued to air nightly.

The California native got his start as a production assistant on *Real TV,* a home-blooper show. In 1997 he borrowed $50,000 on his credit cards to release *Banned from Television,* which featured footage of gruesome accidents. (Francis was later found liable for stealing the "Banned" concept from a *Real TV* colleague.) It was in 1998 that he debuted the first installment of *Girls Gone Wild,* in which he initially offered up videocassettes and DVDs of college-aged girls bearing their breasts for the cameras. As the show grew, he branched out, launching XXX-rated titles and even a *Guys Gone Wild.* (It didn't sell.) Like most infomercial producers, he took shortcuts. The shows are continuity programs—the first title may cost just $9.99, but you continue to receive further titles and get billed full-price—and from the very start there were floods of complaints from people who had difficulty canceling the auto-ship plan or returning the videos.

But it wasn't his shady business practices that set his downfall into motion. It was his outrageous personal behavior. It started in 2003, when he was arrested in Panama City Beach after he was accused of paying underage girls—a sixteen-year-old and four seventeen-year-olds—to make out in the shower while his crew taped them. A search of his home (the evidence from which was later deemed inadmissible) turned up cocaine and other drugs. The case was a juicy one: Francis was initially charged with seventy-one separate counts, including racketeering, drug trafficking, and child pornography. (He later pleaded no contest to one count of felony child abuse and two misdemeanor prostitution charges.)

His brush with the police landed him on the radar screen of just about every law enforcement agency in the country. In December 2003—five years after he'd started selling *Girls Gone Wild* and deceiving people with his sales tactics—the FTC filed suit against his company, Mantra Films, for deceptive trade practices, including shipping videos to people who hadn't ordered them. (He agreed to pay $1.1 million to settle the charges in 2004.) In 2006 the Department of Justice targeted Francis for failing to maintain age and identity records, and he turned over $1.6 million in fines. In 2007 Francis was indicted by a federal court in Reno, Nevada, on charges that his companies claimed more than $20 million in false business expenses. The indictment also alleged that Francis used offshore bank accounts to conceal his income. While in prison, he was accused of attempting to bribe a prison guard (he allegedly offered the man $500 to bring him a bottle of water) and of concealing prescription medication.

Francis is a convenient boogeyman. He's a shameless publicity seeker and former flame of Paris Hilton. (Does it get much worse than that?) He seems to revel in negative attention: when a college student sued Francis in 2004 for allegedly drugging her and raping her in his hotel room in Miami, Francis responded by claiming that the sex had been consensual, and argued that the woman had stayed to order lunch from room service the following day. He later sued the woman for $25,000,036—the

$36, of course, was the cost of the lunch. He's so despicable that when a wannabe thug named Darnell Riley broke into Francis's home and forced him at gunpoint to pose for an explicit extortion video, few members in the media could muster up much sympathy. And he did little to improve his rep in 2006 when he allegedly assaulted a *Los Angeles Times* reporter who was following him around as part of a story and then tried to force himself on her. (He later argued that she had come on to him.)

Yet if you only focus on his business activities—and you remove all the horrific personal behavior—he's not all that different from plenty of other people in the industry. He charges people for things they didn't purchase? He's concealed the estimated $100 million he's made over the years so he doesn't have to pay taxes? He opened up offshore bank accounts? He isn't the only one.

Although Francis is out of prison for the time being, he'll be spending millions on lawyers for the foreseeable future as he deals with a litany of charges. But that's hardly put a damper on his infomercial career. New volumes of *Girls Gone Wild* are constantly in production, and he's now expanding his reach to the U.K., Australia, and France. He's expanded beyond infomercials, too. His company recently debuted a line of loungewear and swimwear and, perhaps taking a page from Hooters, recently announced plans to launch a chain of theme restaurants. One will be located in Cabo San Lucas, a short flight from Francis's fourteen-bedroom, $25 million compound in Punta Mita.

But while dozens of government investigators continue to pick apart Francis' schemes, interview hundreds of witnesses, and comb the world for every last dime he's ever earned, plenty of other seamy infomercial marketers carry on. And they do so without a concern in the world.

CHAPTER 5

Where the Shopping Never Stops

To most people, the idea of spending a day and night affixed to the couch watching nothing but QVC probably sounds like a nightmare, a scenario straight out of a counterterrorism manual. Subject someone to twenty-four hours of nonstop home shopping and you would imagine they'd have little choice but to give the goods up. "Please, I'll tell you everything you need to know. Just don't make me sit through another hour of a pant-suited woman with a blond perm and French manicure breathlessly describing a pair of $69.99 fourteen-karat gold earrings."

Actually, it really isn't all that bad. After a few hours, the perky sales patter starts to wash over you, numbing your brain like a mild anesthetic. Over on CNN, politicians are flinging insults at each other. Investigators on *CSI* are examining the charred remains of a runaway prostitute. Here in the home shopping world, the mood is reliably, refreshingly upbeat: there are no pop stars getting arrested for drunk driving or improvised explosive devices tearing off limbs of youthful American soldiers in the Middle East—just happy shoppers picking up tennis bracelets and weight-concealing dresses.

The excessively enthusiastic hosts go a long way to setting the mood, but every hour brings a fresh batch of uplifting anecdotes from loyal QVC customers, who call in with glowing product endorsements amid news of birthday celebrations, christenings, and upcoming holiday meals. As I take in all the merriment, I also absorb countless bits of knowledge, from just how "chocolate gold" is produced to what goes into manufacturing a Tiffany-style lamp to the fact that female pirates once roamed the seas, a revelation that emerged on a segment devoted to pirate-inspired jewelry. (The line featured little charms made of anchors and mermaids, but the host was careful to point out that none of the pieces "screamed pirate," which no doubt reassured viewers that they could achieve a pirate-accented look without donning an eye patch and replacing their hand with a prosthetic hook.) As day turned to evening and we roamed from room to room in the massive faux house that constitutes QVC's studio in Pennsylvania, I actually found myself tempted to pick up the phone and order something. Anything. It didn't really matter; I just wanted to share in the revelry.

Home shopping has never earned much respect from the fashion mavens who dominate the retail trade, but it's a vast, exceedingly profitable industry. QVC's corporate headquarters, Studio Park, located thirty miles outside Philadelphia in West Chester, Pennsylvania, occupies more than eighty acres and features one of the largest broadcast facilities in the world—a 60,000-square-foot studio (featuring a 20,000-square-foot replica mansion) that hums day and night. More than 17,000 employees are on the company payroll. QVC booked more than $7 billion in sales in 2007, enough to make it larger than Saks Fifth Avenue and Neiman Marcus combined as well as America's third largest broadcaster—just behind ABC and NBC—even though it sells no airtime or advertisements. Close to 200 million calls came in to QVC in the United States alone during 2007. The company can ship out as many as 300,000 packages a day from warehouse space that totals 109 football fields. HSN, the number two shopping channel, is somewhat smaller: located on a sixty-four-acre campus in St. Petersburg, Florida, the company's 4,000 employees racked up more than $3 billion in sales in 2007, which still makes it larger than J. Crew and L. L. Bean combined.

Not surprisingly, the dollars add up at a furious pace. On one day in 2001, QVC sold more than $80 million of merchandise thanks to a promotion on Dell computers; when Michael Dell turned up on the set a few months later, some $48,000 worth of computers were sold for every minute he appeared on screen. When the flamenco guitarist Esteban appeared on HSN, he sold more than $1 million worth of music in four hours, enough product to land him a spot on *Billboard*'s "Top 100" by the time he walked off the set. Both networks broadcast live every single minute of the day and night, all year long, with the exception of Christmas Day, when both HSN and QVC go "dark." (Shoppers determined to pick up the Diamonique Love Knot Stud Earrings or the fourteen-karat tricolor diamond-cut butterfly charm bracelets can always head to the Web, where the computers never take a day off.) There have been only a few instances over the years when the home shopping networks have shut down entirely. Acknowledging that there are times in the life of a nation when shopping for jewelry does not trump all, QVC suspended programming on September 11, 2001, with the following message: "QVC acknowledges today's events and expresses our heartfelt concern with this national tragedy. For more information, please turn to your TV news channel. In light of these events, QVC will be temporarily suspending its broadcast." Only Santa Claus and Osama bin Laden, it seems, have the power to make the shopping stop.

If you haven't taken the time to tune in recently, you may not know just how much has changed since home shopping first arrived on the scene in the 1980s. Not only do the networks generate billions more in revenue, what was once a tacky retail backwater filled with cheap jewelry has morphed into one of the most highly coveted spots in retail. Not long ago QVC had to beg C-list celebs to make the trek to Pennsylvania to appear on the air. Tune in tonight and you may see Heidi Klum of *Project Runway,* skin care guru Dr. Nicholas Perricone, or celebrity chef Todd English. And QVC isn't focused on poor women in the sticks with a hankering for cubic zirconia: big cities like New York, Los Angeles, Chicago, Philadelphia, and San Francisco represent its fastest growing markets. The transformation has been startling. QVC operates one of the most sophisticated inventory management and customer service operations in the world, manages one of the most successful e-commerce platforms, and enjoys vastly superior margins compared to its brick-and-mortar competitors like Macy's, Wal-Mart, and Saks. How on earth did this happen?

Home shopping didn't get off the ground as part of some devilish plan concocted by the world's largest media conglomerates. It was an accident.

In 1979 Lowell "Bud" Paxson, the owner of an AM radio station in Clearwater, Florida, turned up at an appliance store that had purchased commercials on the station, in order to collect on an outstanding debt. The owner of the showroom wasn't in a position to fork over the $1,000 he owed. Would Paxson consider accepting payment in the form of merchandise, specifically 112 Rival olive green electric can openers? "What choice did I have? I could take the can openers, or I could take nothing. So I took the can openers," Paxson later recounted.

The following day, Paxson interrupted the host of WWOT's morning show, Bob Circosta, to deliver a special message. After explaining to listeners that the can openers normally sold in stores for $14.95, Paxson said, "I'll sell these for $9.75, and if you'd like to have one, then call the radio station, and we'll take your name and phone number. But you have to come to the station and pick it up before noon. You also have to come with a check or cash because we don't take credit cards. If you want one, call the station."

Over the next fifteen minutes, all 112 can openers were spoken for. By noon, eighty-five of them had been picked up. Home shopping was born.

Paxson's success with the can openers led him to carve out a daily segment on the radio called Suncoast Bargaineers, a five-minute slot in which the station sold hair dryers, electronics, jewelry, and makeup, items that Paxson picked up at clearance prices. Circosta handled the on-air pitch. Radio listeners bought the products sight unseen, driving over to the station to pick up their purchases, with Circosta occasionally dropping off purchases on his way home from work. "Nine times out of ten, I'd stay for dinner," Circosta says. Paxson's next step was to take his sales shtick to television.

Several years earlier, Paxson had invested in an FM radio station with a lawyer and former prosecutor named Roy Speer. After the duo sold the station in 1982, Paxson suggested they use the proceeds from the sale to start a TV shopping program. In 1983 the Home Shopping Channel debuted on cable as a three-hour block of programming. But it was only a small step-up from what Paxson had been doing on the radio: while people could now actually see what they were purchasing, the low-rent production was aired only on a local cable network on Florida's Gulf Coast. That changed two years later when

Paxson and Speer took it national, rebranded it as the Home Shopping Club (they'd later change the name to Home Shopping Network), and made it available twenty-four hours a day. Bob Circosta, who had been on the air the morning those can openers debuted a few years earlier, was now hawking merchandise from coast to coast.

Paxson and Speer's debut was well timed. They had launched their venture just ahead of the sweeping decision by Congress in 1984 to deregulate cable; if half-hour infomercials were making a killing selling vegetable choppers and hair tonics, why not offer consumers a never-ending stream of merchandise on a dedicated shopping channel? They also emerged just in time for the new cultural trend that was sweeping America. As malls invaded suburban communities and a new '80s materialist ethos emerged— captured by catchphrases of the era like "Shop till you drop" and "I'd rather be shopping"—the sight of a shimmering diamond ring rotating slowly on a large-screen TV tapped into the consumerist moment perfectly.

But although Speer and Paxson had managed to combine two of America's most beloved passions—watching television and shopping—they weren't exactly earning kudos for their tasteful merchandise or refined approach to sales. During its early years, the channel trafficked almost exclusively in close-out merchandise at bargain-basement prices. The cheap jewelry and porcelain knickknacks were available for purchase only as long as they appeared on screen. And Home Shopping Network hosts would stage elaborate countdowns, lowering prices during on-air pitches. Circosta's own signature prop was a rubber-bulbed horn, which he sounded at the end of every call from a viewer. Classy it most certainly wasn't, but it worked. In 1985 the network generated $50 million in sales and had more than a thousand employees on the payroll, most of whom were assigned to man the phones and take orders. A year later, the company went public and became one of the hottest new offerings of the year, gaining more than a one hundred percent rise on the day of its initial public offering.

Paxson and Speer weren't the only savvy entrepreneurs to see the television retail opportunity. Although the Home Shopping Network was the first to enter the market, it was quickly eclipsed by QVC, which was started by Joe Segel, the entrepreneur who had previously founded the Franklin Mint, the direct response giant that sold "collectible" coins and plates. Segel had been motivated to start a home shopping network of his own after watching the Home Shopping Network. Appalled by the tacky products and tactics he'd witnessed, he was convinced there was an opportunity to sell more upscale items with a softer touch. He assembled $20 million in capital to get started, debuting QVC— or "quality, value, convenience"—in November 1986 in more than seven million homes.

While Segel's approach was less heavy-handed than the hard sales ethos adopted by HSN, QVC's products were only marginally more luxe than its Florida-based competitor's. Bloomingdale's it wasn't. Much of QVC's merchandise consisted of inexpensive jewelry, including that home shopping staple cubic zirconia. Yet QVC was an immediate success: the company racked up an impressive $112 million in sales in its first year.

HSN and QVC quickly became the two most prominent companies in the television retail sector, but plenty of other entrepreneurs were making plans to infuse the cable dial with various retail offerings. By the late 1980s, the tantalizing prospect that interactive television would allow Americans to sit on their couches while they perused giant video catalogs led to the creation of more than fifty home shopping ventures, companies with names like TelShop, Shop Television Network, Cable

Value Network, Caravan of Values, America's Marketplace, the Consumer Discount Network, and the Television Auction Channel. Fearful they'd lose out on a golden opportunity to exploit a new market, most major retailers got in on the act, too: Kmart, JCPenney, and Dayton Hudson (now Target) all made attempts to carve out a spot in the television shopping universe. Cable companies helped stoke the fervor, mindful that consumers shopping from their television sets represented one of the most potentially lucrative developments in the history of the medium. The cable giants were the gatekeepers to the viewers sitting on their couches, of course, and they exercised their power accordingly. Not only had they been given stock in QVC and the Home Shopping Network for pennies on the dollar, they also negotiated contracts that granted them a five percent cut of gross revenues, which meant every time a consumer purchased a gold necklace for $39.99, the cable company walked off with $2, a financial arrangement that not only incentivized the cable companies to carry the shopping networks but also gave them a reason to award the shopping networks lower numbers on the television dial.

The home shopping frenzy didn't last very long. The recession of the late '80s and early '90s led to a dip in consumer spending and reduced inventories of discounted goods. The industry's down-market aesthetic grew increasingly passé as consumer trends started to change, and the interactive television revolution that had been predicted a few years before had failed to materialize. When the buzz fizzled, more than ninety percent of the start-ups had either folded or merged with larger players in the industry; the highly publicized ventures that major retailers had embarked upon, such as JCPenney's Telaction, which cost the company an estimated $100 million, were abandoned. Only a handful of major players ended up surviving, including HSN and Segel's QVC, which had expanded significantly with the acquisition of the Cable Value Network for $380 million in 1989.

The shakeout of the early '90s marked a major turning point for the industry. A number of the original pioneers departed the scene, including Paxson, who left HSN in 1990 shortly after experiencing a religious conversion and turning his attention to Christianity. (In appropriately dramatic fashion, Paxson's spiritual awakening took place one evening at Caesar's Palace in Las Vegas when he opened the Gideon's Bible in his bedside table. He went on to start the Worship Network and the family-friendly PAX TV, now ION Television.) Roy Speer left HSN a couple of years later; he was ousted amid allegations of kickbacks, bribes, and improper payments made to a company controlled by his son, charges that eventually resulted in a messy class-action lawsuit. But it was Joe Segel's exodus from QVC that really took the industry by surprise. In 1992 Barry Diller announced his intention to take over the company as CEO and make a substantial investment in the network, news that floored media observers from New York to Hollywood.

Diller, of course, was the former chairman of Paramount Pictures and Twentieth Century Fox, the consummate entertainment insider who had most recently been responsible for establishing a fourth major TV network with programming like *The Simpsons* and *Married with Children.* He was about as far from the world of down-market home shopping as you could get: he shuttled between a mansion in Beverly Hills and a penthouse pied-à-terre in Manhattan; he counted Calvin Klein and David Geffen as his best friends. Suddenly he was in charge of a network headquartered next to a cow field in rural Pennsylvania best known for selling $49.99 cubic zirconia rings.

What instigated the surprising career move? Diller has longtime friend (and now wife) Diane von Furstenberg to thank for introducing him to the magic of television retail. In 1991 Marvin Traub, then the chairman of Bloomingdale's, had suggested to von Furstenberg that she pay a visit to QVC's headquarters to see the network in action. A fashion powerhouse in the 1970s thanks to her now-iconic wrap dress, von Furstenberg's career had taken a tumble in the 1980s, and she'd remained on the sidelines for much of the latter part of the decade. But she was considering a comeback, and so she turned up at QVC's studio one morning to watch soap star Susan Lucci shill for her eponymous line of hair care products. As von Fustenberg looked on with amazement, Lucci sold half a million dollars' worth of merchandise in less than an hour. "Barry, you've got to go there," she reportedly told Diller when she got back from her trip.

He took her advice, arriving at nine o'clock in the morning on Saturday, November 7, 1992, when von Furstenberg was about to unveil her low-cost new line, Silk Assets. Diller stood behind a bank of eighty telephone operators and, much like von Furstenberg, was stunned to see the phone lines come to life. In less than two hours, she'd tallied up 19,000 customers and $1.2 million in sales. "It was the ultimate Nielsen rating. The phones light up," Diller would recount to *The New Yorker*'s Ken Auletta. "You don't wait till you come into the office tomorrow to find out how you did. . . . It was the closest link I've ever seen between action and reaction."

Diller was sold on the concept, but he needed help carrying out the deal, and he partnered with existing QVC investors Comcast and John Malone's Tele-Communications, Inc. to take control of the public company, putting down $25 million of his own cash and assuming the role of CEO in December 1992. Needless to say, taking over a chintzy shopping channel didn't do much for his reputation among his former colleagues in Hollywood. But the news was a massive public relations victory for television retail, delivering a forceful blast of legitimacy to what was then regarded as a marginal and tawdry business.

Diller was not, as some have suggested, the man who turned home shopping into a viable business. It was already booming by the time he arrived on the scene. In 1992 QVC grossed $1.07 billion and cleared operating profits of $118 million. Diller, however, soon charted a new plan for the company as part of an effort to transform the company from hokey purveyor of gaudy baubles into mass-market retail outlet. He upgraded QVC's production sets and began delicately revamping QVC's product offerings, focusing on more upmarket goods without changing things too quickly and alienating the channel's core audience. He brought in seasoned management, including executives who had experience working at high-end retail chains like Neiman Marcus and Bloomingdale's. He used his sway with the celebrity set to recruit more brand-name personalities to QVC's studios, and he insisted that the network hire attractive models to pose on screen with the products. As Diller knew full well, image was going to be everything.

Diller was a step or two ahead of the curve, though, and his tenure at QVC lasted just three years. Much of his zealousness had to do with his conviction that interactive television was just around the corner; he thought QVC had the potential to serve as the crucial bridge between the worlds of retail and entertainment. Viewers sitting at home, Diller reasoned, would use their remote controls to navigate between sitcoms, dramas, and a giant catalog of merchandise where items could be purchased with the simple click of a "buy" button.

Diller wasn't the first—or the last—to see the promise in interactivity. But his enthusiasm for the notion of convergence—and his desire to return to the entertainment industry spotlight—led him to make a series of attempts to marry QVC with larger media companies. After attempting to first merge QVC and

HSN (a deal that crumbled because of the ongoing troubles at HSN following the messy departure of Speer and a misguided plan to revamp the channel in the QVC mold), Diller turned his attention to Paramount, staging a high-profile bid to acquire the film studio. The deal was never consummated. Following protracted negotiations over the course of several months, Paramount's chairman, Martin Davis, accepted a rival offer from Sumner Redstone's Viacom. Diller then turned his attention to CBS, announcing in June 1994 to great fanfare that he'd reached an agreement with CBS's majority owner, Laurence Tisch, to merge the two companies. But Diller didn't ultimately control QVC—his cable partners Comcast and TCI did—and the pact that Diller negotiated with Tisch fell apart a few weeks later when Comcast's chief executive, Brian Roberts, decided he had no interest in merging the burgeoning shopping network with a lumbering broadcast network. Roberts took control of QVC instead, and Diller was promptly ushered off the stage. (In 2003 Comcast sold its majority stake to Malone for $7.9 billion.)

The irrepressible Diller didn't walk away from the industry or, for that matter, his vision of a future of interactive shopping. Less than nine months after leaving QVC, Diller took control of a group of television stations, Silver King Communications, which carried the Home Shopping Network, and later negotiated a deal to acquire HSN in a $1.3 billion stock swap with HSN's parent company, Malone's TCI.

All this frenzied deal making by Diller and the nation's largest cable companies in the 1990s did little to diminish the public perception that home shopping was a fad that had come and gone, a world of cheap jewelry and junky collectibles that were purchased by women with big hairdos living on their Social Security payments. "Trailer-park housewives frantically phoning for another ceramic clown," wrote one reporter. "Home shopping is still basically a flea market and a vehicle for broken-down movie stars," a retail analyst told the *New York Times*. Some experts even suggested that home shopping would disappear entirely and end up a footnote in the annals of television history. But while home shopping didn't earn much respect from elitist media critics in Manhattan or entertainment honchos in Hollywood, the industry's business model was rock solid: in its first ten years, QVC had steadily increased revenue and boosted its profit margins. It was also clear, though, that if home shopping was to have a hope of really branching out and engaging new customers, it had to shake its down-market reputation.

Following Diller's departure from QVC and the arrival of a new CEO, Doug Briggs, the network continued to move away from inexpensive jewelry and expand to new categories like beauty, fashion, and housewares. Home Shopping Network underwent a major transformation, too, although it turned out to be a much rockier process. When Diller arrived at HSN in 1995, the network was in disarray after attempting to follow QVC's lead and upgrade its image as a high-end purveyor of products. As part of the shift, the network had dropped some of its hard-sell tactics (such as selling products only as long as they were being advertised on the air) and radically upgraded its catalog, introducing many new high-end products. But the changes were made too quickly, and loyal HSN viewers, dismayed by the sudden shift, abandoned the ship in droves. Diller and his right hand, Jim Held, managed to get HSN back on track—and back in the black—with a revamped product mix and a more consumer-friendly approach. But while HSN has been profitable ever since, it's never come close to touching QVC. More than a decade since Diller's arrival, Home Shopping Network remains less than half QVC's size.

. . . .

Just as it's been since the 1980s, home shopping is a totally live medium. Tune in to QVC at four o'clock in the morning, and you won't be watching a pre-recorded program that was filmed days or weeks earlier. QVC's 20,000-square-foot "home," which features a working kitchen, home office, garage, and living room with a stone fireplace, broadcasts live twenty-four hours a day. (The only thing that isn't live is the occasional prepackaged product demo.) There isn't even the seven-second delay that major broadcast networks use for "live" events such as awards shows to prevent something embarrassing from slipping by. As the many amusing clips on YouTube can attest, mistakes are occasionally made: products sometimes malfunction, hosts drop items, and every once in a great while a prank call is broadcast on the air.

The advantages of the format more than make up for the occasional flub and the cost of having hundreds of production staffers labor around the clock. Part of home shopping's appeal is that it's happening in the moment. The product you see on the screen is on sale at that very moment; wait an hour to pick up that turquoise handbag for the low, low price of $49.99, and you might just miss out on a great deal. The program hosts—those cheery men and women who mix product demonstrations and call-ins from viewers with a nonstop stream of dim banter— aren't relying on scripts or reading stilted dialogue off a tele-prompter. This is *real* reality television. Hosts riff on the products in front of them, and viewers are assured they'll never see the same show repeated twice, although it certainly doesn't feel that way after you've seen the same presentation for gold jewelry for the fifteenth time.

Broadcasting live gives home shopping networks an astonish-ing degree of control. News of a major snowstorm blanketing the

Midwest might lead a producer in HSN's control room in sunny Florida to devote a few minutes of airtime to a snow blower. QVC employs a staff of PhDs who analyze real-time sales data to determine how many minutes to devote to a specific product based on rising and falling demand curves. Hundreds of small adjustments are made on the fly to maximize sales.

"Pick up the ring again and twirl it around on your finger," a producer might instruct a host through the IFB (for interruptible feedback) earpiece that all on-air talent wears. Because the networks see precisely how many calls are flooding into the network at any given moment—and just how many of those callers are converted to customers—the smallest gesture (such as twirling a ring) can be repeated if they generate a response. Camera angles that result in a call surge can be emphasized, lighting can be adjusted on the fly, and an utterance that strikes a chord with the viewing public can be repeated. For the casual observer sitting in front of the TV at home, the folksy on-air banter often appears exceedingly cheesy. Yet it belies just what a ruthlessly analytical industry it is. After all, the networks cannot manufacture more airtime: there are only twenty-four hours in a day, and there aren't even sixty minutes in an hour since space has to be made to promote upcoming programs. Every second is a precious commodity, and unbelievably sophisticated strategies have evolved to milk each second for all it's worth.

It's not just the producers and executives in the control room who can see how the show is doing. As hosts and guests face into one of the five robotic cameras trained on them, a small screen before them displays the same information telling them just how well—or not well—they're doing. (As if appearing on live television in front of millions of viewers wasn't stressful enough.) A particularly clever form of conditioning, feeding the real-time sales info to hosts and guests allowed them to internalize what triggered consumers and adjust their behavior accordingly, both consciously and subconsciously. Joe Sugarman, the inventor of BluBlocker sunglasses and a staple on QVC for much of the 1990s, started to notice that his sales improved depending on the tie he was wearing—"The louder, the better"—and spent a considerable amount of time before each appearance picking out just the right one. (His decision to wear a tuxedo one day wasn't as well received; while a little showmanship is fine, flashy antics aren't particularly appreciated by network execs intent on portraying a more upscale image.) Ron Popeil said that he noticed the call volume shoot up every time he took a little leap in the air, an enthusiastic gesture that he repeated again and again. Some of the discoveries came as a result of accidents. During a pitch for a basket of diet food products on QVC, a bowl was set out so the guest could empty the box of cereal that came with the package. The bowl was too small, though, and when the guest poured out the box, the cereal spilled over. The response rate immediately jumped: viewers at home didn't realize the bowl was too small, they just assumed the package was a better value for the money and that the diet's servings were larger than they'd imagined. Naturally, only small bowls were used for the presentation from that point on.

It's this incredibly powerful information, distributed in real time to the desktops of senior executives at the networks, that governs the decision-making process. Minutes after a product debuts on the air, execs know whether they have a hit on their hands or a dud, and they can make adjustments to the schedule. It also provides insight into seasonal and cultural trends. QVC and HSN devote more airtime to treadmills, stair climbers, and Pilates courses right after the new year, for example, since they know that viewers at home are looking for ways to fulfill New Year's resolutions like losing weight and getting in better shape.

In the aftermath of the attacks of September 11, 2001, QVC execs noticed that sales of bedding products were rising sharply. The reason? It turned out that stressed-out Americans glued to the round-the-clock media coverage of the aftermath of the attacks wanted nothing more than to retreat to a comfy bed under brand-new cotton sheets and down comforters.

As you've probably noticed, most of the presentations on shopping networks feature two people in front of the camera. (Some jewelry presentations, particularly for those that are part of QVC's or HSN's own line, involve a single host.) As on an infomercial, there's the host responsible for guiding the show and a "guest," who may be the person who invented the product, the celebrity who attached his or her name to the item, or an expert of some sort. The host is responsible for ensuring that each product feature is described in detail, that the guest is sufficiently engaged in the presentation, and that viewers are informed of special promotions like free shipping or the option to pay in installments. It's also the host who makes sure that the show flits along thanks to a constant stream of cheerful patter.

It isn't nearly as easy as it looks. A home shopping host has to be a professional chatterbox, someone who can take the most mundane item and riff for an eternity. Chances are, if I handed you a set of sheets and asked you to spend the next fifteen minutes telling me about them without pausing for more than three or four seconds, you probably wouldn't do very well. Put those same sheets in the hands of a QVC host, and she might start off by explaining that they're made of one hundred percent combed cotton percale. Then she might chat about thread counts and explain why these sheets are particularly soft, stain resistant, or unlikely to wrinkle. Next, she might toss in a brief, amusing personal anecdote about the sheets on her own bed before returning to the item at hand and talking up the various color options and the fact that similar items at department stores retail for twice the price. Between the sales pitch and the small talk, she'll intersperse her presentation with a few calls from viewers. With millions of people watching—and with her producer talking into her ear—she'll be expected to make the entire presentation feel like what QVC calls a "backyard fence sale," a presentation as innocuous as your best friend's daughter selling you a box of Girl Scout cookies. "It's insane. You have to be the multitasker of all time," a regular home shopping guest explains.

Of course, the hosts do a good deal of preparation before they take to the set with a new product. Networks like QVC and HSN have research departments that brief hosts and ensure they're fully informed about a product. Hosts also spend time with the vendor or manufacturer of the product before going on air. (In the case of particularly important items, they may even pay a visit to a company's factory or office as part of a "fam," or familiarization, trip.) The prep work is critical, which is why many of the hosts carve out specializations so they have some comfort with the subject matter, and time is set aside so hosts can run through routines before going on the air. But in the end, the material cannot be presented as if it's written down on a cheat sheet (home shopping hosts hold small cards, which feature the most important bits of info) nor sound like it's been rehearsed. Sales take place only when the host *believes.* Or appears to, at least.

A home shopping sale is about trust. This isn't a professional salesperson lecturing me on 300-thread count sheets. This is a person I respect sharing some ideas on how I can be happier when I climb into bed. It's this folksy approach, which QVC tends to be better at than HSN, that encourages viewers to form bonds with the hosts. Ultimately, shoppers have to be seduced. Research indicates that the first-time QVC buyers spend several months watching the channel before they succumb and make their first purchase.

Creating this sense of trust and community is fomented by the testimonials (or "t-calls") from viewers, which flood into special toll-free lines day and night. People who have purchased the item in the past—and who have already had a positive experience with the product—have the opportunity to offer up effusive praise, share a personal experience (that features the item, of course), and briefly kibbitz with the host and guest. The formula works beautifully. The ability to call in and speak on the air makes viewers feel appreciated and part of a community; they also get to chat with "famous" people that they adore. And hosts do their very best to reciprocate. When a caller tells HSN's Diana Perkovic just how much she adores her presentations, Perkovic thanks her for calling in and asks, "Will you call me again soon?" It's a clever gesture. For a moment, you might have thought that Perkovic actually cares about Gladys from Fresno.

The calls also happen to serve as a potent form of social proof, the disembodied voices of loyal, satisfied customers from all over the country who can confirm that the product is just as good as advertised and reasonably priced. A call isn't really worth broadcasting unless the caller is prepared to praise the product that's currently on the air; even callers who plug other items they've purchased from the network in the past are gently directed back to the item that's currently displayed on the screen. When callers seem more interested in recounting an irrelevant personal anecdote, hosts quickly—and skillfully—extract the testimonial they need before moving on to the next caller: "So what advice would you have for someone at home who's thinking about purchasing the fourteen-karat Double Diamond Cut Wide Band Ring?"

Social proof is also at work when home shopping networks display how many items have been purchased in the corner of the screen. There's no reason, of course, why you should care that HSN just sold 1,268 flat-screen televisions in the last ten minutes. But it suggests the item is in high demand and other shoppers are rushing to the phones to scoop up a great deal. A time counter creates the impression of scarcity and motivates viewers to act now lest they—God forbid—lose out on the chance to buy Joy Mangano's Jeweled Tape Measure for $24.95.

The tactics were even more aggressive during HSN's early days. Counters were used to count down instead of up, and the host would discount the price of an item as the presentation unfolded until the inventory had been depleted. QVC never adopted the hard sell, and HSN reformed its image in the 1990s. The pushy approach is alive and well on other shopping networks, however, where the prices fluctuate, hosts say things like "Going, going, gone!" and lights flash and sirens wail when items suddenly are placed on sale. QVC and HSN moved away from the hard sell because it seemed to undermine the spirit of trust. Today on both networks, the prices of products are discounted as part of an introductory promotion or the daily "special value," which can account for up to twenty percent of daily sales. But once the initial promotion is over, the price is relatively static. QVC and HSN don't jiggle with pricing any more than a mainstream retail outlet, since they know that there's nothing a shopper hates more than to find out she paid $59.99 for something that was discounted to $49.99 an hour later.

False scarcity has also been dialed back a few notches since the early days of home shopping. The time counter now indicates when the host will move on to the next item, not how much time you have left to order the product, although hosts make plenty of references to vanishing inventories, which for obvious reasons is less offensive to the viewers than arbitrarily raising or dropping prices or setting time limits. When QVC or

HSN suggests that it's running low of a particular item, it seems beyond the network's control, although much as with other mega-retailers, it isn't necessarily the truth. QVC isn't buying five hundred pairs of shoes at a time, or even five thousand. But the network is never going to unload all of its inventory in one go. And for obvious reasons they're not especially eager to highlight the fact that the "unique" purse on sale was replicated a quarter of a million times at a factory in Guangzhou. So they carefully ration their inventories in concert with demand curves, making it appear that popular items have run out, and using waiting lists to both conceal their inventory management tactics and to "punish" people who fail to act in time.

A variety of other tactics are put to work. As on infomercials, home shopping networks rely on repetition to drive home the message. Watch an hour-long presentation on HSN and you'll hear many of the same points made again and again, rephrased slightly each time. Just like a knife infomercial that shows a pitchman cutting through everything from a tomato to an old shoe, hosts on home shopping channels often show off a million and one uses for a particular product, mindful that with each successive demonstration, the value of the product rises ever so slightly. A simple black dress isn't just suitable for a night on the town; it can also be worn to work and to church. A bracelet with faux diamond studs is the perfect accessory for a dinner at a fancy restaurant. But reverse it to reveal a plain platinum band, and you can wear it to the office, too. This is why the networks typically seek out multidimensional products. They're looking to appeal to as wide an audience as possible.

Ultimately, QVC and HSN can only employ the sort of tactics that either shoppers don't mind or don't notice. Someone who is "tricked" into buying something will take advantage of the money-back guarantee, which makes the entire exercise pointless. But whatever reservations viewers might have about the sales strategies—or a relentless pitch that can go on for the better part of an hour without interruption—it all goes down much more smoothly thanks to the hosts, who carry out their jobs in such a casual, nonconfrontational way that millions of people are perfectly happy to follow along with the action for hours on end. Indeed, hosts do such a good job charming viewers that the networks have avid fans who don't even call to purchase anything. Like window shoppers at Macy's, many people take in QVC and HSN for fun. (And like sports fans, they have a favorite that they stick to religiously.) For some people—mostly single, older women—the parade of shoes, skin moisturizers, and faux furs serves as a comforting presence, a friend that they can turn to at any hour of the day or night. And why not? The hosts don't come off as salespeople—they're companions and confidantes, people who share bits of info about their personal lives, tell you about their weekend plans, and what they had for dinner last night. They never burden you with bad news or bore you with a long-winded story. They never even frown.

"You have to remember that you're always talking to one person," an HSN regular tells me when I ask her about her on-air approach. "I visualize one person—a wife and mother just like me—sitting on the other side of the camera." Whatever it is that makes the viewers at home feel so special, there's no question that the hosts are capable of touching people in a deep way. "Since I moved, I've been so lonely," a woman confesses to QVC host Antonella Nester late one evening, "but when you come on, you make me so happy." It's a terribly depressing thing to hear amid all the cheeriness, a sudden reminder that millions of people with actual problems turn to this land of retail make-believe for comfort and hope. "I'm here for you!" Nester says with a smile before quickly moving on to the next item, an imitation emerald set in fourteen-karat gold.

Given its negative association, you won't hear the words *cubic zirconia* mentioned much on the air these days. It carries a negative association, not surprisingly. QVC refers to its fake diamond jewelry using the brand name Diamonique, "the world's finest simulated gemstone," although it's made of cubic zirconia, the crystalline form of zirconium dioxide that was first produced synthetically in the Soviet Union in the mid-1970s. To HSN viewers, it's simply "simulated diamonds." ShopNBC is the only major channel that uses the dreaded term. But it's an awfully convincing material: unless someone examines the piece of jewelry closely and knows what to look for (such as the fact that CZ weighs considerably more than a real diamond), there's no real way to tell the difference. Of course, context is usually the most helpful indicator: if your next-door neighbor is driving a 1986 Honda and working at Wendy's, that three-carat "diamond" ring she's wearing probably didn't come from Tiffany's.

Home shopping's transformation from CZ-hawking trailer park favorite to retail powerhouse started in the early '90s, but it took a number of years for the A-list to come around. For much of the 1990s, the networks' lingering reputation as a cheap jewelry outlet proved to be a major deterrent to upscale brands. Placing one's products on a shopping channel threatened to undermine a brand's status as high end. It also had the potential to put off mainstream retail outlets: during the '90s, there were occasional reports that chains like Saks and Neiman Marcus refused to do business with brands that had hawked their wares on networks like HSN and QVC.

Celebrities were equally skittish. Many of the personalities who turned up on home shopping during the early days were either long past their prime or not much concerned with sacrificing any hard-earned cred. Joan Rivers had seen her comedy career tank and was millions of dollars in debt when her collection of jewelry debuted on QVC in 1990. (Her line proved to be an instant hit and generated $30 million in sales its first year.) A handful of equally kitschy celebrities flocked to television retail at the same time: Vanna White of *Wheel of Fortune* fame pushed her Little Miss Vanna line of cosmetics and stamped her name on clothing, shoes, and a teeth whitening solution sold via infomercials. Susan Lucci marketed a line of hair care products. George Hamilton rather appropriately promoted a self-tanning product called Constant Color. The conventional wisdom was that you turned to home shopping when you couldn't get a legit job in television or film or you were so eager to make money, you couldn't care less about the consequences to your reputation.

To some extent, television retail is still a haven for the D-list. Jennifer Flavin-Stallone's Serious Skin Care products might be a huge hit on HSN, but she's not exactly locking in prime space at Barneys. Socialites in Manhattan aren't attending galas wearing pieces from Tori Spelling's jewelry line. You won't find Brad Pitt photographed in *Vanity Fair* wearing a suede "touring coat" from Carson Kressley's QVC collection. But the sheer size of the television retail market—and the networks' efforts to make home shopping more respectable—has started to attract companies that would have never dreamed they'd enter the TV market a decade ago. These days, prestigious brand names like Estée Lauder, Canon, Olympus, Cuisinart, and Reebok all have deals with home shopping networks. So do a handful of high-end fashion/beauty brands like Christian Dior, Stuart Weitzman, Michael Kors, Dana Buchman, and Frédéric Fekkai. More than a dozen celebrity chefs now hawk merchandise on the air, including Emeril Lagasse, Wolfgang Puck, Todd English, and Gordon Ramsay. A decade ago, home shopping networks were awash in $29.99 cubic zirconia rings. Now you might find a critically acclaimed chef cooking up porcini mushroom risotto while he tries to sell you $200 worth of cookware.

Far fewer well-known faces appear on ShopNBC, the number three home shopping channel, which has positioned itself as an even more upscale alternative to QVC and HSN. This wasn't always the plan. When NBC acquired a stake in ValueVision Media in 1999, a home shopping channel that specialized in fine jewelry (and subsequently changed the name), ShopNBC had hoped to leverage its bigger sister's media assets and talent relationships. It would be a cross-promotional hub, suggested NBC executives: you'd watch a drama on NBC, then skip over to ShopNBC to pick up the products that were just featured on the show. This was much the same idea that had led Barry Diller to TV retail years earlier, and once again this marriage of entertainment and retail never came to pass. But even without the stars of NBC's prime-time lineup pitching new products, the network has managed to expand and has slowly transitioned away from jewelry to electronics, beauty, and home decor. The channel is still small potatoes compared to QVC—it generates roughly one-tenth the revenue—but has staked out a strong position at the pricey end of TV retail: the average ShopNBC price point is more than double that of QVC and HSN.

Along with the emergence of higher-end TV retail networks, the demographics of home shopping have shifted in recent years. It's still a market overwhelmingly dominated by women (less than twenty percent of purchases are made by men), and it still skews a bit older (women ages twenty-five to fifty-four make up the vast majority of customers), but the people doing the buying aren't just Midwestern hicks, as so many assume. The average income of a QVC viewer is close to twenty percent above the national average, and the network is seeing major growth in large cities, attracting busy women who may not have the time or patience to shop at a department store. But while the influx of brand-name products, celebrities, and more affluent customers should continue, the stigma of home shopping endures. No one may be surprised when someone like Donald Trump takes to retail airwaves. (In a clever quid pro quo, he worked QVC into an episode of *The Apprentice* and later turned up on the network to market his book, selling 37,000 copies in twenty-two minutes.) You won't, however, see Prada and Louis Vuitton offer their products on TV anytime soon. It's not that QVC viewers wouldn't gobble them up. If QVC shoppers are willing to spend $195 on a 0.5-ounce vial of Neuropeptide Eye Area Contour Cream by celebrity dermatologist Dr. Nicholas Perricone, it's possible they'd also be happy to pay $500 for shoes or $2,000 for a purse. But just as QVC toys with false scarcity by announcing that inventories are running low, ultra-luxe designers know full well that their own strategy of scarcity requires them to eschew the TV retail market, and introducing products to QVC could shatter the perception of exclusivity.

QVC's and HSN's press releases buzz about the famous faces that appear on their networks; in reality, though, glamorous merchandise is in the minority. Sure, there are occasional segments with big names like Bobbi Brown and Dr. Patricia Wexler. But most of the airtime is devoted to (not nearly as posh) products like seasonal sticker kits you can use to "embellish your scrapbook." Home shopping is designed to appeal to as wide an audience as possible, and the truth of the matter is that the average QVC viewer is more interested in leaf blowers and cotton sheets, not Wexler's tiny, one-ounce jar of skin serum for $49.98.

But big brand names and celebs generate attention, and attention generates viewers—and viewers are just what the shopping networks need if they're going to expand. QVC may now appear in ninety-six percent of U.S. homes, but only ten percent of the general public has ever purchased a product from a home shopping channel. Creating "destination programming" such as hosting a concert by Elton John (and selling his CDs and DVDs at the same time) and picking off famous faces from popular reality TV programs—like Heidi Klum, Paula Abdul, and *Project Runway* winner Chloe Dao—help attract a new audience. The celebrity names add some cachet (if that's even possible with Paula Abdul) and help erase the memory of spinning wheels of cubic zirconia. But they don't keep QVC's staff of 17,000 employees on the job. Affordable footwear and tchotchkes for the home—and the occasional porcelain doll marketed by Marie Osmond—do that. It's an approach similar to one Target has pursued in recent years. Lines by trendy designers like Proenza Schouler get the press, but the vast majority of Target's sales come from cheap items that you could find just as easily at Wal-Mart.

One way the shopping networks set themselves apart is that unlike big retail chains, much of their inventory comes from independent vendors who bring items to the network directly. QVC receives more than twenty thousand inquiries every year from entrepreneurs and has a staff of more than one hundred to sift through submissions looking for new items to put on the air; several times a year, one of the company's national product searches packs a convention center with aspiring QVC guests. Of course, this isn't because QVC feels any sort of obligation to help out the small businesses of America. It's simply a matter of filling the product pipeline and differentiating the network from its competitors. QVC introduces about 280 (as of 2007) new items a week, and the items that sell aren't necessarily the ones that you can find at every department store in town. QVC and HSN also thrive on the narrative: the story of a third-generation fisherman from Maine who makes crab cakes using his great-grandmother's secret recipe is a great hook; a product that's made by a multinational food conglomerate in Omaha is not. A sale is infinitely easier when you can remind viewers that this is the only place they can find the product on the screen in front of them.

As you might expect, it isn't particularly easy to get a product accepted by QVC. Less than four percent of the items officially submitted to the network ever earn time on the air. The vast majority of products are rejected outright, and a much smaller percentage is evaluated but ends up failing QVC's stringent protocols. The network can't afford to offer things that can't be easily produced en masse or are liable to break when a UPS driver drops a box on the ground. None of the senior execs want to hear about an item returned in droves. So everything that makes it to the air is subject to an extensive testing process. Even the items that do make it through don't necessarily last: the QVC data machine is ruthless, and products that don't achieve sales targets get dropped and disappear into QVC.com's closeout section.

But for those that turn out to be winners, the payoff can be astounding. Perhaps you've seen a kooky woman named Jeanne Bice on QVC promoting her chintzy line of Quacker Factory sweaters? (She's hard to miss: she wears a neon rhinestone-studded headband when she's on the air and pitches a line of sequined sweaters that feature Christmas trees.) Bice was a divorced mother who was making duck-motif sweaters in her garage in Florida when QVC gave her a shot. She now grosses $50 million a year. Leslie Blodgett operated a tiny California-based chain of cosmetics stores called Bare Escentuals before she first made it to Studio Park. Her eight-minute QVC debut sold out, and when she returned for a second visit, she made more in twenty minutes than one of her stores took in an entire year. Bare Escentuals now grosses hundreds of millions a year and is QVC's number 1 cosmetics brand.

The number of high-end, branded products are few and far between. If it's not provided to QVC by an independent vendor, it's likely something that QVC cooked up on its own, such as its popular line of inexpensive sportswear called Dialogue. This isn't to suggest that what the home shopping networks sell is junk. On average, you're actually likely to find better merchandise on TV than you are at a giant discount department store since the networks have much stricter quality control departments and carefully vet every product before it goes on the air. For the most part, you're getting a decent product for a very decent price. And unlike the infomercial industry, the home shopping networks (and QVC in particular) have a solid reputation for customer service, shipping products in a timely fashion, accepting returns, and refunding money. As for whether you're willing to pay HSN any money at all for a bra created by Dr. Robert Rey, the flamboyant star of E!'s *Dr. 90210,* well, that's another matter.

If you've spent any time navigating the cable universe, though, you know that Rey is downright classy compared to some of the programming on other home shopping channels. If you tune into Shop-At-Home, you might find a group of burly men demonstrating knives used to gut fish or showing off collectible coins. On Jewelry Television, you'll find women with big hair standing on a set that hasn't been updated since the mid-'80s selling pendants and chains for less than thirty bucks. The sales tactics only get more outrageous when you check in on the home shopping networks that don't have the luxury of a dedicated cable channel and lease blocks of airtime from other stations. On the Jewelry Channel, a Texas-based company that sells items on an auction basis, you'll get a glimpse of what HSN looked like at the very beginning. Hosts shout out the names of the people calling in to purchase items, digits spins on the screen like a slot machine, and the entire pitch is accompanied by a pulsing soundtrack. It makes QVC look like a visit to Harry Winston on Fifth Avenue.

Smaller companies like the Jewelry Channel have little in common with their more established rivals, as I learned when I visited the offices of the United Shopping Network, a company that used to sell estate jewelry on local stations across the company before going bust in 2006. USN's offices couldn't have been more different from QVC's vast compound in Pennsylvania: the small studio was located in an office building in downtown Los Angeles, and a bank of phone operators sat several feet from a small, brightly lit platform where the item currently on sale was displayed. There was no set, but that didn't matter much since the entire show consisted of a close-up shot of the ring or bracelet for sale, which rotated slowly on an electric turntable. The host never appeared on camera, which wasn't such a bad thing considering he looked like he'd been physically transported from a casino in Reno in 1979. The only thing viewers could see were his overly tanned hands as he massaged the jewelry under the halogen lights.

After spending a half hour in the studio, I stepped into the control room, where I found a young man was sitting behind the controls, operating the Chyron machine, the device responsible for displaying the graphics you see on the air. Every few seconds, he punched in a number, which was displayed in the corner of the screen under the header that read "Items sold." He was steadily adjusting the number upward in batches of twos and threes: 278, 282, 284, 288, 291.

"How do you know what number to change it to?" I asked naively as he pecked away. He laughed. "It doesn't really matter what I type on the screen. Just as long as it goes up."

CHAPTER 6

Circus of the Stars

It's safe to say that when Erik Estrada was starring in one of the most popular shows on television in the early 1980s, he probably didn't expect the day would come when he'd be standing in rural Arkansas pitching undeveloped land. Back then he was one of *People*'s "Ten Sexiest Bachelors in the World." He was so popular as Ponch on *CHiPs* that NBC gifted him a Rolls-Royce to encourage him to stay on the show. Oh, how times have changed. These days, you'll find him on the air in the middle of the night pitching a "free trip" to visit the community of Bella Vista. "No sales pressure!" he cheerily assures viewers. Stick around after it's over, and you might just catch former CNN anchor Bob Losure pitching a suspicious food supplement or see former *Happy Days* star Anson Williams promoting a skin care line.

Long before VH1's "celebreality" shows came along, infomercials represented the final stopping point for actors on a downward career trajectory. When the studios stopped calling or when your agent dropped you, there were always a few bucks to be made hawking a questionable product in the dead of the night. Judith Light turned to infomercials after her stint on *Who's the Boss?* devolved into tacky movies of the week. Lindsay Wagner, the star of *The Bionic Woman,* hadn't been seen in years when she materialized in spots for the Sleep Number Bed. When Chuck Norris's career as an action star came to an end, he started shilling a home gym. Suzanne Somers was the washed-up former star of *Three's Company* when she reemerged as the face of the Thighmaster. Marilu Henner, Bruce Jenner, Corbin Bernsen, Jane Fonda, Christopher Knight, Larry Hagman, John Ritter, Dionne Warwick: the list of famous people who have appeared in infomercials sounds like the roster of guest stars who appeared on the 1977 season of *The Love Boat.*

Of course, there was nothing new about paying celebrities money to pitch products. Celebrity endorsements have been around forever, even if their value has always been hotly contested by the advertising community. The big difference with stars appearing in infomercials was that it quickly became known as the career move of the last resort—not least because placing celebs in thirty-minute ads started off as a novelty, a tactic that direct response marketers used to momentarily distract channel surfers from switching stations. Infomercial producers weren't terribly concerned *who* caused viewers to stop. In much the same way that early infomercials tried to shock viewers with stunts like setting cars on fire, when it came to bringing in famous hosts, they recruited stars who would make viewers at home pause for a moment and therefore potentially stick around to see what was for sale. Infomercial producers weren't thinking about maintaining a brand. They were focused on bang for the buck, and celebrities on the downward slope were bargains.

While celebrity appearances were a coup for producers, they became something of a devil's pact for the stars themselves. Actors could get away with doing soft drink commercials and even fast food ads, but appearing in an infomercial was quickly perceived as an act of desperation, even if it might have provided a good deal of money for relatively little work. After Cher appeared in several infomercials in the early 1990s, she endured the mockery of David Letterman and *Saturday Night Live* and spent years blaming the dearth of acting opportunities on her decision to dabble as a late-night pitchwoman. "There's nothing like an infomercial to slam-dunk your ass," she later wrote in her memoir.

This has changed to some degree. While many infomercials still function as the province of the B- and C-lists, there are some products that have managed to rope in big names, such as the Proactiv infomercial with Jessica Simpson and P. Diddy. A cultural shift partly accounts for this: in the media-centric, ad-infused world we live in, we've come to accept the fact that famous people sell out. If Rachael Ray can turn up in a commercial for Dunkin' Donuts, and Tiger Woods can star in an ad for Buick, why can't Kelly Clarkson sell an acne product on an infomercial? But budgets are also a major factor: the hundreds of millions that Guthy-Renker now generates from Proactiv allow the company access to the upper reaches of the celebrity universe. Substantially higher production values have helped ease the transition, too.

Still, the number of supremely famous faces who have taken to the late-night circuit is relatively small, and truly famous celebrities still shudder at the notion of appearing on a thirty-minute commercial. A thirty-second commercial for Pepsi might be okay. Hawking a vacuum cleaner on channel 82 at three o'clock in the morning? Not so much. But direct response marketers haven't been particularly eager to hire big-name stars either, especially for certain types of products. Most infomercial producers are focused on moving inventory, not creating a brand, and would have trouble justifying the exorbitant expense. They pay attention to margins and the return on their media dollars, not whether the mention of the product name generates a warm and fuzzy feeling in the hearts of consumers. The last thing they want is a famous face to detract attention from the 800 number at the bottom of the screen. And, really, would you truly be more inclined to buy a vacuum if you saw George Clooney using it?

Consumers are a good deal savvier than they used to be. Marketing research indicates that within seconds of exposure to an ad, consumers form strong opinions as to whether an endorsement is authentic and honest. We size up the star on screen and form an immediate judgment about how likely it is that this person uses the product that he or she is instructing us to buy. (This does little to explain why Erik Estrada is pitching swampland in Arkansas, but there are always exceptions.) Putting a star in an infomercial for a vacuum, blender, or electric drill has never made much sense. Nor will you usually see a star appear in a get-rich-quick infomercial—viewers know full well that the celeb didn't make his or her money buying no-money-down real estate. The goal of these shows is to either show how a product works or demonstrate that it has the potential to change the lives of "real" people. No one is going to believe that someone like Jessica Simpson, who once said that she thought tuna fish came from a chicken, really cares about grilling up shrimp eighteen different ways.

But when it comes to beauty and fitness products, which are fundamentally more aspirational in nature, the opposite is true. Viewers at home are supposed to want to have the skin, hair, and body of Jessica Simpson, Cindy Crawford, and Elle Macpherson, and they're also supposed to believe that there's a "secret" that can account for why these famous women have such luxurious hair, polished skin, and toned bodies, and having a Beverly Hills plastic surgeon and a full-time hair stylist and makeup artist doesn't fit into the equation. Viewers who can clearly see Nick Lachey's abs, Brooke Burke's butt, and Christie Brinkley's thighs are informed that they can achieve the same results—for just three payments of $39.95. Convenience and impulse aren't nearly as important as stimulating emotion. So when stars comes on to instruct you to purchase Proactiv, they not only share their own personal experience with acne, they take out the pictures to prove it. The product has changed their life, they rave—which is why they *just had to* share their experience with you, the viewer.

Of course, the real reason a celebrity is flogging products on TV is the eye-watering paycheck and the chance to earn a potentially stunning windfall from royalties. Back in the 1990s, stars (as well as their agents, managers, and advisers) were shocked to hear about has-beens who'd earned millions by attaching their names to various products marketed on television. In 1996 retired boxer and Doritos pitchman George Foreman signed on with the appliance manufacturer Salton to promote a line of indoor grills, the George Foreman Lean Mean Fat-Reducing Grilling Machine. The product turned into a sales sensation, and Forman walked away with $137.5 million in cash and stock three years later when Salton decided to buy him out of his contract. Suzanne Somers's acting career was nonexistent when she appeared on TV to promote the Thighmaster in the early 1990s. The decision not only put tens of millions in her pocket (more than 110 million units were sold in eighteen months) but also enabled her to embark on a new, fantastically lucrative career as a professional pitchwoman. Guthy-Renker can pay $2 million or $3 million for a celebrity endorsement and can offer up the potential to earn millions more thanks to royalties.

The economics of a celebrity deal—and a star's level of involvement—varies widely. Erik Estrada, didn't wake up one day and decide he desperately wanted to sell property in Arkansas. He's a spokesperson for the company, along with former game show host Chuck Woolery. They show up to read a script, and they walk away with an upfront fee and small royalty. Nick Lachey didn't invent the silver-colored bouncing ball that he says he uses every day to firm his abs. He just tells you to use it.

In other cases, stars are involved in developing the product from the start, and they stand to make much, much more if the item is eventually successful. (They also stand to lose much more in the way of credibility if the product bombs.) Most of the products pitched by celebs on QVC and HSN are of this ilk: home shopping networks have the wherewithal to set stars up with lines of their own and make it worth their while, and they know that getting stars involved in the creation of a product boosts sales. Does that mean that viewers are supposed to believe that Heidi Klum is walking around town wearing the silver Quilted Heart Locket that she sells on QVC for $65? Or that she spent late nights designing sketches of each piece in her collection? Who knows. But it's certainly more believable than if she'd turned up on television to advertise a mop.

Compared to infomercials, home shopping networks tend to be safer outlets for stars looking for cash. Creating a new product gives them a measure of creative control. The fact that the networks now feature more upscale products has helped, too, as has increased media fragmentation. Just as American celebrities can travel to Japan to star in ads for products they'd never be caught dead holding in their hands stateside, Frédéric Fekkai knows he can turn up on QVC with his hair care line and rest assured that his celebrity and socialite clients—who probably don't watch much home shopping—won't even notice. And even if they do, it may not matter all that much. Like designing a Target line, there's a certain degree of kitschy cool that comes from being able to say that you sell your wares to the masses in the middle of the night.

But it's the money that really reels in the big names to QVC and HSN. The royalty rate on home shopping networks can be five to ten percent of gross sales—and the sales mount exceedingly quickly. When Hulk Hogan appeared on QVC and racked up $1 million on his Hulk Hogan's Ultimate Grill over the course of three one-hour appearances, he may have walked away with as much as $100,000. Tying new brands to celebrities also poses a certain amount of risk for shopping channels, particularly since—unlike infomercials—QVC and HSN contracts require the star to appear on the air live. When Paula Abdul turned up for a QVC appearance in 2007, her unsuccessful attempt at formulating a coherent sentence set off a minor YouTube sensation.

You don't have to first hit it big and fall off the celebrity map to carve out a career as a direct response superstar. Some of the most successful players in the world of infomercials and home shopping—from producers to directors to on-air personalities—are people who once nurtured dreams of walking down the red carpet to the Oscars, but have since had to settle for the info-mercial Oscars in Las Vegas. Jim Caldwell doesn't look the least bit familiar to me when we sit down to chat, although he had some fleeting fame in the 1980s as the host of a couple of game shows, including *Tic Tac Dough*. But he's since carved out a lucra-tive career as an infomercial pitchman and producer. (Like news anchors, ex-game show hosts have become popular fixtures on the infomercial circuit: they're universally recognized, gener-ally nonthreatening, and often considerably cheaper than prime-time stars.) While I recognize Forbes Riley instantly, it wasn't because of anything she'd done in the world of legitimate TV or film. I knew her as the woman from the Jack LaLanne juicer infomercials.

Riley has a long list of credits on IMDb, but they're not exactly the sort that will earn you much coverage in *People*. She's appeared in a handful of forgettable cable movies and B films like *Megiddo: The Omega Code 2*. She's landed one-episode appearances on shows like *The Practice* and *Picket Fences* and had short-lived hosting gigs on ESPN, The Learning Channel, and Animal Planet. But while her career as an actress never made her a star, she's managed to become one of the most prolific and successful hosts in direct response. She's been described as the "Julia Roberts of the infomercial industry," a moniker she's happily adopted as her calling card in recent years.

Riley is pushing fifty, but she could easily pass for late thirties. She's tan and trim, with a gleaming smile that looks like it was crafted by one of Beverly Hills' finest cosmetic dentists. When I meet her, I'm reminded of Leeza Gibbons, another talk show host and infomercial staple. Riley, clearly, prefers the Julia Roberts association. She quickly points out that just like the famous actress, she's the mother of twins. "She copied me!" she jokes, grinning at her husband, Tom, who seems to have heard the line more than once before. She proceeds to explain that she's the "billion-dollar host," which is to say that the products she's pitched on the air have collectively generated sales in excess of a billion dollars.

Riley's career as infomercial queen started, as it did for so many others, when she was struggling to earn roles in film and TV. In the early '90s, she appeared in her first half-hour spot, pitching Aromatrim, that strange device you placed under your nose to eliminate your appetite. (She was the woman who trooped up and down the boardwalk in Venice, California, with the Aromatrim in one hand and a plate of cookies in the other.) Later she was hired by exercise guru Jake Steinfeld to pitch fitness products on FitTV. Since then she's established herself as one of the ubiquitous hosts in the world of paid programming. Just don't call what she does "selling."

"I don't sell anything," she says with a mix of mock outrage and genuine annoyance. "I just share passion!"

She sure has no shortage of passions. Over the years, she's appeared in nearly a hundred infomercials, including the Maxi-Glide hair straightener, Pressa Bella dry steam iron, Power 90 fat burning system, Honeywell QuietClean air purifier, Abs of Steel, Wagner Paint Mate, Aerobed inflatable mattress, Abtronic Wonder Massage, Orbitrek elliptical glider, and ProStrong Nail Strengthener. Her longest running—and most successful—show has been the Jack LaLanne Power Juicer and Power Juicer Express. (The show is still on the air more than five years after its debut and has generated more than $350 million in sales, according to Riley.) Her passions aren't confined to half-hour infomercials. She's also a frequent presence on QVC and HSN, where she pitches products like the Barefoot Science Arch Activation System and the Urban Rebounder, a trampoline you set up in your living room to bounce on and lose weight.

"I can't sell. I don't like to sell. I hate salesmen," she adds.

She might not like to call it selling, but whatever it is that she does, she's pretty darn good at it. Hosts who are successful pitching products are hired again and again; one successful show leads to another, which goes a long way to explaining why Riley is such an inescapable presence on late-night cable TV. (It also explains why she's done so well for herself. With the royalties she earns on gross sales, her successes on the air have minted her a small fortune.) But Riley doesn't want to be considered purely an infomercial phenomenon. She's quick to point out that she landed a Fox pilot not too long ago, and she says she's regularly in discussions with TV networks and studios about "exciting new opportunities." Given her age, though, the chances of a big Hollywood breakthrough are remote. But she fits perfectly into the demo that home shopping networks and infomercials target, which is why her paid programming career is as busy as ever. And while Julia Roberts probably wouldn't switch places with Forbes Riley for all the money in the world, in the fame-obsessed world we live in, plenty of people would be thrilled to get paid to pitch insoles on live television.

Every year, the home shopping networks receive thousands of homemade audition tapes from aspiring on-air presenters; QVC even occasionally hosts an open call to look for new talent. (You can call their audition hotline at 1–800–422–7805 to find out about the next event in your area.) So how do you pick out a good home shopping host? You hand them something, anything, and ask them to sell it. You don't really need to be armed with much knowledge to riff on a product, inject a little cheer, and tug on a few heartstrings.

When Kathy Levine, who spent close to twenty years at QVC, turned up at her audition in the mid-'80s, she was given a pencil: "If you have long nails and don't want to wreck them, you can use the pencil to push the numbers on your phone. Pencils are incredible because you can erase all your mistakes. And don't forget if you get angry, you can break a pencil in two; it makes you feel so much better. Then you can give the extra piece to a friend, making you resourceful!"

Forbes Riley took a more emotional approach to the pen she was given by Jake Steinfeld: "As long as you've got a pen, you can touch someone's heart, no matter how far away they are." Touching, isn't it?

Few of the people who audition for on-air positions make the cut, of course. Not only do potential hosts need to be able to sell just about anything that falls into their hands, they also have to exude warmth and approachability. They have to be likable, trustworthy, funny, and attractive. (Not *too* attractive, though. The middle-aged women watching at home have to be able to relate, which is why the hosts of home shopping shows are a diverse lot.) It's a tall bill of goods. But for those who pass muster, it's a comfy job. Hosts are well paid—some of the more seasoned hosts make on the order of a half million dollars a year—and the job comes with a certain amount of celebrity status.

Like soap opera stars, home shopping personalities don't generally spur much ink in the tabloids, but they have dedicated fan bases of women who congregate online and exchange gossip about their favorite on-air personalities. Outfits are dissected, and details from their personal lives are unearthed. Sometimes even scandal ensues: when two QVC hosts, Judy Crowell and Jeff Hewson, were briefly married in the early '90s, fans followed the resulting breakdown of their months-long marriage religiously, from the moment the two started wearing wedding bands on the air to the moment when the rings came off. Hosts—particularly the ones who have been around since the early days, like Bob Bowersox and Mary Beth Roe—are regularly stopped by eager fans when they're in public. And some of the ladies of home shopping have emerged as middle-aged sex symbols to a certain male demographic. (The husbands of avid viewers, perhaps?) Moments when a QVC or HSN host has bared a bit of skin are well documented online, and there are active discussions about them on sites with names like legsandheels.com.

One of the most popular pitchmen on television in recent years has been Anthony Sullivan. Sully, as he's known to everyone in the biz, is inescapable on TV these days: he's been the face of Swivel

Sweeper, One Sweep, the Smart Chopper, Taplight, Foodsaver, and First Alert Alarm System, among others.

When I meet Sullivan, he immediately reminds me of Ron Popeil in that both have an intense energy that almost compels you to pay attention. But while Popeil doesn't come across as the jovial sort, Sully, it's quite clear, is the life of the party. If he hadn't made it in sales, he might very well be entertaining a tipsy crowd in a pub in the south of England. His arms flail about as he explains to me the secret to a successful pitch. His words fly a mile a minute. He's even more manic than he comes across on TV.

Sullivan is also something of a celebrity. As we chat at an infomercial industry gathering, someone stops by every minute or two to shake his hand or pat him on the back, which he reciprocates with a big grin and a thumbs-up. In fact, he's recognized almost everywhere he goes.

"People stop me in airports and say, 'Aren't you that guy who sells the mop?'" Like a small group of other late-night pitchmen, he's become something of a pop culture phenomenon. The Fox show *MadTV* spoofed him in 2004, although the actor on the show who played a character named "Roland Backinson" used a thick Australian accent, much to his dismay. The actor demonstrated a home alarm system, a riff on the First Alert spot that Sully's promoted for the past few years.

A native of Devon, Sully follows in a long tradition of pitchmen who moved from the street fairs of England to the much more lucrative confines of cable television. He first found success as a teenager pitching products on the streets of London. It was thanks to fellow Brit pitchman John Parkin that Sully arrived in the United States to pursue a career in TV. Television pitchmen, it turns out, recruit other pitchmen, passing the torch to the next generation who invade your living rooms in the middle of the night with their over-the-top shtick. And they stick together.

Sully was introduced to his wife by Billy Mays, the bearded pitchman for OxiClean, Kaboom, and OrangeGlo. Mrs. Sullivan just so happens to be Mays's cousin.

Like others who have come before him, it didn't take long for Sully to realize that instead of earning a fee to host a show, he could earn much more producing the program from the start. He's since founded Sullivan Productions in his adopted hometown of Tampa, where he's close to the studios of HSN. (Quite a few infomercial hosts live in the Tampa area, including Tony Little and Billy Mays.) He often teams up with Mays to produce and direct TV spots.

Nowadays Sully is focused on finding people to replace him in front of the camera so he can concentrate on producing shows. "It's isn't easy anymore," he explains when I ask him how one goes about finding the next infomercial star. It usually requires turning up at the occasional state fair or convention to see people in the act. Like Ron Popeil, he sees the pitch as an art form. He also seems to share Popeil's disdain for high-priced celebrity pitch people. "They don't know how to sell," he says. "You can't just have someone with a pretty face. You need someone with a story! Drama! There needs to be personality."

It was precisely that intangible factor—personality—that originally led me to tune into infomercials back in the day. Almost everyone who appeared on television in the late '80s and early '90s had it in spades. Tony Little, Susan Powter, Richard Simmons, Matthew Lesko: their crazy antics and absurdly high energy levels compelled you to pay attention. (That their careers coincided with the crack epidemic was totally accidental, naturally.) It was also their offbeat, campy personalities that later earned them their stars on the pop culture walk of fame.

Of course, at the time I wasn't thinking about how ironic it was to tune into these shows—nor did I have any idea who Susan Sontag was, who defined camp culture in her famous 1964 essay, "Notes on Camp." ("Camp is art that proposes itself seriously, but cannot be taken altogether seriously because it is 'too much.'") I just thought of them as amusing. But it's clear that infomercials were part of a broader generational affection for kitsch. Along with lava lamps, superhero lunch boxes, Chia pets, mood rings, Spam, porcelain figurines, and Twinkies, infomercials became funny precisely because they weren't supposed to be.

Infomercials and home shopping shows continue to amuse three decades after their arrival. The tacky conventions—the wacky demonstrations, hard sales tactics, seemingly scripted testimonials, and cheesy graphics—remain the source of their enduring comedy appeal, while also being the reason the industry has had such a difficult time shaking its down-market reputation. Many of the parodies still reflect the gimmicks from the golden age of the infomercial, those days in the 1980s and early '90s when you could turn on the TV and see a silly man with a British accent and a bowtie setting a Rolls-Royce on fire. Few infomercials are as outrageous these days, but we have a nostalgic connection to the kitschy formula. And the people who starred on the programs have since become pop culture icons. Remember the *Saturday Night Live* skit from the 1970s in which Dan Aykroyd appears as the inventor of the Bass-O-Matic, a device that allowed you to make a tasty bass smoothie?

How many times has this happened to you? You have a bass. You're trying to find an exciting new way to prepare it for dinner. You could scale the bass, remove the bass's tail—head and bones—and serve the fish as you would any other fish dinner. But why bother now

that you can use Rovco's amazing new kitchen tool, the
Super Bass-O-Matic '76. Yes, fish-eaters, the days of
troublesome scaling, cutting and gutting are over, because
Super Bass-O-Matic '76 is the tool that lets you use
the whole bass with no fish waste, and without scaling,
cutting or gutting.

Aykroyd was spoofing Ron Popeil, of course, whose two-minute spots for various "O-Matic" inventions were all over the air at the time. (After turning the fish into a nasty brown-colored liquid, Aykroyd hands the glass to costar Laraine Newman, who proceeds to gulp it down. "Wow, that's terrific bass!" she says.)

Aykroyd parodied the ubiquitous pitchman several more times, and infomercial-inspired skits have been a staple on the show ever since. David Spade memorably spoofed Don Lapre on a couple of occasions, Steve Martin pitched a product called "Steve Martin's All-Natural Penis Beauty Cream," and Chris Farley played cosmetics infomercial queen Lori Davis. Ben Stiller did a brilliant imitation of Tony Robbins on his short-lived Fox skit show. ("I hypnotize you with my teeth, and you pay me money!") When he was a regular on *In Living Color,* a hyperactive Jim Carrey did an impression of the equally hyperactive pitchman Jay Kordich, better known as the Juiceman.

The send-ups continue. Steve Martin returned to *SNL* in 2006 and parodied the direct response pitches targeted to people in debt. (The skit featured a book called *Don't Buy Stuff You Cannot Afford,* which included such nuggets of wisdom as "If you don't have any money, you should not buy anything.") Then there's the slew of homemade spoofs that have been unleashed by sites like YouTube. You'll find people who invented silly products and filmed their "pitch," as well as people who turned ordinary household items into an infomercial-style commercial, like the guy who took a pair of household scissors and created a show called "Amaze-O-Cut." You'll find faux infomercials used to promote God, too. Several Christian evangelical groups have used the familiar and amusing format of an infomercial to "pitch" the Bible. And late-night TV figures have popped up on dozens of shows, movies, and commercials. Ron Popeil played himself on *The Simpsons*. Tony Robbins made an appearance *Shallow Hal*. (Not surprisingly, he played a self-help coach.) Geico used Tony Little and the guitarist Esteban in a couple of its ads. Little also turned up in a campaign for Microsoft's MSN service along with pitchmen Matthew Lesko and Anthony Sullivan.

That they usually end up the butt of the joke doesn't seem to bother them that much. "It's nice to be recognized, quite honestly," Sullivan tells me. "Think about it. I started off my career demonstrating mops at fairs in England. And I still demonstrate mops for a living. Getting stopped for an autograph—an autograph!—at the mall in Tampa was really the last thing I ever expected to happen in the world."

CHAPTER 7

Remote (Control) Dreams

The dream of interactive television has been floating around for almost as long as the medium itself. In the 1950s, CBS aired *Winky Dink and You,* a children's series that allowed kids to send away for a kit that contained a set of crayons; a "magic drawing screen"—a piece of plastic that adhered to the TV screen thanks to static electricity—allowed them to draw on the screen during each episode to reveal a set of secret messages. But while children grew fond of the format, their parents were considerably less pleased, particularly since many kids dispensed with the screen and special crayons and simply drew directly on the screen. (It seems parents were also a bit perturbed that their kids were parked about six inches from their television sets.)

The notion that the television could function as a two-way medium gained new momentum in the late '70s when Warner-Amex Cable debuted QUBE in Columbus, Ohio. QUBE was a system that permitted viewers to access thirty channels—a considerable improvement over what was available at the time—as well as order movies on a pay-per-view basis and participate in polls and auctions. It was unusually advanced for the era. But these were highly unusual times. The system emerged during the so-called cable franchise wars, a time when media companies were furiously competing for the rights to establish cable beachheads in local communities across the United States. To sway local officials, aspiring franchisees made grand pronouncements about the services they planned to offer to residents, and QUBE was intended to showcase exactly what a high-capacity, interactive cable system would look like.

Most of the lofty promises made by emerging cable companies never came to pass. As soon as the lucrative franchises were handed out, the cable companies backed away from their elaborate—and expensive—plans to construct such advanced systems. QUBE, which had been popular with viewers but had never turned a profit, was eventually phased out.

The idea that the TV could do much more than simply deliver entertainment hardly faded. Interactive television ended up becoming one of the most overhyped technologies of the 1980s and '90s. With each passing year, consumers were assured that a host of exciting, new services were on the way, and industry analysts made bold predictions about what lay ahead: viewers would be able to pick and choose what they watched and when they watched it. They'd be able to play along with game shows and gamble from the comfort of the couch. A giant catalog of merchandise would allow viewers to purchase a barbecue grill or hair dryer with the click of a button.

Dozens of companies hoping to capitalize on the iTV revolution came and went during the 1980s and '90s. Even Barry Diller's decision to purchase a $25 million stake in QVC in 1992 was predicated on a vision of the future of interactive shopping, as he made quite clear to Ken Auletta of *The New Yorker* shortly after he took over the shopping network:

*As Diller envisions it, the customer will say, "I want
a raincoat. Instantly! I want an umbrella," and it will
figure out the cheapest ones, and deliver them to the
door. He predicts, "Three years from now, you'll say,
'I want shoes.' You'll press a button and see yourself
in various shoes on the screen." From their homes, he
says, consumers will be able to roam the aisles of Bloomingdale's; avoid the last-minute Christmas rush by
calling up a special selection of gifts for the "special
person," choosing one, and having it delivered the next
day; find a hotel in the Caribbean, inspect its rooms
and amenities on the TV screen, and then press a
button to make a reservation.*

In 1994, when Time Warner trotted out an interactive cable
system in Orlando, Gerald Levin, then the CEO of the company, told reporters that he expected to soon see the day when
viewers would use their cable systems to order pizzas and renew
their driver's licenses in lieu of waiting in line at the DMV. You
know the rest of this story: it's been fifteen years since Diller and
Levin made these pronouncements, and while you can order a
pizza, renew your license, and roam the aisles of Bloomingdale's
from the comfort of home, you do it via your computer, not your
television.

In theory, these newfangled cable services sounded de-
lightful. Making them happen was another matter. Interactive services couldn't simply be turned on with the flick of a
switch. The cable networks that had established a foothold in
three-quarters of American households during the 1970s and
'80s hadn't been built as a two-way communication medium.
Cable's "tree-and-branch" architecture was designed to deliver

the same programming to every subscriber in the neighbor-hood, not let lazy couch surfers send in their orders for pepper-oni pizzas. To support new features like pay-per-view movies and home shopping, the cable companies would have to invest billions in new infrastructure. Coaxial cables lines, which connected the cable companies to nearly every community in America, would have to be replaced with high-capacity optical fiber. New software and security protocols would have to be designed. And the cable companies would have to install new, digital set-top boxes in subscribers' homes. Who was going to pay for all this?

The cable companies sure didn't want to. After all, they en-joyed one of the most lucrative monopolies in America. Con-sumers couldn't go out and pick another provider or simply pick up another set-top box at an electronics store. There was no choice in the marketplace: the government-regulated franchise system allowed local municipalities to pick a single cable pro-vider, which would dig up the city streets and wire the com-munity—and pay the local government a five percent fee—in exchange for exclusivity. What incentive did they have to pour billions into building out new infrastructure?

They would have gladly spent the money if they knew that consumers would pay for these services, but that wasn't necessarily obvious at the time. Accessing a mall from your TV set sounded great, particularly to wide-eyed entrepreneurs, but it was hard to assess the level of public demand and even harder to figure out just how the exorbitant costs associated with constructing such a system would ever be covered. When Time Warner wired 4,000 homes in Orlando with interactive cable, it spent tens of millions to do so; each set-top box alone cost $5,000. Yet viewers turned out to be slow in embracing the high-tech functionality at their fingertips.

Industry analysts were quick to point out that many of these new features violated the basic tenet of television that TV is a "lean back" environment. Our consumption is passive: we sit back in our La-Z-Boy recliners and take in the entertainment and advertising as it flashes before our eyes. Did Joe and Jane Consumer really want to do more than sit back, relax, and enjoy the show? It wasn't clear. And since viewers had little notion what interactive television would entail, it wasn't as if the public was rioting in the streets, demanding that the cable companies provide them the ability to freeze live television and order cubic zirconia necklaces with the click of a button.

The tide started to change in the early 1990s when new competition emerged on the horizon. In 1991 the FCC startled the cable industry when it proposed that phone companies be permitted to transmit television programming. But other threats loomed as well. In the early '90s, digital broadcast satellite companies like DIRECTV and EchoStar started arriving on the scene with the promise of more video and audio channels than consumers had ever seen before; there was also the nascent Internet to contend with, which was poised to emerge as a potentially disruptive force. In 1996 Congress passed the Telecom Act, which had wide-ranging effects on the entire broadcast media sector, unleashing unprecedented deregulation on the industry and providing a road map to a digital future. The force of regulatory change, the threat of increased competition, and a sharp drop in the costs associated with replacing legacy technology spurred the cable companies to take action; all the major multi-system operators (or MSOs) responded by aggressively upgrading their networks and accelerating plans to roll out interactive systems.

They faced no shortage of challenges. Most critically, the industry had no established technology standard. Each cable company operated a proprietary system, purchased set-top boxes from one of several manufacturers, and relied on software provided by dozens of smaller firms. There was no way to create any sort of interactive platform that would be compatible with all of them. And because each functioned as a closed network, not a single bit of content could be delivered to subscribers' living rooms without the blessing of the cable company.

Things couldn't have been more different on the Web, of course, which was accelerating at a blazing clip in the late '90s. The Internet was predicated on open standards and designed from the very beginning to be a fully interactive medium. There was nothing to prevent scrappy entrepreneurs in Silicon Valley from experimenting with new services and rolling them out to the public at large. The Internet had no gatekeepers or near-monopolistic forces that could squelch innovation. So while the dysfunctional cable industry sat back and mulled over its technological limitations and what seemed to be a lack of consumer acceptance, all the fuzzy dreams about interactivity migrated to the Web in the late '90s. Amazon.com showed the world that people did, in fact, want to buy products from home. Search engines like Yahoo! demonstrated that people wanted access to local information. Millions of consumers flocked to eBay to buy and sell goods. The notions of what you'd use your television to do back in the 1980s had been transferred to a new device: the personal computer.

It certainly didn't bolster iTV's chances that many of the early experiments generated a tepid reception from the public. Attempts to add interactivity to entertainment content in the late '90s proved disappointing: when NBC offered interactive clues to its hit show *Homicide,* few people accessed the service, leading to the conclusion, once again, that television viewers weren't terribly interested in diverting from the entertainment programming on their screens. Another blind alley was the premise that the computer and television would converge, leading to the launch of services like WebTV, which allowed viewers to browse the Web and check their e-mail using their television sets. It quickly became evident that the TV wasn't well suited to either application since you don't sit close enough to your TV screen to type e-mails, and you needed additional equipment to do both, namely, a keyboard. The one thing that did seem to work, of course, was the sort of functionality that television could do best—giving viewers the ability to control what they watched and record their favorite programs. It was also something that had an obvious business model. Few had any clue if consumers would pay for access to sports scores or for the ability to order a pizza, but video on demand promised to be a clear moneymaker: if consumers went to Blockbuster to pay four bucks to rent a movie, wouldn't they pay the same amount to do the very same thing without getting off the sofa? The cable companies quickly focused their attention on the services guaranteed to earn them a profit, like pay-per-view movies.

Interactive shopping raised a series of complex challenges. Despite all the hoopla about its enormous potential and the exciting prospect that you'd be able to use your remote control to purchase what your favorite sitcom star was wearing or a news anchor's tie, in practice adding those functions promised to be a nightmare. What if, instead of buying the bracelet that Jennifer Aniston was wearing on *Friends,* viewers wanted to buy her dress? How would the shows make it clear which items were for sale and then manage the inventory? What would happen when the episode appeared as a rerun years later? And would people even be interested in this? In those days, many people doubted that TV viewers really wanted to interrupt their viewing to go shopping. Product placement was one thing: they were subtle brand messages, and there was no direct response component to it. Asking viewers to break out of entertainment mode and switch into shopping mode was another proposition altogether.

Home shopping was a much more obvious opportunity. Viewers of QVC weren't watching a show with a narrative. They were watching a program designed precisely to sell them goods, which viewers appreciated full well. What better way was there to get someone to purchase something than to make it as easy as a click of a button? Developing the technology to support these services wasn't a trivial matter, however; each cable system would require a customized platform, and there were complex security and billing issues to contend with. And neither the cable companies nor their home shopping partners were particularly focused on the subject at the beginning of the twenty-first century. MSOs were directing their attention to proven revenue opportunities like video on demand. Home shopping players like QVC and HSN were enjoying enormous success online, which provided them with a chance to sell direct to the consumer without giving up a cut to their cable partners.

This wasn't the case in Europe and Asia, however. Interactive television was embraced in places like England and Japan much earlier on, the result of fewer system operators, fewer technology platforms, and fewer consumers willing to conduct commerce online. In 2001 QVC launched its first interactive purchasing system in Britain in partnership with BSkyB; it now processes more than a million orders a year thanks to the "buy" button on remote controls. But these services should finally debut in the United States over the next few years. In 2006 Time Warner and HSN unveiled a "buy" button in Hawaii, and it's only a matter of time before the technology is integrated into cable systems nationwide. Equipping infomercials with this sort of click-and-buy capability is a longer way off, but it will arrive one day, too. The conventional wisdom that we want to sit passively in front of the TV no longer necessarily holds water. The Web has introduced us to interactive services we couldn't imagine living without. The time-shifting capabilities of personal video recorders has turned us into our very own programming chiefs. A rising number of people watch TV and surf the Web simultaneously, gossiping about plot points on message boards as they watch shows unfold. And there is little doubt about the connection between TV programs and merchandise sales. A product mention on a TV show can lead to an almost instantaneous sales response on the Web.

In the meantime, the direct response industry has been aggressively expanding its efforts to build robust businesses on the Internet. QVC generated more than $1 billion in revenue from qvc.com in 2007, and all of the major shopping channels now actively encourage viewers to conduct their purchases online, where customers can view a much larger catalog of inventory and where the costs associated with processing transactions is substantially less than having viewers speak with a phone operator. Both HSN and QVC have been actively incorporating new features and functionality: customers can access video clips, post product reviews, and chat with other customers. And both companies also have plans to unveil mobile shopping platforms in the United States in the near future. (In Japan, QVC makes ten percent of its money from mobile commerce.) Infomercial marketers have been busy exploiting the Web, too: some products now generate as much as half of their sales from transactions that are conducted online.

But the Internet isn't a substitute for interactive television. Much of what's advertised on TV, after all, is designed to capitalize on our impulses, and while viewers can now head to the Internet and spend a few minutes entering their credit card information to purchase a product, it's easy to see how an interactive platform would make buying a new barbecue grill or treadmill a two-second process. You'd click a bright red button on your remote control, a message would ask you to confirm the purchase, and that would be that. Your credit card on file—or your cable bill—would be charged accordingly.

There will be challenges, of course. More than a few parents will inevitably have to deal with their kids who rack up thousands in charges, repeatedly clicking the "buy" button with each successive demonstration.

Even diehard home shopping fans are concerned about the prospect they'll turn into compulsive shoppers. When I polled a half dozen longtime fans, they all said they hated the concept, not because they thought it was a bad idea, but because they all thought they would have trouble resisting temptation. "I really can't imagine what would happen," said one such woman. "I have a feeling I'd go from buying items once a week to buying things daily. I might have to throw out my TV and go back to listening to the radio."

CHAPTER 8

But Wait, There's More!

Every fall, the infomercial industry convenes in Las Vegas for its annual convention, a three-day extravaganza that culminates with the industry's equivalent of the Oscars, where attendees nibble on lobster and filet mignon as statuettes are handed out to winners and moving montages to now deceased industry legends are broadcast on a big screen on the stage. Unlike the Oscars, though, where the awards are ostensibly handed out to recipients based on artistic quality, the statuettes at this ceremony are awarded to winners based on the only metric that counts in this business: revenue. Proactiv took home the top prize in 2006. It was a moving moment, I assure you, although I must admit I was a little bit disappointed that Vanessa Williams didn't appear in person to deliver the acceptance speech. I'm guessing she was out shopping, spending her hard-earned infomercial millions. In 2007, Sheer Cover, which is also manufactured by Guthy-Renker, took top honors.

It's appropriate that the industry gathers in Las Vegas. Much like the glittering casinos, infomercials have used the illusion of hope to tap into the hearts and minds of the American consumer. Like the gambling business, it has a much darker side that few in the industry want to talk about. For every Bill Guthy and Greg Renker—who have reputations for honestly using the medium to purvey products—there's a Kevin Trudeau or Donald Barrett. Or a William McCorkle, who will be sitting in a jail cell in Georgia until 2016. At least McCorkle seems to have learned his lesson: in recent years he's reportedly become an evangelical Christian and redirected his life to serving Jesus.

The convention provides a window into the industry's split personality, the divide between the companies that provide legitimate products and services and the shysters out for a quick buck. In the convention hall, hundreds of companies have set up booths, and they illustrate just how sophisticated and disciplined the business has become. There's a long row of companies that are offering telemarketing, product fulfillment, and inventory management services. There's a mammoth UPS booth with a giant sign that reads WHAT CAN BROWN DO FOR YOU? and dozens of reps from Google and Yahoo! are on hand to discuss marketing partnerships. Yet the very first infomercial entrepreneur I meet inside the convention hall isn't quite as reputable. He's perfectly nice, and his company sounds reasonable enough. It's only later, when I search for his name on the Internet, that I discover his previous career as a "performer" in the adult entertainment industry.

The infomercial industry is at a crossroads in more ways than one. It still has yet to shake its unsavory reputation and technology threatens to make direct response television a thing of the past. Thanks to personal video recorders, we now have the freedom to pick what we want to watch and when we want to watch it; there's no longer any need to channel surf and hunt for something decent to watch. We now have hundreds of stations to choose from, plus thousands of hours of on-demand content. We don't have to decide between an old rerun of *I Love*

Lucy and an amusing infomercial with Ron Popeil. Infomercials thrived on our lack of options. But what happens when every television show ever created is available at the click of a button? Would you really spend your time watching meat sizzle in a TurboCooker?

The infomercial entrepreneurs on hand for the convention are all smiles. Privately, though, they express a little bit less optimism. Infomercials are no longer the moneymakers they once were a decade or two ago. In the early days, marketers could assume for every product that failed, there'd be another that would rack up the big bucks in increments of $19.99. That's no longer the case. Nowadays, for every late-night success, more than fifty end up losing money. In addition to the countless technological changes and the advent of the Internet, they have to contend with the fact that people don't trust the products advertised on TV like they used to. Years of deceit by unscrupulous marketers has taken its toll.

Don't reach for your Kleenex just yet. The people who populate the world of direct response advertising are nothing if not practical. They figured out how to slip direct response spots past the FCC when they weren't yet even legal. They figured out how to get viewers signed up for continuity plans so they'd become customers for life. And they also happen to have sold the masses on the most ridiculous products ever invented. These are the people who managed to convince us that we'd enjoy dehydrating our food; that there was nothing more enjoyable in this world than making homemade beef jerky; and that in lieu of purchasing a new toothbrush for two bucks, we'd be better off investing $50 in an electrical toothbrush sanitizing machine. In a nation of fickle consumers with short attention spans, the men and women of direct response television managed to amuse us *and* talk us out of our money.

"People used to go to the state fair. Why did they watch the guy with the kitchen knives? It's not that they didn't have kitchen knives. It was entertaining for people to watch him slice and dice and chop," says Jack Kirby, an infomercial and home shopping veteran and a former chairman of the ERA.

We're sitting in Kirby's enormous suite at the top of the Mirage. Although all of the big shots are in town for the event, most are content to remain far from the fray of the convention floor and the seminars and sessions that have been convened to address topics like outbound telemarketing and product patent law. They stay in their rooms, where they negotiate the deals that will result in the ab device you'll see advertised at three o'clock in the morning sometime next year.

"Some guys will fall by the wayside," Kirby says. "But those who truly are clever and observant of the changes in society and technology will be able to capitalize on it."

Just how the industry will see its way through the thicket is still up in the air. With the success rates falling—and with new technology threatening the very existence of the industry—the time may come when they have little choice but to seek out new ways to sell product. As people bypass infomercials, and as the thirty-second commercial becomes increasingly irrelevant, the line between entertainment and advertising will blur further. Instead of a stale infomercial for a toaster oven featuring a pitchman with an enthusiastic audience, you may see a faux cooking show that's filmed with a new guest star each week. A home improvement show may feature offers to purchase the furniture and appliances via an 800 number, Web site, and interactive TV menu. Product placement is already a booming business, of course, but the shows don't ask the viewer to take immediate action. They will. And traditional ad agencies won't be able to do it alone.

The only people who seem to be capable of getting us to act on our impulses are the direct response marketers, something that Madison Avenue, awash in brand advertising, has never had to concern itself with. And the power of an uninterrupted block of programming remains as powerful as ever. Look no further than Barack Obama's half-hour infomercial in October 2008, which was broadcast simultaneously on CBS, NBC, Fox, BET, Univision, MSNBC, and TV One. The $4 million campaign gave him the opportunity to share an extended personal narrative with the American public, something that had not been possible within the context of the thirty-second spots that had blanketed the airwaves in the months leading up to the election. More than thirty million Americans tuned in, making it the most-watched piece of paid programming in U.S. history.

But it's also clear that if direct response television is going to survive and adapt, it's going to have to do a better job keeping the scam artists out. There have been far too few consequences for people who cross the line, and those that do so often repeat their crimes again and again. The industry is going to have to clean up if it's going to transition to the mainstream and shake the cloud over its head.

As I wander the convention floor, I see the vestiges of the days of old. There are eccentric-looking inventors and aggressive entrepreneurs with jars of (unlabeled! patent pending!) skin creams they'd just *love* to demonstrate. Many of them are too tan and wear too much gold jewelry and are filled with the sort of bug-eyed, nervous energy that isn't terribly reassuring, particularly when they tell you they can only discuss the product "in secret" for fear of "spies." At the coffee bar near the convention floor, there are men in cheap suits talking about instant fortunes and millions made overnight, clutching heavy briefcases that contain "prototypes."

It's more unlikely than ever that the solo inventor with a dream will hit it big here. While the industry titans who made their fortunes in direct response were, in many cases, just that—dreamers with few resources who paid $100 for a half-hour slot on cable to tout a new product—twenty years later, that same spot may cost $20,000. The average infomercial costs hundreds of thousands to produce and millions more to promote.

That hasn't deterred many of the people who have arrived in Las Vegas. On the main convention floor, there's an area reserved for "inventors," people who have turned up to demonstrate the exciting new product they've designed. Their purpose here is clear. This is an industry of innovation, the official pamphlets remind the crowd, a business about novel ideas. Infomercials represent the American dream. Anyone can come up with a good idea and make a mint.

When I enter the area, I notice the inventors immediately glance down at the badge I'm wearing around my neck. The badges are color-coded by occupation, and they're looking to see if I'm a producer, someone who might be interested in turning them into the next Tony Robbins. A press badge isn't quite as exciting, but they're still happy to show off their creations. One woman shows me what she describes as a "hands-free fashion bag," which strikes me as a slightly more fashionable version of the fanny pack. A grandfatherly man in a sweater vest demonstrates the keyless door lock he's invented, which allows you to get into your home with an automated code. It's a great idea. Except I've seen the identical item at the hardware store, and what he's showing me is a rudimentary prototype. I don't have the heart to bring up the topic as he launches into his pitch and confesses he's spent years working on this concept and has sunk his savings into making the venture a reality. I tell him he's brilliant and that the product will probably make him millions and move on. There's an energetic duo showing off a next-generation bagel slicer. It's big and clunky but, as the makers of the product explain, has been proven to reduce BRI. (That stands for bagel-related injuries, I soon find out.) I can't help but think of Ron Popeil, who was selling a bagel slicer three decades earlier.

This is an industry rife with products that are simply updated versions of products that have been sold for years. True inventions are few and far between. The lack of innovation is abundantly clear when I spot several ab devices, a product that has been so thoroughly exploited that I can rattle off a list of names as long as my arm: AbLounge, AbRoller, AbScissor, AbSlide, AbRocker, and AbRageous.

And if anyone had anything truly unique, I can't think of a worse place to show it off. Pity the entrepreneur with a clever item who catches A. J. Khubani's eye. In six weeks, he'll have the same product on the market for two bucks less, and he'll spend $25 million blanketing the airwaves with ads.

Why come up with anything new anyway? Americans know what they like. They want to make more money, have rock-hard abs, and cook and clean their homes in half the time. And so here at the convention the mops have gotten more technologically advanced, and in place of the blender that had six settings that could spin at 14,000 revolutions per minute, a new, updated model now has eighteen settings and can spin at 20,000 revolutions per minute.

Although the industry titans stay far away from the newbie inventors, they all turn up for the awards show. All the greats have assembled in one room, people who have spent the last quarter century promising millions of sleep-deprived Americans that they can make millions, cook in half the time, get along with their spouses, regrow their hair, and, yes, have gleaming, white teeth—just by picking up the phone. They're having a grand old time. Everyone is dressed up. Esteban is the featured entertainer. The ceremony pauses briefly for a charity segment—some disabled kids are getting new wheelchairs, a speaker announces. The crowd claps enthusiastically. Everyone seems pleased to have done their part to help society. Several more awards are handed out, a final speech is delivered, and the attendees drink their final glass of wine and finish off the last of the assortment of chocolate desserts. Out in the hallway, the younger members of the audience are making their plans to hit the casinos. The infomercial moguls quickly head for the exits. They've got business to do tomorrow.

ENDNOTES

Introduction

Page xi. is a $300 billion dollar industry: Figures regarding the size of the industry should be taken with a grain of salt. Most estimates regarding the size of the home shopping and infomercial industries are provided by industry trade groups, such as the Electronic Retailing Association and Direct Marketing Association. The $300 billion figure, for example, includes all forms of "direct-to-consumer" sales and also includes Internet commerce, even though a relatively small percentage of online selling features a television or radio direct response component. Throughout the book, sales figures for individual products were generally provided by the people involved in marketing these products. Program rankings are from Jordan Whitney Inc. and Infomercial Monitoring Service, Inc., two firms that rank top-selling infomercial products and track their respective advertising budgets.

Chapter 1: County Fair to Cable Fare

Page 1. Popeil recounts his early years and familial connections to the business in *The Salesman of the Century* (New York: Delacorte, 1995). A lovely profile of Popeil can be found in

Malcolm Gladwell, "The Pitchman," *The New Yorker,* October 30, 2000. For more on Popeil's products and design influences, as well as photos and illustrations, see Timothy Samuelson, *But Wait! There's More!: The Irresistible Appeal and Spiel of Ronco and Popeil* (New York: Rizzoli, 2002).

Page 9. men like John "Doc" Healy and Charles "Texas Charlie" Bigelow: For a scholarly review of the early days of medicine men, see Stewart H. Holbrook, *The Golden Age of Quackery* (New York: Macmillan, 1959). A fine summary of the historical material can be found in Joe Nickell, "Peddling Snake Oil," *Skeptical Briefs* (Committee for Skeptical Inquiry), December 1998.

Page 9. was produced by a quack named John R. Brinkley: For an impressive survey of Brinkley's career, see Pope Brock, *Charlatan: America's Most Dangerous Huckster, the Man Who Pursued Him, and the Age of Flimflam* (New York: Crown, 2008).

Page 11. His ties to pitching date back two generations: Popeil recounts his history in his autobiography, but a more comprehensive (and amusing) account of the Popeil–Morris clan is featured in Stanley Jacobs' superb documentary, *Pitch People* (SJPL Films, 1999). The classic knife demonstration by Lester Morris was transcribed from Jacobs's film.

Page 15. "At some magical point in the 1950s": James B. Twitchell, *Lead Us Into Temptation* (New York: Columbia University Press, 1999).

Page 16. The Montana-born Eicoff: For more on Alvin "Al" Eicoff, see his book *Or Your Money Back* (New York: Crown, 1982).

Page 18. The groundswell culminated in 1961: A detailed account of this period can be found in "Station Brakes: The Government's Campaign against Cable Television," *Reason,* February 1995.

Page 18. named the show's ill-fated ship the SS Minnow *in his honor:* An account of Schwartz's decision to name the boat in

Minow's honor can be found in Robert M. Jarvis, "Legal Tales from *Gilligan's Island*," *Santa Clara Law Review*, 1998, 39, no. 1.

Page 20. people like Arthur Schiff: For more on the life of Arthur Schiff, see Paul Farhi's "He Sliced and Diced His Way into Pop Culture," *Washington Post*, September 2, 2006. For more on the Ginsu phenomenon, Ed Valenti and Barry Becher recount their story in *The Wisdom of Ginsu: Carve Yourself a Piece of the American Dream* (Franklin Lakes, NJ: Career Press, 2005).

Page 23. Ronco was forced to file for bankruptcy: See "It Slices! It Dices! It Goes Belly Up!" *Newsweek*, February 13, 1984.

Page 24. "a toaster with pictures": See "Under Fowler, FCC Treated TV as Commerce," Peter J. Boyer, *New York Times*, January 19, 1987.

Page 25. Accounts of the rebirth of the infomercial industry have been given in trade publications such as *Response* and *Electronic Retailer*. A number of the details in this section also come from my conversations with early pioneers such as Frank Cannella and Nancy Marcum.

Page 26. Beckley would later turn out to be one of the industry's first scam artists: See ' "Millionaire Maker' Ed Beckley Sentenced to 15 Months in Prison," Associated Press, November 20, 1998, and ' "Millionaire Maker' Beckley Trying to Get Away from 'Get-Rich Shtick,' " Associated Press, May 19, 1996.

Page 26. Murphy, too, ran afoul of the authorities: See *Federal Trade Commission v. California Pacific Research, Inc. and Robert E. Murphy, Jr.,* U.S. District Court for the District of Nevada (1991). A federal judge later ordered the company and Murphy to pay $2 million plus court costs for false and deceptive advertising. See "Firm Fined for False Hair Growth Claims," United Press International, September 10, 1991.

Page 28. Sugarman ran afoul of the FTC: See "FTC Chides Sugarman for Misleading Ads," *Ad Day*, November 3, 1988.

Page 32. His countdown in the final seconds of the show was sales magic: I suggest viewing this for yourself, since a transcription can hardly do Popeil justice. A clip of Popeil's Showtime countdown can be found on YouTube.com.

Page 34. "If you can sell in Atlantic City, you can sell anywhere": This quote is from Marco R. Della Cava, "The New King of TV's Soapbox," *USA Today,* October 25, 2004.

Chapter 2: Late-Night Carnival

Page 39. This American quest for self-fulfillment: In *Sham: How the Self-Help Movement Made America Helpless* (New York: Crown, 2005), Steve Salerno provides an excellent overview of the early self-help movement and its explosion during the latter part of the twentieth century. An account of the motivational business can also be found in Jonathan Black's *Yes You Can!* (New York: Bloomsbury USA, 2006).

Page 40. this problem–solution dynamic: Many of the strategies used in infomercials were described to me by leading figures in the industry. A number of details were published in several industry trade books, such as Steven Dworman's *$12 Billion of Inside Marketing Secrets Discovered through Direct Response Television Sales* (Los Angeles: SDE Publishing Inc., 2004), which contains two dozen lengthy interviews. Also particularly useful was Timothy Hawthorne's *Complete Guide to Infomercial Marketing* (Chicago: NTC Business Books, 1997) and Nancy Marcum's *Do You Want to Make a Million?* (Phoenix, AZ: Marcum Publishing, 2003).

Page 43. impulse buys: See Tom Agee and Brett A. S. Martin, "Planned or Impulse Purchases? How to Create Effective Infomercials," *Journal of Advertising Research,* November 2001.

Page 45. Created by Rick Hunt, a San Diego carpenter: An amusing account of the Flowbee can be found in "A Hair Raising Scheme," Salon.com, January 6, 2000.

Page 50. Most "storymercials" or "sitcommercials" have been fail-ures, too: An overview of various infomercial formats and their history of success (or lack thereof) can be found in Hawthorne's *Complete Guide to Infomercial Marketing.*

Page 52. Dozens of strategies, many of which are relatively subtle, are employed to stimulate sales: Many of the psychological tactics used by infomercial marketers are cogently described in Dr. Robert B. Cialdini's *Influence: The Psychology of Persuasion,* revised ed. (New York: Collins, 2007). The book is a longtime favorite of infomercial producers, and much of Cialdini's work has been adapted in various trade books.

Page 53. Paco Underhill, *Why We Buy: The Science of Shopping* (New York: Simon & Schuster, 1999).

Page 57. The laugh track: For an interesting history of the laugh track (along with audio and video clips), see Drake Bennett, "Don't Make Me Laugh," *Slate,* September 19, 2007.

Page 59. James Surowiecki, *The Wisdom of Crowds* (New York: Doubleday, 2004).

Page 60. Research has demonstrated that this subtle repetition is highly effective: See Mandeep Singh, Siva K. Balasubramanian, and Goutam Chakraborty, "A Comparative Analysis of Three Communication Formats: Advertising, Infomercial, and Direct Experience," *Journal of Advertising* (Winter 2000).

Page 62. "odd-even pricing": Much has been written on this subject. See Mark Stiving and Russell S. Winer, "An Empirical Analysis of Price Endings with Scanner Data," *Journal of Consumer Research* 24 (June 1997).

Page 67. Returning a product purchased on television can be a compli-cated process: This was something I discovered myself after ordering numerous products as part of a test. With many of the relatively inexpensive products I purchased, there was no customer service information included with the package.

Page 68. is that the host communicates authority: This is rather obvious, but it has also been widely proven by researchers over the years. See Robert R. Harmon and Kenneth A. Coney, "The Persuasive Effects of Source Credibility in Buy and Lease Situations," *Journal of Marketing Research,* 19, no. 2 (1982).

Page 69. why English pitchmen have been used so frequently over the years: For more on this phenomenon, see Oscar W. DeShields Jr., John Tsalikis, and Michael S. LaTour, "The Role of Accent on the Credibility and Effectiveness of the Salesperson," *Journal of Personal Selling and Sales Management,* 11 (1991); and Oscar W. DeShields Jr., Ali Karab, and Erdener Kaynak, "Source Effects in Purchase Decisions: The Impact of Physical Attractiveness and Accent of Salespersons," *International Journal of Research in Marketing,* 13, no. 1 (1996). Interestingly, the same does not hold true for English television viewers: British cultural attitudes toward Australians undermine their credibility in the U.K. market.

Page 70. That's just the sort of cheery person she is: The URL of her Web site makes this clear: wonderfulwriter.com.

Page 74. the reason Proactiv was often displayed against the background of running water: Guthy and Renker mentioned this in an interview in *Palm Springs Life* (April 2002), and Renker later confirmed this in an interview.

Chapter 3: The Kingpins of Paid Programming

Page 79. it wasn't such a stretch for the company to pay Combs $3 million to show up: This is an estimate based on conversations with industry insiders. Guthy and Renker would not discuss specific compensation for its spokespeople.

Page 79. An account of Renker's and Guthy's early days in the industry was published in *Response* magazine (May 2001).

Page 84. Originally crafted by two dermatologists, Katie Rodan and Kathy Fields: To avoid confusion, although the women created

Proactiv and are still used in the product's advertising material, they have since launched Rodan + Fields, which is unaffiliated with Guthy-Renker and competes with Proactiv.

Page 87. Ajit (A. J.) Khubani, the founder of Telebrands: Khubani's early career history is detailed in Steven Dworman's monthly newsletter, *Infomercial Marketing Report,* and republished in *$12 Billion of Inside Marketing Secrets Discovered through Direct Response Television Sales.*

Page 91. His most brazen knockoff, though, came when he launched the ThighShaper: An account of Khubani and Peter Bieler's feud is included in Bieler's *This Business Has Legs: How I Used Infomercial Marketing to Create the $100,000,000 ThighMaster Craze* (New York: Wiley, 1996). Amusingly, Khubani suggested to me that he hadn't heard of the book.

Page 93. The government hasn't been quite as timid: The various actions taken by the FTC against Khubani can be found online at ftc.gov. For the most recent round of litigation, see *Federal Trade Commission v. Telebrands Corp. et al.,* U.S. District Court, District of New Jersey. (Khubani's wife, Poonam, was named as a relief defendant.) Khubani later appealed the ruling in *Telebrands et al. v. Federal Trade Commission,* U.S. Court of Appeals, Fourth Circuit. The court upheld the decision on August 7, 2006.

Chapter 4: Crooks and Liars

Page 96. Steven Feder and Peter Stolz, were busted as part of an investigation into fraudulent business practices: See Beatrice E. Garcia, "Operators of Miss Cleo's Psychic Hot Line Settle Federal Charges," *Miami Herald,* November 15, 2002, for details of the federal proceedings, and David Ho, "'Miss Cleo' Psychic Hot Line Forgives $500 Million in Customer Debts," Associated Press, November 14, 2002, for an account of the settlement. Settlements were also reached with various states, including Arkansas, Illinois, Indiana, Kansas, Oklahoma, Pennsylvania, and Wisconsin. In Missouri, Feder and Stolz were charged with two felony counts of unlawful merchandising practices. The two entered Alford pleas, allowing them to maintain their innocence while acknowledging there was enough evidence to convict them. Their convictions were later expunged. See Michael D. Sorkin and Valerie Schremp, "Official Defends Expunging of Records in 'Miss Cleo' Fraud Case," *Port St. Lucie Tribune,* October 9, 2002.

Page 96. The ensuing investigation uncovered a litany of devious ways that gullible callers had been scammed out of their money: For a more detailed account of the Miss Cleo scam, see CourtTV's investigation into the case, "Seeing the Future—or Just Dollar Signs?" from January 17, 2002, online. Another insightful piece is Dahlia Lithwick's "With Psychic Friends Like These . . . ," *Slate,* March 26, 2002.

Page 98. the list of offenses is so long and the number of products that have generated legal action so numerous that it makes your head spin": Dr. Stephen Barrett has done an excellent job archiving the various FTC and FDA actions mentioned here on his Web site, Quackwatch.org.

Page 99. A Mayo Clinic study published in 2002: See Bratton et al., "Effect of 'Ionized' Wrist Bracelets on Musculoskeletal Pain: A Randomized, Double-Blind, Placebo-Controlled Trial," *Mayo Clinic Proceedings,* 77 (November 2002).

Page 100. Robbins (or Anthony Mahavorick, as he's legally known) recounts much of his personal past in his dozens of books, CDs, and DVDs. For a more balanced look at Robbins's methods, see Salerno's *Sham* or Black's *Yes You Can.* Amusing accounts of Robbins's lectures—and a detailed critique of his tactics—can be found on noted paranormal skeptic James Randi's Web site, randi.org.

Page 101. his tendency to go after his critics: In perhaps the most notorious case, Robbins filed suit against the *Vancouver Sun* after the paper reported that he had "stolen away the wife" of a Canadian businessman. (She later married Robbins.) See "Robbins' Libel Trial Begins; Motivation Guru Alleges Articles in *Vancouver Sun* Harmed Reputation," *Globe and Mail* (Canada), June 20, 2005. Robbins later won a partial victory and collected CAN$20,000 in damages. He's also been involved in several high-profile business disputes. Guthy-Renker filed suit against Robbins in 1994, the details of which can be found in "Suit Hits Self-Help King Robbins," *Variety,* August 3, 1994.

McGraw's seamy past is described in Sophia Dembling and Lisa Gutierrez, *The Making of Dr. Phil* (New York: Wiley, 2003).

Page 104. The billionaire mogul had merely licensed his name and collected a fee—a Donald Trump trademark: For more on Trump's licensing business, see Stephane Fitch, "What Is Trump Worth?" *Forbes,* September 21, 2006. Details about his licensing ventures can also be found in Timothy O'Brien's *TrumpNation: The Art of Being the Donald* (New York: Warner Books, 2005).

Page 105. NGC has a checkered legal past: For details of NGC's most recent settlement with the state of Vermont, see the attorney general's official statement on the matter: "Attorney General Sorrell Settles 'Government Grants' Lawsuit," December 28, 2006.

Page 105. For an interesting account of a Milin seminar in the early '90s, see Art Levine, "Money for Nothing," *Washington Monthly,* April 1993.

Page 114. Vu racked up millions in sales before he ran into legal trouble in the early '90s with Florida's attorney general: The Florida investigation into Vu's business activities is addressed in Jane Bryant Quinn, "This Suit's for Vu," *Newsweek,* April 13, 1992.

Page 114. After he was the target of an FTC suit: See "TV Pitchman Accused of Misleading Viewers; FTC Alleges 'Cash

Flow System' Spots Have False Information," *Washington Post,* April 23, 1993. For details of his settlement, see "David Del Dotto Agrees to Settle FTC Charges He Misrepresented 'Money Making' Real Estate Program," Federal Trade Commission, October 2, 1996.

Page 114. Today he oversees Del Dotto Vineyards: See for yourself at deldottovineyards.com.

Page 115. He took home $364,761 for second place at the World Series of Poker in 2007: Vu's poker career can be tracked on sites like pokerlistings.com. Videos of his performances in the World Series of Poker can be found on YouTube.

Page 115. a man named William J. McCorkle: Much of this account relies on the fine reporting by the *Orlando Sentinel* and *Dateline NBC*'s investigation into McCorkle from 2001. Unfortunately, McCorkle did not respond to my interview requests, and his attorney declined to comment. A good deal of press related to Chantal McCorkle can be found on a Web site dedicated to securing her release, freechantal.com.

Page 125. His program, however, quickly ran into trouble: Much of Lapre's checkered past is laid out nicely in Leigh Farr's "Don Wan," *Phoenix New Times,* January 13, 2000, and the *Arizona Republic* has done a fine job of reporting on his more recent travails. Lapre and I played a cat-and-mouse game for months: although he initially agreed to speak with me, he later only agreed to answer questions in writing, and then later decided against cooperating altogether.

Page 126. when Grant was charged with first-degree murder: Grant's murder trial began in May 2008.

Page 127. Get-rich-quick guru John Beck nearly ruined Gabriel Ruiz's life: Gabriel Ruiz is a pseudonym. He asked to not be identified by name, as his family and friends are still not aware of the events described in the book.

Page 134. In 2002 the duo—along with several others—were sued:
See the FTC's official statement on the matter: "FTC Flexes Its
Muscles in AB Energizer Case," April 26, 2005.

Page 136. The FTC took action against the company: A May 2000
final consent order prohibited Enforma and Grey from making
unsubstantiated claims for weight loss products and led Enforma
and Grey to agree to pay a $10 million settlement in consumer
redress. In 2005 the Federal Trade Commission announced it
had filed a second civil contempt action against Enforma and
Grey for continuing to violate the terms of agreement.

In 2000, the FTC filed suit against Garvey, charging that
he misled consumers and also crossed the line between being
an actor and becoming a product promoter. The FTC argued
he demonstrated "a reckless indifference to the truth," a legal
standard that would make him liable for the claims; for his part,
Garvey maintained he was an actor reading a script. Although a
lower court agreed with the government in *FTC v. Garvey,* the
Ninth Circuit Court of Appeals in Pasadena later ruled that he
was not liable for the statements he made, affirming the U.S.
District Court for the Central District of California's finding in
favor of Garvey.

*Page 136. In 2005 a man by the name of Stephan Karian paid the
largest settlement in infomercial history:* For details, see *FTC v. Great
American Products, Inc., Physician's Choice, Inc., Stephan Karian,
and Michael Teplitsky,* U.S. District Court, Northern District of
Florida. In January 2008, the FTC alleged that Karian et al.
violated the terms of the court order entered against them two
years earlier.

Page 138. A good deal has been written on Trudeau over the
past few years. See Libby Copeland, "Wait, There's More," *Washington Post,* October 23, 2005, and Christopher Dreher, "What
Kevin Trudeau Doesn't Want You to Know About," Salon.com,

July 29, 2005. Documents related to Trudeau's two previous criminal convictions can also be found on thesmokinggun. com. Trudeau did not respond to my repeated requests to be interviewed.

Page 141. "Dr." Robert "Bob" Barefoot, a quack who describes himself as a doctor despite the fact he never even graduated college: Barefoot supposedly earned a two-year diploma from Canada's Northern Alberta Institute of Technology. His questionable qualifications are described in Judy Packer-Tursman, "Many Experts Don't Swallow Extraordinary Claims for Calcium Supplements Derived from Sea Coral," *Washington Post,* May 20, 2003. He has faced legal claims as well. See Carolyn Susman, "Coral Calcium Proponent Barefoot Charged with Making False Claims," Cox News Service, July 1, 2003.

Page 144–45. In the past, Trudeau's companies have been incorporated offshore, in places like the Isle of Man in the British Channel Islands, a well-known tax haven: This fact is addressed in various court documents, including *FTC v. Kevin Trudeau et al.,* U.S. District Court, Northern District of Illinois.

Page 146. a former physician named Lorraine Day: Day's support for Ernst Zündel is documented on his Web site, zundelsite.org, as well as her own, drday.com. The description of her relationship with Zündel is contained in a letter she wrote in 2003 to Dr. Dean Edell from KGO-TV, which is archived on drday.com. Day's virulent anti-Semitic views can also be found on the Web site goodnewsaboutgod.com, which is operated by Day's Spencer Publishing. For more on her role in defending Zündel in court, see Adrian Humphreys, "Zundel Expected to Take on New Lawyer: Torontonian in Court," *National Post* (Canada), September 24, 2003.

Page 159. The posts from disgruntled former employees: This text has been edited to correct spelling and punctuation mistakes.

Page 161. An account of Video Professor and John Scherer's background and legal troubles are recounted in Michael Roberts, "Prof Positive," Denver *Westwood,* April 20, 2006.

Page 163. The California native got his start as a production assistant: For a lengthy account of Francis's background, legal ordeals, and altercation with the LAT reporter, see Claire Hoffman, "Joe Francis: 'Baby, Give Me a Kiss,'" *Los Angeles Times,* August 6, 2006.

Page 163. Francis was later found liable for stealing the "Banned" concept from a colleague: According to the *LA Times,* Les Haber, a producer who had worked with Francis on *Real TV,* sued him in 2000 for breach of implied contract, breach of confidence, and unjust enrichment. A jury found Francis and his company liable for $3.5 million; the two sides later settled for an undisclosed sum.

Chapter 5: Where the Shopping Never Stops

Page 170. Lowell "Bud" Paxson, the owner of an AM radio station: Paxson recounts his experience in a memoir, *Threading the Needle* (New York: HarperCollins, 1998).

Page 171. "Nine times out of ten, I'd stay for dinner": See Eloise Parker, "There's No Place like Home Shopping," *New York Daily News,* June 27, 2007.

Page 175. he was ousted amid allegations of kickbacks, bribes, and improper payments made to a company controlled by his son, charges that eventually resulted in a messy class-action lawsuit: For more on Speer, see Barry Meier, "A Hard Look at Home Shopping's Family Ties," *New York Times,* April 26, 1993, and Alan Goldstein, "HSN's Roy Speer Out of Daily Grind, Still in the Fight," *St. Petersburg Times,* May 16, 1993. The lawsuit was later settled by the company out of court. See Mark Albright, "Home Shopping to Settle Shareholder Suit," *St. Petersburg Times,* October 11, 1995.

Page 176. Diller has longtime friend (and now wife) Diane von Furstenberg to thank: An account of Diller's visit to QVC and

Diane von Furstenberg's experience on the air is detailed in Ken Auletta's "Barry Diller's Search for the Future," *The New Yorker,* February 22, 1993.

Page 181. what a ruthlessly analytical industry it is: A fantastic analysis of the quantitative processes used by home shopping networks—and QVC in particular—can be found in Jeffrey F. Rayport and Bernard J. Jaworski's *Best Face Forward* (Boston: Harvard Business School Press, 2005).

Page 182. Joe Sugarman, the inventor of BluBlocker sunglasses and a staple on QVC for much of the 1990s: Sugarman's experience on the air is described in his self-published book, *Television Secrets for Marketing Success* (Las Vegas, NV: DelStar, 1998).

Page 182. During a pitch for a basket of diet food products on QVC: This is recounted in *Uphill All the Way* by Marvin Segel (New York: Newmarket Press, 1999).

Page 191. It's still a market overwhelmingly dominated by women: For research concerning the demographic makeup of infomercial and home shopping viewers, see Naveen Donthu and David Gilliland, "The Infomercial Shopper," *Journal of Advertising Research,* 36 (1996). Recent gender data are from the Direct Marketing Association.

Page 193. much of their inventory comes from independent vendors who bring items to the network directly: For more on this, see Corey Kilgannon, "Oh, to Be Discovered by the Folks at QVC," *New York Times,* November 15, 2006.

Page 194. a kooky woman named Jeanne Bice: Bice's path to TV glory is recounted in her book *Pull Yourself Up by Your Bra Straps: And Other Quacker Wisdom* (New York: Hyperion, 2005).

Chapter 6: Circus of the Stars

Page 201. Foreman walked away with $137.5 million in cash and stock: See Patrick McGeehan, "Salton Pays $137.5 Million for George Foreman's Name," *New York Times,* December 10, 1999.

Page 206. When Kathy Levine, who spent close to twenty years at QVC: A personal account of Levine's career as a home shopping network host is included in *It's Better to Laugh . . . Life, Good Luck, Bad Hair Days & QVC* (New York: Pocket, 1996).

Page 207. dedicated fan bases of women who congregate online and exchange gossip about their favorite on-air personalities: Sites like televisionwithpity.com feature active home shopping bulletin boards. For an amusing account of how fans congregate at QVC, see Dan Shaw, "For Sleep-Deprived Shoppers, a Pilgrimage to QVC," *New York Times,* September 6, 2002.

Page 210. Infomercials and home shopping shows continue to amuse three decades after their arrival: A long list of clips have been posted online in recent years. Paul Lucas's amusing Web site infomercial-hell.com features a bunch of early favorites.

Chapter 7: Remote (Control) Dreams

Page 213. CBS aired *Winky Dink and You":* The early days of interactive television and an account of *Winky Dink and You* are detailed in *Interactive Television Production* by Mark Gawlinski (St. Louis, MO: Focal Press, 2003).

Page 213. Warner-Amex Cable debuted QUBE: See Andrew Pollack, "New Interactive TV Threatens the Bliss of Couch Potatoes," *New York Times,* June 18, 1990.

Page 215. Diller's quote is from Auletta's "Barry Diller's Search for the Future."

Page 216. When Time Warner wired 4,000 homes in Orlando with interactive cable: "I-Way or No Way for Cable?," *BusinessWeek,* April 8, 1996.

Page 218. Things couldn't have been more different on the Web: For more on the subject, see Darcy Gerbarg, *The Economics, Technology, and Content of Digital TV* (New York: Springer, 1999).

INDEX